MISS
CHLOE

ALSO BY A. J. VERDELLE

The Good Negress

MISS CHLOE

A Memoir of a
Literary Friendship with
Toni Morrison

A. J. VERDELLE

AMISTAD
— 35 —

An Imprint of HarperCollins*Publishers*

Page vii: "We Are Each Other's Harvest" excerpt from "Paul Robeson" by Gwendolyn Brooks. Reprinted by consent of Brooks Permissions.

Page 18: Excerpt from *I Dream a World* by Brian Lanker. Used by permission of Lanker, Inc.

Page 357: Excerpt from "After Storm." Copyright © 1989 by Rita Dove, from COLLECTED POEMS: 1974–2004 by Rita Dove. Used by permission of W. W. Norton & Company, Inc.

HarperCollins books may be purchased for educational, business, or sales promotional use. For information, please email the Special Markets Department at SPsales@harpercollins.com.

FIRST EDITION

Designed by Nancy Singer

Library of Congress Cataloging-in-Publication Data has been applied for.

ISBN 978-0-06-303166-1

22 23 24 25 26   LSC   10 9 8 7 6 5 4 3 2 1

Ailey

We are each other's harvest:
We are each other's business:
We are each other's magnitude and bond.

Gwendolyn Brooks
from the poem "Paul Robeson"

Do You Know Where Your Wisdom Lives?

When you open the door to Toni Morrison, you look genius in the face. She was a legend while she lived. Now that she's gone, she's a literary monument. A beacon. An ancestor. An everlasting eidolon, thriving in a weightless world. A woman and a writer who left a voluminous legacy. A woman who lived through incarnations we can only conjure. Consider:

Chloe Ardelia Wofford was born colored, in Lorain, Ohio, in 1931.

Colored was the term of the time. "Colored" is what her birth certificate says. Mine says "negro." Morrison was twenty-nine when I was born. So, in those three decades, we made our first naming transition. Officially. From colored to lowercase negro. More name changes have come, as we stopped accepting definition solely as a racialized opposite.

Toni Morrison lived a dozen years short of a century, but she researched, thought about, and reimagined all four centuries of our experience here in this country we call America. This little girl from Lorain made books covering all our eras. She focused on our positions under the low sky of our lives: first as colored, which was originally an "emancipated" moniker; then as negro; then as Negro; then as black; then as Black; then as African American—which brings us, through self-definition, to now. Her books about us—about people living under unseemly, outrageous, and callous conditions—managed to capture our persistence and stamina and aliveness, regardless of how our country left our future for dead. Written from *inside* our culture, her characters and their struggles ring true to our experience, even when her invented scenes or situations were improbable or impossible.

Morrison's works are soaring, towering accomplishments. Some of her sentences vault high as church steeples; her word choices ring with musicality; her constructed scenes or chosen names can give you pause. In *Beloved*, Sethe's dog is named Hereboy, which is canny and a linguistic reference at once. Through her characters and their situations, Morrison considered multiple positions; her works start and settle debates. People become seriously motivated after reading Toni Morrison; I have seen folk take definite action, in their own best interest, as a result of a Toni Morrison book. I read an article about a successful African American businesswoman who read a Toni Morrison book and then took the leap into entrepreneurship. People everywhere are changed after reading Toni Morrison. Though Morrison credited everyone with their own choices, that her works were transformative did not escape her and did not displease her.

CHLOE WOFFORD MADE TONI MORRISON of herself. She pursued the highest heights, throughout the arc of her experience—staring, glaring, working, peering, writing, imagining. Pencil in hand, she watched her country writhe, be vile, throw up waves of consistent and insistently revived ignorance and hatred. She herself defied derision. She refused to be a victim. This refusal was part of what set her free. Toni Morrison's intense attention to her talent, her genius, set her mind aloft—and set her work a-sail in the free air. Morrison famously pronounced racism "a distraction." A system that forces people to argue about their value or viability, as opposed to focusing on their own lives, their own gifts, their own hopes. Racism sucks energy from human development. Rather than succumb to the distraction of responding to what others thought she, or we, could not be, Toni Morrison refused to race-splain. Why argue our humanity to obstinate people who are, at their most benign, terrifically unaware? Toni Morrison spent her time on earth being and becoming and developing who she was, which was genius.

Not everyone who faces racism is unvictimized or, like Morrison, unvictimizable. Not everyone can make that *decision*. You have to have some chops, some cash, some wherewithal, *to refuse*, as she describes it. One of Toni Morrison's key positions was that you work with what you have. She had the goods.

Unchecked greed and ruthless oppression combined to deny our presence, our humanity, our capability, and our accomplishments, but Morrison understood these behaviors to be unjustifiable and patently ridiculous, if at the same time painful. She chose consistently to lean into her own legacy, to cultivate her own confidence, to live in the landscape defined by the truth of her strengths, including language, including the strength of her culture.

As a young Black girl in America, I was already in Morrison's debt. This I was aware of. Morrison belongs to a rare club of writers who have changed literature, popular culture, and Black women's views of themselves—like Zora Neale Hurston, Maya Angelou, Paule Marshall, June Jordan. Women and readers of this time, of this era, will elect the changemakers of their time. During her era and mine, Morrison accomplished an enormous tour de force: by relentlessly stripping the hegemonic gaze, Morrison made us and our human complexities so visible, in language so eloquent and deep, that the whole of world literature could not deny her innovation and brilliance. When I met Toni Morrison in person, I had been her reader and her cheerleader for dozens of years.

Morrison's fame is far-reaching. You can find Toni Morrison quoted here, there, and everywhere. Translations abound. YouTube has scrolls of clips of her. There are articles galore. There are hundreds of published interviews. She talked about writing, she talked about race, she talked about racism, she talked about motherhood, she talked about history and social justice, about who had the problems and what were the salient questions. Her commentary tended to be targeted. Her narratives created characters we can call by their first names, and can remember, and *can quote*. In some circles, Toni Morrison quotes are flung about like Frisbees. If you have readers in your life, it might take you twelve minutes to find somebody who can quote Baby Suggs's Sermon in the Field. Some folk can quote Joe Trace sitting around sorry after he murders his little girlfriend. Women can quote Sula and Nel, BFFs whose luck with each other runs out—sort of. Other women can tell you when they are a man's third beer.

For some of us, Morrison evoked mighty changes in our

vision, by her work and her writing and her piercing, unrelenting insight. Her writing covered innumerable facets of our lives—so many that were her books brilliant gemstones, the carats would be uncountable.

Toni Morrison's oeuvre is still shimmering. Her books are time-centered and timeless simultaneously. Though some of her books are more than forty years old, they read as contemporary. Her narratives contain generations that invoke whole swathes of our culture, if not its generalized totality. Her willingness to reach across time and age met no limits in chronology. Most of what we think about, worry over, consider, ponder, wrestle with today, decades into the twenty-first century, Morrison has covered, in one book or another—set at whichever time in our long chronology of yesterday she happened to be staring down. Her subjects reference theories of life, and philosophy, and violence, and Black people, and our interiors. Her narrative crises magnify our social and familial challenges—which have not let up for centuries. Morrison reimagined a history that only our ancestors have lived. Morrison's novels are specific and sweeping and rattling; her works are read and read again.

We reference her narratives by those moments that shook us. And there are plenteous moments to be shaken by, to choose from. Her ideas are debated and argued over, written about and reified—in colleges and universities all across this nation and the world. I know this. I teach college students. I teach graduate students. I meet and speak to students and writers from all corners. Morrison's work is studied and parsed in multiple languages and in an array of disciplines. Literature first. But also history, sociology, women's studies, magic/occult, religion, Black women's studies, Black/African American studies, American studies, rhetoric, architecture, civics, the history of cities.

Toni Morrison published eleven novels, including *Beloved*. After the publication of *Beloved*, her fifth novel, her body of work won her the Nobel Prize in Literature, in 1993. Morrison was the first African American woman to receive this highest international literary honor.

Her first novel, *The Bluest Eye*, was published in 1970, when Morrison was thirty-nine. To know she started publishing nearing what we now call midlife stood as encouragement to women and writers like me, who came to writing late. Morrison's fiction is everything. Massive. Voluminous. Voluptuous. Substantial. Omniscient. Prescient. Provocative. Correct. Erudite.

Eleven novels. Qualifies as a library.

Morrison's nonfiction is equally keen, though not a whole library like her fiction. Jimmy Baldwin holds the gold standard for our nonfiction: between his collected short essays, *The Price of the Ticket*, *The Fire Next Time*, and *Nobody Knows My Name*, Baldwin stays out in front for real-time, anti-racist, enduring commentary. You see film of him speak, once, and you realize you are looking at a rare genius. His work also creates a mighty chronology in its own frame.

Reading Morrison's ideas stripped of fictive aim, we meet strong, elegant examinations of the enduring and understudied facts of our lives. Her nonfiction (essays, speeches, and reflections) foreground her social justice insights and concerns. When her first nonfiction book, *Playing in the Dark: Whiteness and the*

Literary Imagination, was published in 1992, her ideas blew the lid off many a jar. It's a little book, but it's lean, revelatory, and explosive. Her arguments reference how much American literature and art rely on us Black folk, poking further holes in the gauzy imaginary of Black marginality. The truths of the American conflict are seeable and not subtle. Morrison's work argues that our centrality is inarguable. Morrison contends, and our culture demonstrates, that Black genius exists and can be met walking down the street. You can see what she sees if you will read history honestly, if you will look at culture with unbiased eyes.

Street is a loaded word, not just in our culture, but also in America. In our culture, the word *street* is no joke. But I do mean to use the word *street*, here, and I use *street* very sparingly. The way America works, the street is the whole landscape of life for some people. For others, their feet barely touch a street. The word *street* has many connotations, and multiple definitions, but none of its definitions or references is ambiguous.

In 2019, Morrison published collected essays, *The Source of Self-Regard*, which holds a special place as the last publication during her lifetime. It collects speeches, essays, and more important, Morrison's reflections on the writing and construction of her works of fiction. This pink-jacketed book creates one volume of decades of sharing, philosophizing, pontificating, urging, considering, critiquing, calling out. My favorite of her nonfiction is a sleeper, and is ekphrastic: *Remember*, a book of photography and text published in 2004, covers segregated and then integrated schools. *Remember* is little known and not much discussed, yet it's one of the books I carry around to introduce Toni Morrison to people who might not yet be her readers.

WITH HER YOUNGER SON, Slade Morrison, who predeceased her, Morrison published reimagined children's fables—short, illustrated children's books. Since the stories reference fables, in a way they add a tone of nonfiction, commenting as they do on stories many of us know. The stories have long, language-heavy titles, which suggests that adult engagement might be required. Morrison always spoke of Slade wistfully. I never met her youngest son.

THE LAST TIME I SAW filmmaker Arthur Jafa, before he left New York, we were talking about how we wished we could keep up with the musicians. Musicians are always generating. Practicing. Talking to each other across the bars. Of course, novelists work with the full chorus of human behavior, and so on a canvas constructed to represent the world, Morrison worked like a musician. She studied, she practiced, she performed. Her performances were her books.

Study. Practice. Perform. Repeat.

Research inspired Morrison. Few endeavors jazzed her more than reconsidering, reimagining, resurfacing, reexamining the openly overlooked, intentionally buried, or understudied facts of the past. The author from Lorain brought Black communities to the page. Morrison replayed us back to ourselves. She held up the mirror. Showed us struggling and surviving, thriving and testifying. Self-governing. Doing the work that she was doing: making change, making home, making trouble, making money, making history, making art.

Jazz musicians have the expression "going deep in the shed." This expression references study time, practice time, focus time, time musicians take to study the music, to work on improvisation, to work on transcriptions, to work in preparation for performance, emergence, or laying down tracks. When a musician is "deep in the shed," that means you're not likely to hear from them, they're not likely to be playing around. They're getting ready, usually with a new body of material. Morrison took a shed approach to her writing agendas. She'd think, and study, and read, and research, and practice, and perform, and repeat. For Toni Morrison, performance was setting to the page the story she was imagining. Even though her shed was palatial, the work was still hard.

IF YOU HAVE NOT READ Toni Morrison, you cannot know who she is. This seems important to acknowledge at the outset. The work introduces the author, and then the author arrives to support her work.

Reading Toni Morrison—not necessarily all, but some—presents her register, her language, the grand and impressive sweep of her imagination. The unshakable, grounded wisdom of her critique. You cannot situate Morrison in her rightful place in the canon and in the arc of social thought without experiencing her consistent and often devastating breadth of insight, which she brought equally to narrative and to her sometimes blistering nonfiction.

Morrison's works are dense and driving and drenching. Individually and cumulatively. Watch out you don't drown. Each person who ever interviewed Morrison about any of her works came with a whole array of different questions about the same work. In her books—rife with culture and allusion, family and physicality, magic and flowers—readers find infinite ways of responding, thousands of emotional entry points triggered by velvet, or by a leap, or by a flame, or by a beer. Or by a river spitting up a breathing child.

GETTING OVERWHELMED READING MORRISON IS EASY. Whole historical eras rise up in baby towns and living rooms; premeditated murders happen in the backyard; women go without men their whole lives and then, when the drought ends, sometimes they bite. Twins are lost to each other all the way into the afterlife after getting their feet shot at by marauding whites.

Any narrative about Toni Morrison that did not foreground her work would not meet with her approval and would be roundly denounced. I promise. I was her friend, and this, too, applied to me. Cryptically and possibly "churlishly," she might say, *My work is the only reason anybody knows anything about me. Without my books, nobody knows my name.*

JUST AS TONI MORRISON WAS known for her work, Toni Morrison knew me because of my work. The galleys for my first novel, *The Good Negress*, were sent out by my publisher, Algonquin, as a holiday gift in the season before the book was to be released. A friend of Morrison's on the board of the National Humanities Center read the book and asked for another copy, to send to Morrison. Morrison read the novel and sent back a note commending the novel. The spring after the novel was published, I was invited to teach at Princeton. The summer before I started at Princeton, Morrison asked me to come visit her in New York. That first meeting, in the summer of 1997, launched a long friendship that, in her new absence, played out before me like silent films.

My relationship with Morrison lasted a third of my life and was not wholly intimate and not fully professional. Our relationship had its flares and embers, its low heat and occasional blaze. This happens in the arc of relationships of all kinds, especially those that endure. In the twenty-two years we knew each other we had two and a half spats. A low, respectful number. And thankfully, or mercifully, we got to the other side. Friction is temporary, we acknowledged like grown-ups.

Always, we were part mystery to each other. Being surprised by each other infused the time we spent together. Sometimes the surprise was how well we understood each other. We could rely on each other in certain foundational ways. Black ways. Folk ways. Linguistic ways. We viewed history similarly: as understudied and so one-sided as to be often untrue as promoted. Morrison's work did not present "negro" characters as intellectually deficient, which buoyed and encouraged me as a young person and then again as an aspiring writer (in my skin). Her stories were populated by protagonists and antagonists, powerful forces of all persuasions—good, bad, smart, sophisticated, confused, befuddled, nosy, mean. In her fiction, white people receded into the background; Black people ran their own families, their own shows. By foregrounding our power, by depicting our promise, Morrison's works skewered the culture that rendered us repeatedly opposite her vision. Her novels showed how our lives really worked. In many respects, Morrison's books created a whole new landscape for what Black people see, in literature, as home. We see ourselves as much in the mind as in the streets. By the late 1970s, when I was heading toward college, Morrison was in her late forties; she had published three novels and had been editing for decades by then. Morrison was bringing Black publishing into the real world. Morrison was bringing Black life into the light. Complete with all its "myriad subtleties," as Paul Laurence Dunbar so sweetly and gracefully referenced.

No one was more surprised than I that I got to know Toni Morrison in this life. We had one of those classical relationships between women: crossing generations, spanning several cycles in life, exhibiting high and low notes, reaching and dipping and finding its way. Our friendship involved a studied and charismatic personality, famous enough that her appearances needed curating. Our shared experience staked in the trajectory of a wobbling, waffling, acerbic nation.

WOMEN DEPEND ON EACH OTHER here and everywhere. We rely on each other to model, to trailblaze, to hold up the other end of the banner, to bring up the rear, to second-line, to cheerlead, to affirm, to caution, to rally. Complexities, eruptions, laughter, awe, and joy—all presented. Our relationship was ultimately, to me, an alchemy of season and light, often agitated by our opposite stages in life and by the unarguable presence of genius, the unyielding pressures of time. Our exchanges were soothed by keen imagination and sometimes serrated by the heft of her expectations. Nonetheless, we graced each other with what we had to give. We applauded our mutual offerings.

I Dream a World

My first novel, *The Good Negress*, taught me that our knowledge is dated to the age of our parents. We know their music, their heroes, their ideas, even dances popular in their time. Because I was partly raised by grandmothers, my early knowledge dates even further back. I know my parents' and my grandparents' era, too. The further back we go in our history, the fewer celebrations or ceremonies we were allowed. In our family, we celebrated birthdays as if cake and candles and presents were indicators of self-possession and a familial locus of control. My sisters and I always reference our birthdays as touchstones of our family life and childhood. Our earliest knowledge was imprinted at birthdays; we had a celebration, even on weeknights, for every birthday in the family. Our creed: little brown children will be celebrated, serenaded, routinely informed of their value and specialness. Ditto for the elders. Full stop.

We called one of our grandmothers "Ma Howell": she was both the queen and the general of birthday party celebrations.

In our family, because of Ma Howell, *everybody's* birthday was roundly, soundly acknowledged. Dinner, punch, cake, candles, the birthday song. Even the adults were treated to their favorite meal. Cakes so loaded with candles that the whole room flickered with flame. Around birthday dinner tables, we young people learned who we were and who we came from. Consider the candles torches; consider the knowledge passed.

As a very young child, unaware of whose birthday had arrived, I looked most forward to the punch and the brightly colored aluminum cups. The cups were my signal that there was a birthday, before I could make sense of time and date and age. We celebrated our birthdays at Ma Howell's house, where she lived with her elderly parents. Choosing our own cups represented the same agency as choosing crayons, though rarer and more festive. A cold cup, a bold color. That the temperature of the cup was so like winter fascinated me, as most of our birthdays are in warmer weather. Ma Howell would settle her entire aluminum ice tray down into the pitcher of punch, on the birthday table—the whole ice tray, with its pull-up handle undisturbed. I don't know why the pitcher did not fall over.

Toni Morrison's parents were dated to Ma Howell's age and era—so, I would argue, her wisdom would be sourced to that time, too. Our grandmother Ma Howell graduated from Howard in 1932, about twenty years before Morrison arrived there. Ma Howell taught me things that I later learned Morrison understood. The word *negress*, for example—so rarely used—is from her parents' (and my grandparents') era. Most of the fun we had and the jokes we made with each other, Morrison and I, began with some date-referencing language.

Words carry luggage, and for us, playful uncovery of the luggage of language inspired our conversations.

My grandmothers represented living history to me. Their era happened to coincide with Morrison's lived experience of her past as well. I was the anomaly, because I had two grandmothers and three great-grandmothers. My lived experience included references far behind my birth and awareness. My great-grandmothers—who helped raise me—were born in the nineteenth century. They struggled through youth in a handmade time, with Jim Crow hovering and hassling them and chasing them away from self-possession and from freedom. And still they made their way, they made a way for us. I defined my whole cohort of grandmothers as wise women, women in the know.

IN THE LATE 1980s, WHILE I was in graduate school, Brian Lanker published a photography book, *I Dream a World: Black Women Who Changed America.* I counted up my quarters and bought a hardcover copy. You talk about a book to change your life! Everybody is in this book. Full-page black-and-white photographs. Facing pages contain life stories and advice written by the women. All the women still alive who cut a path or paved the way or made a way from none: Gwendolyn Brooks, Dorothy Height, Toni Morrison, Angela Davis, Alice Walker, Wilma Rudolph, Leontyne Price, Eleanor Holmes Norton, Beah Richards, Sherian Cadoria, Johnnetta Cole, Barbara Jordan, Rosa Parks, Maya Angelou, Sonia Sanchez, Elizabeth Catlett, Oprah Winfrey, Maxine Waters. This is but a subset; the list goes on. Each woman writes or submits what she has to say about life or about something inside life. Often, the women explicate their career choices, their trajectory, their accomplishments.

Lanker's photographs are phenomenal, mostly because of the beauty and intensity and power of his chosen subjects. The book approaches the ascendant, the wildly inspiring.

In her section, opposite her fierce photograph, Toni Morrison writes:

> *I remember myself as surrounded by extraordinary adults who were smarter than me. I was better educated, but I always thought that they had true wisdom, and I had merely book learning. It was only when I began to write that I was able to marry those two things: wisdom and education.*
>
> *. . . When I turned in the manuscript of* The Bluest Eye *in 1968, there was a lot of interest in certain kinds of black expression. But I had written something separate from the harangue and the confusion.*

This. This encapsulates our lives, our home experience, our ventures out into the learned world. In our homes, in Black America, herculean efforts are made to keep wretched oppression at bay, to keep the oppressors and their insanity outside the door. In the larger world, only the struggle, only the insanity, only the harangue is "of interest." How we wrestle with this harangue is how our country likes to watch us. Seemed sadistic to me—how our nation entraps us and then ogles our struggles.

Toni Morrison recognized the interior wisdom—the work of smoothing, of soothing, of making hard lives bearable in an unbearable nation. Wisdom in works, wisdom in action, wisdom under warm hands. Wisdom from successful survival. She recognized herself as well-read, as literate, but as possessing information that could only stand still and hold a flickering light to the real work of self-preservation, of nurturing the continuance of life.

Morrison's locus of wisdom is a site I totally recognize. My life and my experience, in that regard, was just the same. A whole corps of wise women participated in my raising, and we girl children learned exactly where our wisdom lived. An understanding of the source of our strength, of our past, and of our future was the knowledge that launched us. We could ignore our speaking, protective, wise antecedents at our own peril. Few of us were dismissive. Mostly we watched, studied, learned. Emulated.

Wise Old Women

A Black woman who has lived to her wisdom years has been through some things, some thickets, has likely been witness to a whole host of crimes. An aged Black woman peers at the world from the corner of Seen Before and For Shame. A Black woman in her wisdom years sees and speaks shrewdly. She may shriek. A silver-haired Black woman has met peril in the daylight, has stared him down, and has strode on through. You have to march to keep up with the program. She knows what's important. Keeping the pace—persistently—must be part of how we play the game. Life gives us teams, but there are few substitutions. A Black woman who has lived to her wisdom years knows what's important. She has hidden from and stood up to the harsh realities of scarcity, refusal, race prejudice, gender mistreatment. She has often grown into sweet serenity or fierce toughness. When I met her, Morrison was learned and literate and ascendant—and entering her wisdom years. Reaping the rewards of decades of work—imaginative writing, dogged revision, ruthless historical queries. She had demonstrated devotion to the grace of creativity and dedication to the tasks at hand. Either she was deferential to her blistering imagination, or her imagination made demands. Morrison showed the world what Black America makes.

Compared to Morrison, I was a young'un. But I learned about women of Morrison's age growing up with my chorus of grandmothers. My sisters and I were girl children, cooking in a wisdom stew.

Those children whom people called old souls—I was not one of those. I was precocious, rambunctious, curious, and occasionally querulous. I asked questions and "created theories," using surprising vocabulary for a child. I made arguments no one expected. When I was very young, I mixed up the creative and the true—until I understood fiction defined. And then I realized that fiction is a whole world, a matrix, an industry, a whole set of strategies separate from, but similar to, reality. Fiction is far more than telling stories. Fiction is architecture, daily visitation, imagination brought to the table and given soup and a crown.

Until I was thirteen, my mind lived on a diet of books and the advice of old women. Voluminous years for learning and for learning how. Years of raw, tender, full-open consciousness. Eons in a child's life. I grew up reading and learning and trying to peg reality, with no locus for the language my beloved books revealed.

Our three great-grandmothers and two grandmothers stood up as our pep squad, government, nutritionists, and personal trainers. We referred to the whole group of them loosely and inaccurately as "grandmothers." All of them but one aged in place and said what they had to say, either by food or by phone. I grew up on a soundtrack of folkways—commentary on the bridges we needed to cross from here to there. In time, Morrison enters this trajectory—a woman bursting with book learning, enlarged by big ideas, formed by contentious experience, and adept at laying down language for any complexity, any simplicity, any inanity.

Morrison and I worked on the same faculty, at Princeton, and that's when we got to know each other. For a few years after Princeton, I traveled to see her when I could. I met her either at one of her houses or somewhere she was traveling to. When Morrison stopped traveling, and I moved back to DC, we saw each other infrequently, but we talked on the phone consistently. Calling her in those years was like talking to my grandmothers; all of them were gone by then. I don't know, but I had the sense that Miss Chloe carried her phone around in her pocket. I had the sense that phone conversation was all the same to her. Less movement involved. Less planning involved. More leisure, more *flânerie*. No need to go open the front door.

The soundtrack of old women that seemed a familial and specific circumstance opened up to Morrison as if there were still a party line. She listened to my brief history, and I listened to her meanderings. For Morrison, her history included what she'd written. She loved her work; her work was a huge part of her past and present tense. For me, my history included the women who preceded me, the hopes I had for language, the hoops I'd jumped through until then.

MY FATHER'S GRANDMOTHER LOUISE, we called Grandma—because that's what our dad called her. Louise Smalls Young—she was the last of our chorus of five to go. She was in her seventies and eighties during my childhood—still caretaking, still cooking, still going up and down stairs. She was the eldest of three sisters. She took care of everyone and their children. When we disagreed with Grandma (which was rarely), and she didn't feel like arguing (which was always), she would light a cigarette, blow out her match, look winsomely at us, and say quietly, "You don't get old being no fool." That was her final line of defense, her rock-bottom bona fides. Take it or leave it, smarty-pants.

Her daughter, my father's mother, we called Ma Jones. She taught us to work, and she taught us to be kind. She predeceased her mother, dying at sixty-five. All the time I knew her, she had three jobs. She loved Al Green. We took her to see Al Green live when she was in her sixties. As part of his concert, Al Green tossed out roses, and our grandmother kept trying to catch one; she smiled deliriously the whole night.

My mother's maternal grandmother we called Ma Viola.

She rarely left the house. Ma Viola sat in a chair in her bedroom most of the day. After school, when my sister was in first grade and I was in preschool, Ma Viola made us walk down the street to the middle of the block, so we could cross the street where she could see us. The crossing guard at the corner was belligerently unhappy about our crossing down the block. But Ma Viola wanted to stand at the bottom of the steps in front of her house and watch us cross the street when she said go. The person at the corner was outside Ma Viola's line of sight, and so, for Ma Viola, that was disqualifying.

My mother's paternal grandmother buried only her son, my mother's father. She lived double his life after him. She was a cook, a neat, quiet cook. She could feed people full dinners and have a clean kitchen the whole time. We called her Ma Goldie, and she had plenty to say.

My maternal grandmother is where I get my name. Ultimately named Jimmie Verdelle Williams Howell, my grandmother Ma Howell (the birthday queen) was born to parents who wanted a boy. Viola Moore Williams and James Franklin Williams loved the daughter they were given and decided to use a version of the name they'd planned. You can call a girl child Jimmie, and so they did. Her generation and her parents called her Jimmie; in her work life, she went by Verdelle. Jimmie Verdelle lived a life characteristic of the 1940s and '50s, when Black people learned and earned and saved and proved and tried to stay away from white venom and white ugliness and white violence. She never mentioned that raging Jim they called Jim Crow. I remember wondering about the name, Jim Crow, the first time I saw it written. Had Jim Crow been a name? Where had that name come from? This name for white racism. The whole world of striving Black people in our emancipated past worked to free themselves from the vile meanness of white racism. Such an enormously tragic way to spend (or waste) lives—trying to dodge the vile rancor of people who hate as routine and who murder as entertainment. Black people who could insinuate themselves within communities so that their lives and their savings and their hopes for their children were out of reach of irrational, rancorous white pursuit. Within our own enclaves, which were as protected as we could arrange, we organized our lives around our natural humanness, which seemed then (and now) beyond the capacities of white racism to acknowledge, observe, or let be. Morrison erected dozens of these communities in her works.

Addison Scurlock, "Negro photographer," took a portrait of my grandmother Ma Howell in the early 1930s. We grew up looking at this portrait, marveling at its grand, historic, and stylized tone. It was sepia, it was romantic; Ma Howell's hair was a wonder of straightened and loose curls. She looked like someone from a book about Negroes. It was a classic portrait with a circle surround; this was nothing I knew when this portrait was a fixture in their house.

Addison Scurlock was the James Van Der Zee, or the Roy DeCarava, of Washington, DC. Jimmie Verdelle was probably a student at Howard when the Scurlock portrait was taken; or it could have been a graduation photo taken shortly after 1932. A studio photograph was precious and expensive then, worth preserving and worth personalizing. Jimmie inscribed the Scurlock photograph, which was the convention in those days, "To my dear mom and dad." She signed her name, "Jim."

WE CALLED JIM'S PARENTS Papa and Ma Viola (pronounced VY-luh). Both of them were born in the 1800s—a fact both stunning and endlessly mysterious once I could finally figure out centuries and dates. The use of a boy's name for their daughter was further amazement. I could not help but think that having a boy's name must remind you all the time that the boy thing must not be everything. That being a girl and then a woman holds power, too. You can't forget about power when somebody is calling you Jim, or Toni, or Bob. I imagine Papa explained to his daughter, Jim, that she could learn as much and do as much as any boy.

Papa was the oldest person alive as far as I knew. I can still see him from my earliest childhood: small, focused, frail, peering, proud. Barely able to see. For Papa, a great-grandchild was a wonder of the world. He leaned over us and watched us as if every day we were hatching. He sang to us: *Papa's little bright eyes / Papa's little doll.* There is a famous family story that one of us did something wrong one evening, and my father promised a spanking once we got home. Papa objected but was ignored. So, after my father piled us in the car to drive us clear across town to where we lived, Papa called a cab, because he could not calm his distress. And so, my great-grandfather, close to sightless and infirm, and in his eighties, got into a cab to follow my parents clear across town. He wanted to make sure no little doll got hit.

Papa worked as a cook on the Southern Railroad—for decades. Cooking food for whites who could ride in the comfort Jim Crow had arranged and violently perpetuated, while men and women his color crowded into "Colored" cars and shared aging food from greasy bags and shoeboxes—if they could manage to take a train at all. Papa's job kept him on the road—or on the rails, to be precise. His income established and maintained a household within walking distance of Howard University. His wife, Ma Viola, and his beloved daughter, Jim, maintained the house he funded, receiving a stream of cousins from "down south" over the years, serving as a family nexus in the interest of the Great Migration.

Once, on the railroad, Dwight Eisenhower ordered a steak cooked according to instructions. After receiving and enjoying said steak, General Eisenhower asked to see the cook, who was Papa. After dutifully reporting to Eisenhower's private car, Papa was commended for the steak and given a ten-dollar tip, almost ceremonially. A legendary story in the family. A routine of our history, being "tipped," our centrality unrecognized, our caretaking disregarded. What does it mean when your food is cooked and set in front of you? It means you have money. It means you are not feeding yourself. It means you summon a colored man wearing chef's whites, and you ceremonially offer him a gratuity to the general and a small fortune to the negro cook. A commendation that must be a public ceremony.

JIM MET MY GRANDFATHER Ted Howell at Howard. My grandfather, whom I never met, became one of the first Negro policemen in Washington, DC. In the late 1940s and early 1950s, a Negro

26

policeman was a new possibility and a rarity. My mother continues to express awe and great pride that her father donned the uniform before he left the planet prematurely, when she was twelve.

As is true of most Black men in America, my grandfather's life span was short. Jim, mother of three, became a widow in 1951, at the age of forty-one. She did not marry again. Instead, she began a long-term love affair with travel. Ma Howell had been an English teacher, but she stopped. Once a widow, she worked for the IRS in Washington, DC, for thirty years. Every year, Ma Howell took a trip to someplace far: China, Cuba, Mexico, Spain, Hawaii, Japan, England. Tchotchkes from her trips included plates with her image and marked with the name of the country. I remember registering, *These plates are not for food.* Photographs of her show her well groomed and Scurlocked and world-traveling; photographs of her husband show him eternally young, in his dress uniform. Ma Howell, during her grandma years, stood on foreign steps or shores or monuments in formal lady's traveling clothes—no pants in her era, which, like her boy's name, mystified me.

PRESIDENTS AND PLAYGROUNDS, STEAKS AND HIGHWAYS

The name "Eisenhower" I learned from Papa's perfectly cooked steak story. Only much later did I learn that Eisenhower became president. The first president I could identify was Kennedy. One of my earliest memories is of my mother waking us up, alarming us, in the dim light of morning, to meet mourning in our house. Kennedy had been shot and killed. We woke up to a miasma I still recall: a heavy, weeping sadness that was curious to me and also impossible to understand. Having grown up looking at a kajillion Kennedy images, I imagined the assassination was televised. The cameras were rolling; no one expected him to be shot down—waving, charismatic, sitting confidently in an open car. A charming and telegenic president. Brains blown out as the parade rolled along.

Shock ripples through families as if the family shares a stomach and the stomach is upset. Regular diets are altered, routines go awry, people are short-tempered or morose. Shock rose and rumbled throughout the country, too—as if in the cities the streets were trembling and, in the midland, the wind kicked up. Our family did not mourn alone. The whole country went akilter after the assassination of the president. The shooting was discussed and wept over, in my memory, for years.

FORWARD FOUR YEARS, I HAVE started to notice words and memorize how to spell them. *Playground* is within my powers. To enjoy as a destination, and to spell. My paternal grandmother, Ma Jones, took us on the bus across town to the brand, spanking new John F. Kennedy playground. New swings. The kind of carousel that kids pushed and then hopped on. A safe jungle gym, free of chipping and rust. Fresh paint. A fence surround. A soft landing. And so, with a new playground, this Kennedy president was again commended to us children. Here was a man who, though gone, could see our side, could make something new for us, from his televised grave. You learn early, and from direct experience, that being deemed deserving, martyr, a "hero," gets your name on streets and parks and buildings and statues and schools and playgrounds.

At the Kennedy Playground, I am swinging gleefully. Nothing for the colored had ever been new. I am five or six years old. My ruffled socks and Keds are framed by sky and clouds as I try to pump myself on the swing, higher, skyward. I am in a zone. Ma Jones stands far below my reaching, probably pushing my little sister in a satchel baby swing. "Don't go so high, Angie," my grandmother would urge protectively. In fiction, her spoken words would have to be a portent, a projection, more than just a caution in the wind. After you start writing, you learn the dangers of reading your life as fiction. But you don't know this as a child dreaming fiction in a swing.

Such an early memory. Long after I graduated from ruffled socks, the new playground went to seed. Back to unpainted, unfenced, ill-equipped, and dangerous. Over time, I began to suspect that the Kennedy Playground was segregated. Local news reports of the moment, dug up online, referred to the Kennedy Playground as built for the "children of Shaw." This neighborhood naming signals segregation, but only if you know. "Children of Shaw" meant "Negro children." Negro children are, incidentally, very very young. Once you're ten or eleven, if Negro, you are hardly considered a child anymore—that is, outside your family. You are grown and punishable on the cusp of adolescence, if you are alive and colored in this vitriolic culture, which can be downright anti-Black.

ONE OF MA HOWELL'S MOST enduring characteristics was also her most enraging: you could not complete a spoken sentence if you made a grammatical mistake in her presence. As an English teacher, Ma Howell defined her duty as ensuring that, when we spoke, what she called "the King's English" emerged fluidly from our mouths. We learned grammar by ear.

Ma Howell did not do a lot of explaining why. She simply interrupted you, retorted the correction, and expected that we would restate what we'd been told. We dutifully repeated, interrupted ourselves, until her expectations moved in concert with our thoughts. Ma Howell halted us and badgered us and basically refused to listen until we spoke the English she demanded. "The King's English" meant little to me as a naming phrase. As a child, I had no experience with any king of any kind. Now, after many years, countless students, and rich life experience, I understand Ma Howell being obsessed and nearly possessed by the apparent future of our speech.

Language is cash, I tell my undergraduate students. Language is the one conduit, I tell my graduate students. Both these notions of language were birthed with our Ma Howell, even though it took me decades to become so blunt.

MANY TIMES, IN THE INTIMATE interiors of African American communities, the language of commerce is not spoken. In our communities, especially in intimate spaces, communication value resides in code, in muted tone, in secrecy, even in mumbling and wordlessness. Centuries of ruthless bondage demanded that Black people communicate with intimates while being constantly and inhumanly surveilled. Nefarious and combative people, driven by a manufactured notion of race, behaved viciously, relentlessly, as arbiters of our survival.

The goal became to communicate secretly, on the down-low, saying just enough to stay alive. Violence, murder, torture, and theft of shared language were all written into law and supported by convention. Enforced languagelessness raised the value of communicating in terms that could not be easily or speedily understood. Surveillance and intrusion were constant enemies of our survival; these behaviors and incursions needed to be foiled.

Ma Howell graduated Howard in English, became an English teacher, constantly referenced the King's English, and turned her emphasis on language mastery onto her growing granddaughters. Ultimately, you cannot escape this truth: education is protection. Ultimately, Ma Howell's emphasis on language secured our futures; cost us little and gained us much.

Twenty years after Ma Howell graduated, Chloe Wofford graduated Howard in English. Both became English teachers, as did I. Chloe Wofford started on the road to shaping Toni Morrison, modeling how to sculpt and curate the burgeoning and possibly genius Black mind.

How early in my life my concerns over language were shuddering and roaring. My grandmother was correcting and sensitizing me, and I was reading hungrily in tandem. The language I was learning from the pages of books bore little resemblance to the language spoken round my eager ears. Literature, unvetted, also rattled me, especially in my tween years—the advent of the age of independent choice. When you are curled up and engrossed in a book, and when you turn a page and see some caricature of yourself, or some imbecilic you, or some dead you—hanging from a tree; strung up by a rope; attended to by weird, unreasonable, murderous mobs; burnt; mutilated; impoverished; made fatherless—their lives or spirit or future or family destroyed, it's hard to fall asleep. Black people traumatized everywhere—in the story, in the South, in my youth, in the realm of money.

Eventually, of course, I developed acuity enough and autonomy enough to choose more deliberately, more cautiously. I chose Morrison frequently, and from a thrumming list of others: Maya Angelou, Alice Walker, Julia Peterkin, Gayl Jones, Toni Cade Bambara, June Jordan, Paule Marshall, Zora Neale Hurston. Much later, I read Ann Petry and Nella Larsen. Reading this roster of Black women helped me understand that Morrison was not writing alone. Morrison was, however, singular in her aggressive imagining and ineluctable mastery of language. Morrison's work had depth, saturation, and *shake*, where other writers relied primarily on story. Morrison became my go-to early on; her books I reread.

WE ARE SO YOUNG AND uncritical when we first learn. Life is all about continuing to learn. Life is all about uncovery. When you first encounter a person, a history, a concept, you think you know something or have discovered something. But life and artistic work require that you draw back the duvet, you draw back the drapes, you let the shade roll up and rattle. Nothing is as it seems. Every surface is shallow. The artist's work starts underneath, or behind, or before you begin uncovery. Art demands natural light and a sightline. Art is made from the days we all live, stripped back to their shimmering, original promise. First, the artist makes it plain, and then she makes it pretty.

32

The first time you learn or encounter or discover or un-cover, you haven't really even started. Learning takes repetitive motion, reexamination, peering, scouring, turning inside out, review. The peering yields a pattern, an insight, an appropri-ate palette. Learning takes continuous energy. The outcomes of learning are draped over raw living and inform what we see when we see art. Not having a practice of learning or uncovery can turn your embers cold. The only way to fan the flame is to keep working, keep learning, keep wrestling with old ideas ex-cavated and with new ideas unleashed. Shovel and shout. Tell the story of how your house is bulldozed, your neighborhood is obliterated by a freeway.

Turns out Eisenhower was the highway man. So many African American communities, both struggling and thriv-ing, were riven by the paving and the ramps and his National Highway Development Plan. "The plan" either ignores or de-stroys the lives of Black people. The plan proceeds to serve white interests and to otherwise foster disregard.

Even for those of us whose home lives and business entities were wrecked by Eisenhower's highways, learning from this rupture provides some value. We know from the freeways that our economic progress is still being sabotaged.

Uncovery I: We have not been left alone to build our own, even given that the nation kept us segregated by law. Our thriving and our causes have been violently and vehe-mently bruised and reduced. Segregation is handled on the ground, but collective poverty and sabotage are accomplished by documents, configured in offices and courtrooms. Over our heads, these codes are written. Our economic progress must pass through white coffers, in order that we remain controlled.

Uncovery II: Segregation is less about racial distaste or discomfort and much more about a means of control. How could one possibly destroy a neighborhood with a highway if the neighborhood were not fully Negro? How could one possibly keep Black people from becoming lawyers, and daring to read and write laws, if the schools were not fully Negro? How could you target Negroes at all if they were all mixed in with white people?

Uncovery III: All of us can formulate questions, and our minds are primed to answer.

Morrison asked questions, and then answered, by gracing our lived experience with her sprawling imagination and sense of resonance. The Eisenhower highways, built by General That-Steak-Was-Delicious, represent the same bulldozing destruction as Morrison's "Medallion Golf Course." In fiction and in life: *Just build over the Negroes, raze their lives. No problem.*

Birth of a Writer

For most writers and scholars and readers, library experiences rise up as brain baptism. We don't know the significance of these edifices and institutions when we're first encountering them, when we're young. But even as children, we *feel* the power of these repositories. When our language catches up to our experiences, we are able to describe the indescribable: libraries as hallowed ground and sites of awakening.

My mother—my stake in the ground—had a small but

potent book collection in the house. New titles, mostly. The emerging array of contemporary Black books. I read indiscriminately. My mother's library was where I first encountered Toni Morrison. The mother-curated reading shelf in our house offered exponentially more entertainment than dictionaries or cereal boxes, *Weekly Readers*, or the pale and tepid Scholastic selections we were set up to buy. Books I loved the most: the *Negro Heritage Library* (ten volumes)—a gift from Ma Howell; *The Black Book*, which I did not yet associate with Toni Morrison; and my all-time childhood favorite, *Manchild in the Promised Land*, by Claude Brown. I did not associate Claude Brown with Morrison, either, but time told the truth: Morrison was editor for both *The Black Book* and Claude Brown. Decades will pass before I learn about editing as an activity or about Morrison as an editor. I learn the former first, which helps prepare me for my encounters with Toni Morrison.

Claude Brown passed in 2002. I was elsewhere—chasing a leaping toddler and paying in sufficient attention. I do not remember Morrison mentioning this to me, but I wish I had known to mention this to her. We could have raised a glass to dear Claude. I would have loved to hear her stories about launching his important book. *Manchild in the Promised Land* has sold four million copies. I hope he had heirs. I could have told Miss Chloe how many times I'd read his book while a babe cavorting in brand-new words.

MY MOTHER RECOUNTS HAVING GONE to see Toni Morrison in person when *The Bluest Eye* was first published. They attended, at Ma Howell's insistence, and because Ma Howell refused to learn to drive, my mother always played chauffeur. Morrison skips no generations in her character construction, or in her appeal. Ma Howell was a driving intellectual force in our family. She was older than Toni Morrison but identified intimately with Howard; her alma mater anchored her neighborhood. My mother and Toni Morrison are near the same age. So, I imagine that my mother might have been more aligned with Morrison's books. I was not of an age to discuss my mother's book collection with my grandmother, though Ma Howell did call us on the phone every day. I might have been more likely to talk about books with my mother, but with three daughters and a job, my mother was busy, busy, busy. So, I read on my own and judged the books on my own. I was not much of a judge.

Because it was in the house, on the shelf, I read *The Bluest Eye* too early, really. I read *Manchild* prematurely as well. I read *Song of Solomon*, too, there at home. I did not encounter *Sula* until after I left for college, though it was released years before. As a tween and teenager, I was convinced my mother didn't notice me reading her books. But there having been no *Sula* on the shelf makes me wonder. I'm not sure I was as unmonitored as I presumed.

Sula is Morrison's fire book, her wanton logic book, her sex book, her "these folks are crazy" book. My college students respond so much more passionately to *Sula* than to *The Bluest Eye*. When I mention the word *self-loathing* to my students, that's a guaranteed shutdown—sometimes, for the rest of the semester. After all these years, the notion of self-hatred remains unexamined and, therefore, feels abrasive and shocking and abrupt. So, in the interest of a responsive class, *The*

Bluest Eye was removed from classroom rotation. *Sula*, my students can talk about until the cows come home. They get into arguments. They raise their voices. The energy they bring to *Sula* makes it worth choosing that novel. These are first-year students; sometimes we tussle to get them to read.

In *The Bluest Eye*, Morrison wrote of a young girl's extreme vulnerability among the vicious (private and public) forces of our time. ("Public" includes Hollywood.) When you have learned to read but are just learning about life, print equals truth. A book has always been holy to me—holy and tangible and real and sometimes, not always, predictive. Books certainly cast a warning shot. Seriously, books shape your mind. All children should read as thoroughly as is possible. The muscle of the mind needs development in everyone. And then, as the child ages into older childhood and adolescence, they start to question and compare. Knowledge travels with them from one book to the next. The landscape of life awaits discovery in books. African Americans were forbidden from reading—to prevent eventualities like right now, when the oppressors can be out-read, outreasoned, and outrun by the oppressed. *The Bluest Eye* offered me an education at a very early age; protected me, therefore. Education is insurance against stupidity and also against being caught unaware.

The Bluest Eye raises the "white doll" question. Now, it's hard to imagine the universe of toys without Black dolls, but we're looking at progress. During my childhood, toy manufacture did not include or consider us. White dolls were the only dolls (except for rare, handmade collectibles) when I was doll age. Since a very young age, I was uncomfortable with white dolls. Never liked them, never wanted them. This was a personal issue for me. I was even destructive to my sister's white dolls—which I regret. But the words for this were laid out for all takers in *The Bluest Eye*. Morrison spoke my language, and I grew up learning hers.

THE YEAR AFTER *THE GOOD NEGRESS* was published, I was invited to the Bunting Institute, at Harvard; in 1996–97, when I was there, the Bunting Institute was still a program for women scholars and artists. Now the program has been rebranded and also invites men. Dr. Mary Bunting, who started the program, had been president of Radcliffe, and engineered the merging of Radcliffe and Harvard degrees. I wonder how Dr. Bunting would view the erasure of the women's emphasis.

During the fellowship year, I spent much time in the Harvard Library, driven to contemplation in advance of climbing those august stone steps. Specific libraries define certain eras of my life. The Harvard Library was my stomping ground when I moved to Cambridge for the Bunting Fellowship. I cannot resist libraries. I compare them; I love them. I always have to go, and see.

The Harvard Library was built in memoriam to a Harry Widener, Harvard class of 1907, who died on the RMS *Titanic*. Since learning this from a plaque inside the stone entrance, I tell the Widener Library/*Titanic* story often in my courses. When I think of Harvard, the Widener/*Titanic* story comes to mind first—partly because of the library and the story told in the entryway and partly because of the gilded tragedy.

Wealth predisposes folk to expensive forms of danger, wild risk taking, classically risky pursuits. The *Titanic* was on her maiden voyage. And John F. Kennedy Jr., so early in his flying career, flew when he could not see the horizon. Inviting spatial disorientation, which is a rookie mistake. We don't speak of wealthy accidents in ways that point to error or hurry, hubris or pathology. We overlook rushing and grabbing and greed. Dying with the champagne and freedom that wealth provides is more deserving of sweet and sorrowful language. Dying with the risk and randomness that come with dogged poverty does not often merit notice. Better an iceberg than a gun. Better a plane in the sea than a car crash at an intersection. Better an untested ship than a corner store.

Of course, no buildings memorialize the expired poor. No endowments make permanent the young and the Black. Just as Morrison so famously wrote, not even a "bench by the road" honors the lives lost to slavery. The work of the Toni Morrison Society has since changed this absence of memorials. The Society has carefully arranged benches, at dozens of key sites across the country, that commemorate sites of enslavement, or of African American resistance, as a response to Morrison's recognition that money won't memorialize us.

I accomplished so much reading and study and writing in Widener Library. The Morning Prayers I delivered in February 1997 at Harvard's Appleton Chapel were revised in the Widener Library. Morning Prayers have been conducted every day in the Appleton Chapel since the opening of Harvard, in 1636. I was so happy to be included in that number of people selected to read morning devotions. Compared with the many students and fellows arriving, year after year after year, the number of readers for devotions at Appleton must be comparatively few.

My mother rode the train all night from DC to be there. I read from "Six Prayers," a set of spiritual works I wrote (and hope to publish sometime, with paintings). "Six Prayers" is a practice at philosophic, rhythmic writing, prose poetry about subjects that endure and are less culture bound. Morning Prayers was the perfect occasion for reading these meditations.

My mother insisted that I didn't realize what was important when I told her, "It will last fifteen minutes; you don't have to come." She would not hear me. Miss her daughter's insertion into that tradition of olde Harvard? Miss the chapel bells? My mother said basically, "Quiet, child; don't tell your mother which end is up." Of course, she was right. I found out, after crossing the campus in the dew of early morning, that the reading was significant and memorable. You could feel the lean determination, the unbroken tradition. I met my mother at the chapel; she came by taxi from South Station. We had breakfast after. Satisfied, she took the train home. Sixteen hours traveling for a fifteen-minute witness. My mother headed back to Washington as the workday was starting; you could see how morning devotions were designed to set the stage for a day just beginning to unfold.

Even with the resonance of my reading Morning Prayers, the Widener/*Titanic* story comes to mind first, when I think of Harvard. The *Titanic* engaged a grief that birthed the Harvard Library and those incomparable stone steps. Harvard offers edifice education, which I would learn Princeton offers, too. Harry Widener's is an economic and intellectual story. The RMS *Titanic* carried some of the richest people in the world. Harry and his father perished, but his mother survived. How smoothly his gilded life moved from ease to ease, unto death, and on into the perpetual afterlife of the named library of the greatest of America's universities!

BOOKS MADE ME AWARE OF how my life was different, offered lessons that became practical really only once I was outside my parents' protection, once I arrived at the University of Chicago and started to face life in full form. My mother's library prepared me well, and I proved my commitment to books so completely that books became my birthday joy. One year, my aunt gave me *White Rat*, which led me to hunt down *Corregidora*. Gayl Jones: What a mind. What a story. What a life.

No book can be unread. Tom Wolfe ended up among my options, but I was too young to distinguish; too young to logically foreground race, really; too young to imagine what was happening with that one central Black character. And I was entranced by the novel's sheer size. Wolfe stood on the bookshelf solo among a regiment of Black women; I cannot say he held his own. I can say I read the thick book, cover to cover, and though I did not know the word *salacious* then, I put the book in that category—along with *Sula* and *Corregidora*. Books that did not shy away from raucous, incoherent, sometimes violent intimacy. I wondered about what I was reading, but without any words to shape my queries into questions I could actually ask. I don't think I'd even understood the word *literature* yet, at the tender age of twelve.

Once I had pulled Toni Morrison and Claude Brown and James Baldwin off my mother's shelves, my vision could not go small again. There was a vaster community, a luscious linguistic community, beyond the crosswalks where I lived. I didn't know where this bigger world was located, but I began to focus on finding that geography. Where were the people like the people who lived in the books? Where were the people who spoke the language on the pages in the books? Where were the people who wrote the books? They had to be somewhere.

TONI MORRISON WAS STILL CHLOE WOFFORD when she started working at the library in Lorain. She was in high school. Morrison reported that she was not good at the job, because she read instead of reshelving. I can totally understand why. In Morrison's life and in her youth, books were rare and very expensive. Books have never been inexpensive, but books are most always extra. So, inside the vast building of books, I'm sure Chloe read greedily and with great delight. She could read without bothering anyone. She could read without being bothered. She could learn beyond her daily experience and be presented with a world "out there."

My high school job was French fries, but once in college, at the University of Chicago, I got my first amazing library job. At the beautiful and august Harper Library, deep in the interior of the U of C quad, I started working in the stacks and at the library desk, and I met the me I would become: A book person. A knowledge person. A woman unafraid of quiet, who would amass a fine library of her own. A reader devoted to the experience of the book.

I took up near residence in the majestic, beautiful, monumental Harper Library. Because I worked there, I learned the best seats, the hidden places, the alcove with the least traffic.

Sheltered back in a corner, off the Main Quadrangle, that library was so gorgeous, it can hardly be explained. The tables were old, centuries old, it seemed. Slabs of wood so thick they hardly seemed possible. They certainly seemed immovable. The tables were dozens of feet long; the carpet in the great hall was silencing, thick, and frequently vacuumed. Traffic was usually light. The noise was sucked out of the air by the architecture; the windows were so tall and high, you needed to be airborne to look out or in. And yet, the slabs of sky-high sunlight that came through the high stained glass reminded me of church, or of heaven, or of the holy place where I worked.

Mysteries are revealed in libraries: private or public, massive or minuscule, or found. Ideas and arguments and records of the past emerge from the necessary dialogue among the mind, the page, and ink. You learn to ask questions, even if your first question is: "What?" You go from there to "I didn't know that . . ." to "Really, back then they . . . ?" to the best signal of curiosity: "Did you know . . . ?" Records of discovery or of perception or of loss are also by ink preserved.

You cannot use a library without hearing your own voice. What to read or whom? What and how to choose? How much time will this take? Can you protect the book(s) you borrow? Will you bring the books back?

I learned to cover dust jackets in plastic protective film. I learned to reinforce paperback corners with cut cardboard; to protect paperback covers themselves with clear contact paper, carefully applied. Pressing out air bubbles and reading titles, charging books and checking them in. I was so carefully schooled in the perils of inaccurate reshelving that I was assiduous, and I also had nightmares. A book could be forever lost, reshelved in the wrong call sequence. Library work educates you about the hallowed categorizations of the printed word.

In little places like Lorain, Ohio, and in the era of Miss Chloe's youth, libraries were buildings constructed so mightily that they functioned almost as town centers, town monuments. Libraries were institutions on which citizens relied. Libraries housed books and also other artifacts.

I started out, much younger, with books in quotidian, non-monumental libraries—little suburban branches, some store-fronts; outposts and not monuments. My mother had the grand idea that she could drop us off at the library and go shop for groceries in peace. I looked forward to Wednesday night with unchildish anticipation. Because the libraries I encountered as a young person were neither town centers nor built like vaults, I had little attraction to the buildings themselves. I was fixated, positively riveted, charged, and shot aloft by the stacks within.

Carla Hayden, who is the fourteenth Librarian of Congress, currently holds the top librarian job in these United States. That has to have some standing, beyond the world of books. Dr. Hayden is both the first woman and the first African American to be appointed and sworn in as Librarian of Congress. Since 1802, we've had Librarians of Congress, but we have our first actual, professional librarian in Dr. Carla Hayden. The Library of Congress has grown during her tenure—more resources are reachable by digital connection; and young people and varied audiences are encouraged to come to experience the astounding brick-and-mortar main building—named for Thomas Jefferson, who donated his personal library as the foundation for the Library of Congress collection. His books are still there, encased and observable from a distance.

At Morgan State, where I teach, we have a program, funded by the Mellon Foundation, named after African American historian Benjamin Quarles. Dr. Quarles wrote Black history when we were barely writing; he was a pioneer uncovering our true American history, and committing his discoveries to print. Dr. Quarles taught history at Morgan for decades, and the Quarles program helps prepare students for possible application to PhD programs. They are a small, energetic, intellectually dynamic group of students. As part of their fellowship year, we traveled to DC, to the Library of Congress, to meet with Dr. Hayden. She is a real raconteur, quiet as it's kept.

When she was looking for her first job after college, Carla Hayden spent her days in downtown Chicago to interview, to take employment exams, and to study listings in the newspapers. Between appointments, she would go to the downtown library. While there, wearing her interview attire, she would scour listings for additional opportunities. After seeing her over a period of time, dressed and poised and consistent, the librarians who worked there inquired about her project, or activities, or intentions. Because of her presentation and consistency, she was invited to apply to the library. They hired her there.

That Chicago Public Library job changed the trajectory of Carla Hayden's life. And now she directs the most important library in the nation. She has jokingly referred to herself as an "accidental librarian," though of course she has been intentional from the Chicago hiring moment on.

Dr. Hayden has been at the helm of multiple local or municipal libraries throughout her career. She directed the Free Library system in Baltimore (where I live and teach) before ascending to the helm of the Library of Congress. Appointed by President Obama, Hayden has led the library to better mirror its collections and its constituents. In LOC auditoriums, my Morgan students have seen Joy Harjo, Tracy K. Smith, Jacqueline Woodson, Jason Reynolds, and Amanda Gorman when she was National Youth Poet Laureate—unabashedly Black and brown writers, ambassadors for reading and for books and for children reading, and for all people being present, especially in a library, where historical truths are housed.

Dr. Hayden revealed to my students that you can borrow much more from libraries than books. At some libraries, she reports, you can charge out a suit, or an umbrella, or even decks of cards. You can borrow what the library has to circulate, if you will but find out.

IMPORTANT LIBRARY STORIES BACKDROP THE lives of writers and readers and scholars and regular people everywhere. These stories, too, should be collected, curated, published; libraries change lives. In Hayden's era at the LOC, "ambassadors for young people's literature" model how libraries can welcome and invigorate young people, even with screens as competition. Children and young adults need to pass through those massive, open doors. Even in the twenty-first century, young people deserve the critical experiences of finding, exploring, and confronting knowledge; finding ways to advance themselves (without needing a credit card); exploring ideas on their own. Knowledge always beckons, if you know what *beckon* means.

A library aligns with the human mind. The internet aligns with keystrokes. There is no comparison. The human mind is organic, energetic, and infinite. It takes a human mind to tame or loose a human mind. The internet is young and relates to the mind in only the narrowest ways. A library demands that you learn your sources, their finding tools; you have to think, and wade through material, in order to find exactly what you're looking for. The internet is vast, but not processed and not vetted. Using the internet for all questions is like researching by putting your hand down into a dark barrel. You may retrieve a dill pickle. You may retrieve a frog. You may encounter a sleeping snake. Now, what were you looking for?

At the library, when you go for pickles, you will find instructions for brining, commentary on cucumbers, a treatment on the process of preserving. You will be told what kind of barrel you need, if you need one. You will likely be told how to keep animals out of your pickling juice. At the library, the emphasis is on expertise, classification, and untangling truth. The internet is barely classified and is definitely unmoored. The internet coughs up information with the randomness and uniformity of polka dots. The library will hold things down for you: the only way you get a frog, or a snake, is if that's what you go searching for. You will find these materials in subject order, and alphabetical by author within.

If you let a Black girl loose in a library, you may not recognize the woman who emerges. The lives and the language

47

I encountered in books stirred me by way of their hyper-precision and make-believe. Unparalleled experiences of escape and learning. I started to dare to dream of making books, though I hardly knew the word *writer* then. I was just a regular (Negro) kid who had (mercifully) found books to poach from my mother's shelves; who had found old books to leaf through and wonder about at my grandmother's house; and who, on grocery nights, explored and uncovered the great wonder of the library while my mother shopped in peace. I privately pledged my allegiance to the library and vowed always to engage. I learned early that serendipity and soul, power and laughter, grit and grace, expansion and expression, were all mine to be had if I read. Books and language exploded my understanding of what it meant to be alive.

Awakening to, and in, libraries was a slice of lived experience that Toni Morrison and I shared and revered and felt defined by. We/I owe so much to books. Books changed my sight lines, my expectations, my sense of the enormity of time and the complexity of humanity. Our humanity included.

Oeuvre Is a Word We Need to Know

Toni Morrison's book covers now are one uniform design—a brand, a style made consistent to be easily recognized. Early on in her career, though, her covers were illustrated. Black women on book covers were rare and immensely alluring. Today, not so rare, but equally attractive and just as mesmerizing as in the past.

To see a dreaming Black child on the cover of a book was cause for handling, inspection, possession. It's thrilling to remember this innocence. I recall studying the picture of Pecola with her head tilted, and her bangs. Holding a white doll. How damaged that little girl will become is public knowledge now. Coveting a Shirley Temple teacup. We readers are aware of at whose hands, by whose dicks, by which poverty. We hold racism responsible for her crazy, devalued father, and we wrestle with what her mother knew. On the cusp of my wisdom years now myself, I saw these bad male behaviors as of a piece—domination, engineered poverty, excessive force, rape, racism, greed, lying, and all the other offshoots and outcomes of wanton immorality and the reckless pursuit of personal gain.

Though they are often in the background, Morrison situated men who are blind to others, bereft of insight, and bottomlessly greedy. Men driven to incoherent distraction by their own unchecked impulses. Morrison confronted historical crises one after the other; the unfettered pursuit of male-centered agendas could rightly be considered a continuing crisis of historic proportion. Morrison did us the great favor of suffocating erasures by laying words of beauty and keen insight across the salvage of our lives. She refused to let the printed page continue ignoring and misreading us. She brought power and pizzazz to our place on the page.

WHEN I WAS YOUNG AND reading Morrison—never imagining I would know her—I could envision myself as some of her characters. The girl runaway role, in *Sula*, that we also see in Hurston's Janie, in *Their Eyes Were Watching God*. Don't all teenagers think about running off? Most come to realize the fantastical or financial aspect of the imagining, and so they don't depart. But Sula, in the fiction that is her story, modeled running away and hypothesized that heights could be attained if you did. Sula cautions us, too. Your flight might not be all it seems once you return. You might end up back home, sick and tired, looking at a boarded window, dependent on old friends.

The story in *Sula* seemed to feed bluntly into a "never trust another woman with your man" blues trope. So caught up in sex and stereotype, I almost missed the journey story, the hard Black mama love story, the fatalities of fire, the meditation on the importance of easing folk out of this world.

Between *Song of Solomon* and *Beloved*, I matured. I began to understand deviations: Our lives are nowhere near as hard or as malleable as fictive blunts and bruises might suggest. There are folk for whom life is even harder than the turbulent trials in story. And yet, many ordinary, perceptive, overlooked young Black girls in life and in Morrison's fiction have minds that leap and leapfrog. Her women solve problems, teach children, and fight to preserve possibility. Completely opposite of dull and imbecilic, Morrison's characters vibrantly and sometimes virulently differ from the lazy and unexamined stereotypes that drive how Black people in real-life America are perceived and received. Sad Black girls and their siblings and their uncles and aunts are too often constructed in stereotype and in literature as inert, uninformed, immobile. Morrison presented an alternative agency. Black women in her stories get mad enough to wither antagonists, to stop time. Black women fend for themselves. Black women see beyond craziness and do all they can to make pie from mud. See Frieda. See Claudia. See Eva Peace. See Pilate. See Denver. See Sethe. See Florens. Even see Sorrow. This list could go on.

As a YOUNG-ISH READER, I approached fiction as almost objective truth, which meant I often looked in the stories I read for the mild child. I would identify/place myself there, making the mild child me. Checking the story in the story against the story I was living. This little strategy of literary empathy and sympathy taught me about protagonists, about minor characters, about margins, about antagonists, about the chorus, about the forces in society that leak water and drench our houses and apartments and hopes. Without the appropriate vocabulary, I found myself accidentally launched by reading into a deep, if wordless, study of perspective and point of view.

What a book contained, in my adolescent mind, could not be erased. Pecola's father, who should have been her protector and her champion, was led stupidly into Hades, following his mean, predatory member—a behavior I came to associate with most men, fictive and real. *The Bluest Eye* showed me that I was at risk, though it also showed me how roundly and decisively we have survived. I did not have the blue eye–envy problem, but don't all adolescent girls face Pecola's problem of being confronted with aggressive, lecherous, self-serving men? Certainly, Nel and Sula faced the same. The long catcall near the beginning of *Sula* is a slow-motion transcription from the street. The most lecherous man of my own youth eyed and cajoled me; he was smart and funny and handsome. A photographer. There are pictures of me at twelve that I still can't bear to look at. Pictures that are decent and modest and suitable for families, but behind that lens was a tooth-licking man who reduced me to #MeToo in a time before hashtags. Between my sisters and Morrison, I came away from my teen years mostly unscathed, ready to grow, and ready to go. Bless my sisters' hearts. Bless Toni Morrison's heart and smarts. Was Morrison sending a message? Sending a flare out to preyed-upon adolescent girls? When you read, you get to decide.

Loner that I was, I believe I read both books twice. Books were such great company; they did not misunderstand me. And though some authors (whose books I usually put down) insulted and defamed people colored like me, Morrison's books did not defame. Her narratives rendered wild edges of good and bad, of determination and dreaming, of steely seriousness and gummy insanity, of our trained divergence between speech and thinking, of Black people I had known and seen. Although all her people were made up, I saw parts of my life in parts of the novels she published. Like most readers, I created a self-defined relationship with Toni Morrison, the author I was so devotedly reading. I read her novels twice before I even learned that this is how you study. As Farah Jasmine Griffin argues, you read until you understand.

WHEN I SAW THE NAME "Cholly" in *The Bluest Eye*, I could not have been more than eleven or twelve. "Cholly," I read. "Chol-lee," I said aloud. A Cholly Rich lived three houses away from Ma Jones. I knew Cholly. And then I thought, *Oh, this lady knows us.* Of course, her Cholly and my Cholly were both formally named "Charlie," or "Charles," but Morrison made her phonetic point. And I hopped on that train.

My sisters and I saw Cholly often, while he lived. Cholly was a Vietnam veteran and a stutterer. An African American. A man. He was one of the first personality curiosities of my childhood. Every kid has those people they remember watching and wondering about and not really understanding. Cholly Rich was my grandmother's neighbor and not somebody in my family. So, I saw him, I recognized him and felt somewhat fond of him, but he does not know my middle name; he did not know my address, across town. After I finished *The Bluest Eye*, I could see for sure that this lady's Cholly was not the Cholly I knew. Cholly Rich was more like Shadrack than he was Pecola's maligned, marauding father, also called Cholly.

Seriously. By writing "Cholly," not "Charlie," this writer revealed that she spoke my language, heard my tongue, considered our speech worthy of the printed page. Morrison spoke the big language I was determined to locate, but she also presented the insular words that defined my little world. Surely, she must speak a broader truth, given that she articulated small truths I knew and heard and spoke myself. And yet, she wrote books. I have a vague memory of a moment when I briefly wondered, and looked round to see, if there was a Pecola lurking in our grandmother's neighborhood. Some young mother staggering under the weight of a caustic society and a mean man. Within a couple of years, I learned that Pecola was purely figurative, or representational. I was disappointed yet relieved. I learned that novels reference truth but mix things up; I learned that authors make things up and that the relationship between truth and fiction in a story is real, if indirect.

Turns out, Morrison did not know my Cholly. My Cholly had no children that I knew of—and besides, Cholly Rich would never do any kind of bad thing to any little girl. Our Cholly was somebody who would look out for me, for us—kids on the block. Cholly Rich was a grown man with a good heart and hesitation in his speech. He told jokes. Sometimes you had to hang on for the punch line. We were expected to be warm and kind and respectful to Cholly Rich. He was harmless, like Shadrack—and like Shadrack, he had served our country in uniform. A young man from a segregated neighborhood, battling for American interests on foreign shores. A regular story, usually marked by rough reentry. Cholly, our neighbor, seemed less disturbed than Shadrack. Our Cholly was better able to live in stream with others. Compared with Morrison's Cholly, our Cholly was genuine, and genial, and not vile.

MORRISON IN THE HOUSE

Before she wrote, Morrison brought keen and substantial critical and narrative sensibilities to editing. She moved mountains of resistance and disregard, ushering in modern African American publishing. By documenting the movement and thinkers involved in social critique and literary production in the era before we bloomed into the canon, Morrison nurtured the renaissance that flowers around us now. Before we sprouted, we were seeds.

Before emerging into literary stardom, Morrison made big changes to Black literature as an editor at Random House. Black publishing made big strides, with Toni Morrison quietly and intelligently steering her ship. Her roster of authors carefully selected; their manuscripts by her wise hand groomed. Morrison plied an intellectual currency that her industry had been indifferent to. A state of blindness that rendered her white colleagues bluntly unavailable to the authors she published and celebrated. The nation was sizzling and popping hot grease. Kitchen help were hanging up their uniforms and starting books, when they could. Poets and storytellers labored stoically in secrecy, or silence, or stewing with rage; they tossed words in the air, pages carried on tailwinds. Black wordsmiths and theoreticians found their way to her—a woman who could execute contracts, help turn a phrase, recognize power and purpose, and lay a hand on the future. Why shouldn't we stand on shelves in libraries? Why shouldn't our spines be straight? Why shouldn't we, why couldn't we, make books? Why wouldn't she change which books were published? She attracted authors who were attracted to her brilliant mind. After all, who wouldn't want her editorial acuity and care? Morrison shepherded into print fiery records of real life, of real triumph, of real daring. Autobiography, fiction, poetry, revolution—Morrison made books that documented the ideas and pursuits of Black people who had plans and thoughts and who refused to mute or hide them. Women and men who were changing our world and our country and our understanding of our Black selves.

Morrison had a hand in unerasing us. Black people were shaking up, blowing up, glowing up. Wielding words in the arena as if in bloody bouts at the Colosseum in old Rome. Morrison presented a whole range of new Black thought, making scintillating new paradigms available for allies, and admirers, and posterity. Morrison put new ideas, new strategies, and shifts in thinking on record. Morrison drew back the drapes on foment, expressed in argument, packaged in literature's most respected form, the book.

BECAUSE OF MORRISON'S EFFORTS, Black fury and Black logic stood together, arms crossed, placing a new-ish spotlight on our wise, if wailing, words. Because of her era, and because of the content she selected, and because of the authors she brought along, and because of the context in which she published—Morrison's editorial oeuvre stands as another form of triumph. I was reading her work without knowing she worked. She was an engine behind their names. She was editing them and awakening me. They were important; she was calculating and industrious; I was young and invisible. Henry Dumas, Claude Brown, Angela Davis, all the people rescued from erasure in *The Black Book*, June Jordan, Lucille Clifton, Muhammad Ali—this list, too, could go on.

Language, fluency, and access to knowledge, to the ballot, to books, to land, to safety, to homes, to money, to banks, to organizing, to understanding policy or politics or literacy or counting—all these capitalist and intellectual prizes were bluntly denied us, regulated by law and hotly contested. Delivered through the one conduit that is language. In Morrison's era, Black people were hot, and the temperature felt both unbearable and justified. Black people remain hot now. Cooldown will require parity and respect. We were a far cry from that then, and we are a far cry from parity and respect even now.

I MISSED THE MORRISON EDITORIAL ERA. Most of what I learned about Morrison as editor I learned after I became a professional writer myself. This was not information I had before I knew her, and this was not an era she discussed as if it applied to the present tense. Toni Morrison seemed rigorous, putting the past to sleep. The vast majority of her work reinvigorated our past, but her approach to life demanded that yesterday be treated as done and irretrievable. Morrison was willing to consider history, review history, but there was no redoing history. Looking backward makes you salty and ineffectual. Reconsidering history, intellectually, can be visionary, she proved.

In 1974, Morrison changed our knowledge and understanding of our culture in one sweep. She edited and published *The Black Book*, which mesmerized a whole cadre of stealth African American readers. Not everyone knew about *The Black Book*, but those readers who did were often obsessed. I was.

The Black Book centered our history, using only replicas of historical documents (advertisements, photographs, sales records, album covers). No added narrative, no contextualizing—just presentation of the previously recorded and reported. Curated old news. Replication of artifacts from the slanted, erasure-driven historical record. Anthropology. History. Excavation. Liberation.

Stealthily influential and enormously important, *The Black Book* presented evidence of the long and tense and caustic arc of our past. The book functions like a consolidated encyclopedia, except that by eschewing narrative and confronting the artifacts of the past, you realize how much "knowledge" is filtered, processed, guided. *The Black Book* was an "in-your-face" monograph. Full stop. The book spoke to us: *Here's some information for you, knowledge seeker. Here. Be a witness to your past.*

The Black Book was not alphabetical, was not indexed, and had no chapters. You observed what was delivered. You had to dive in and think for yourself. You had to be willing to go through the whole monograph in order to discover what there was to know. *The Black Book* did not alert you to what you would encounter—no table of contents, either. *The Black Book* did not offer you a map to its pages—no back matter, no notes, no footnotes. You went to the book, and you turned the pages. Your intellectual or emotional reaction was the only organizing principle. There was a loose chronology.

We were children studying Morrison's amalgamation of our history. I would call the strategy patchwork, but that's too soft a word. Unannotated and unadulterated, *The Black Book* cut through our prior ignorance with intellectual blunt force. *The Black Book* confronted, forcing you to face a history that had been blacked out, brutally and deliberately erased by racist premeditation. *The Black Book* was simultaneously ebullient and effervescent with Black survival, resilience, and creativity.

Even in the internet age, when so much has been reduced to obsolescence, *The Black Book* maintains its particular relevance: white racism on artifactual display; early Black accomplishment on artifactual display. *The Black Book* argues with, and corrects, the obscured historical record, page after page after page.

In spite of the intentional tone and strategy for *The Black Book*, which I understood, I remember being young and wanting an index so badly that I started wondering whether "an indexer" was an actual job in the world. I asked my mother. Like Morrison, my mother suggested that I make for myself what I did not see. Sheltered in place as a latchkey kid, I made a youthful attempt at indexing *The Black Book*, projecting myself in the language industry, stumbling toward the applicable words. My amateur index work was laborious and unparalleled, written searchingly and haltingly by a tweenager. I do remember learning then that the plural of index is *indices*. Big knowledge, young girl.

When I was examining and indexing and hovering over *The Black Book*, I had no idea the book was associated with Morrison. Had I realized, as a young teenager, that Miss *Bluest Eye* was behind *The Black Book*, I might have levitated. I might have learned then that there was such a thing as an editor; that there were archives, records, places where manuscripts were preserved and stored. I spent countless hours confronting our buried, scattered history with *The Black Book* in front of me. Looking at all that survival and invention called into question for me the ubiquitous narrative of Black incapability. Again, without the words, I could see that we were uniformly uninformed. None of what I encountered in *The Black Book* was being said to me in school or anywhere else. Our suffering was fetishized, and our achievements and inventions were flatly denied. I was being lied to, and I therefore questioned everyone. Especially people teaching.

Morrison's writers were her earliest flowers—selected and cultivated blooms fed and pruned and monitored through seasons. Morrison invested in her writers, helped them grow up and show up. We were less than a century from the illegality of Black literacy, which continues, even today, to be held brutally out of reach for some of us. But where language was livelihood, where the language of the book was understood and deployed, Black writers were teeing up to tell our truth. Howling, in impressive prose.

WHOSE LANGUAGE?

Growing up, I was just a geeky kid running around reading. Looking for a corner where I'd be left alone. Trying out the vocabulary I encountered. Trying not to lose or break my glasses. Trying to follow the shifting rules of my society— strict for me, lax for others.

Toni Morrison said that she decided to go to Howard because she wanted to go away, to a place where she could read. Her mother wanted her to go to Oberlin. The illustrious Oberlin College, critical to our history, was just eleven miles from Lorain. Morrison thought she would be constantly interrupted. If you want to read, you have to have time alone.

Reading changed my sense of reality: books stood up invention and storytelling as a part of real life, daily life, planned life. Even with all the confounding activity before me, in books there were real and pretend people living countless kinds of lives, suffering and surviving unspeakable struggles. As my childhood years progressed, I would come to understand that people actually did live like people on TV, just on the other side of town from me. But visiting the library once a week kept me reading and helped me understand that TV lives had counterparts, or forebears, in books. Books rendered people more complexly than TV, gave them more words and more time, mightier problems to solve. Whatever we have, or work through, that we call ours, rises no higher or descends no lower than the trials and triumphs of millions of other lives.

Fiction and biography taught me that there could be metaphors of doors and windows. Every window shines daylight on someone, or on some resting furniture, or on a precious or random or disposable collection of things. Just as doors open, doors also seal people off from the street. Doors keep you contained. Doors act as gateways to the beyond, or to another side. *Doors*: such a strange spelling for its pronunciation. Doors were the first metaphor I understood.

How little you know, books said to me.

Who is using all these words? I said to the books.

I CAN REMEMBER BEING STILL in the single digits—under the age of ten—and realizing that nobody around me was saying the words the books laid down. I felt an unbalancing feeling, to know that there was language being spoken, being used, named the same as the language I spoke, but with a vocabulary that was far different, more distinct, approximating infinite; more continuous than any series of words I was using or hearing on my daily trip from sun to moon.

Many of my childhood years I spent with the dictionary; that book was my bible of language development. The first dictionary I remember had a list of names at the back. My name, "Angela," means messenger. I remember thinking, *I'll take that*. Not all dictionaries, I discovered at the library, had the same supplements, or appendices, or stuff in the back. I developed a fondness for particular dictionaries, at so young an age I defined them by color. Our big household dictionary was blue, and not carryable. My father bought the dark-blue library-size dictionary, thinking (erroneously) that we would never need another dictionary until we three daughters were done with school. I cajoled him, when I was in fifth grade, to buy me a dictionary I could carry around. Fortunately, paperback dictionaries were not yet much in vogue. And so, I got a red cloth–covered, illustrated *Merriam-Webster*, an adult dictionary that served me beautifully during my intermediate years.

One year, I looked up the word *mortarboard*. I must have been about ready to graduate from eighth grade. I found in my new language bible a sketch of an African American boy in a graduation cap. I remember. First, I went agog, and then I closed and hugged the dictionary to me. Embracing my friend, the dictionary, I reveled in what I probably couldn't yet articulate: few books in that era were progressive enough to associate Black people publicly with good things. There were three categories of Black people then:

1. slave/subservient/service worker;
2. basic 'bot (head down/grateful/simpering);
3. exception.

Morrison would have been in the third category, probably along with the activists and writers she was publishing. As a child, as a young student, I was in category three, too, except between the school and society, the powers were insisting that categories one or two made more sense for children like me. Although I was increasingly discerning, I was still a child. *Activist* as a word associated with a concept was still somewhat beyond me then. But *mortarboard* was in my immediate wheelhouse. In my romance with my red *Merriam-Webster*, I actually looked forward to searching for *mortarboard* anew. Proving to myself that, yes, I had seen what I remembered: a shaded face under a graduation cap. A nod to Black people—boys!—graduating. The nation's insistent low regard for shaded kids like us was almost second-nature understanding to me by then. I thought of myself pretty decently, thanks to my family's encouragement, but I was routinely being assaulted—by language, by commerce, by America, by school, and also by literature.

It is impossible to count how many times I tucked myself into bed with my light shining on some canonical novel, to turn pages and find some simpering Negro, some drooling Black man lacking competence, shucking, jiving, shuffling, gangrene toes floating off in a water soak. Literature could shoot or kill or have characters enjoy the lynching of a Negro with no warning for the child reader. I became for a time suspicious of a kind of book I couldn't really name. Later, I learned to avoid reading books by white men (unless recommended), as a front line of protection from literature's low regard.

I've never lost my wonderment at the revelations a good dictionary can provide. Every five to seven years, I've found a new favorite dictionary relevant to the demands on my life at the time. *All writers must have a favorite dictionary*. The dictionary is the writer's friend. I still mimic this gesture, the hug, the moment of discovery, when I talk to my creative writing classes, trying to deliver the truth unto their understanding: Not every dictionary is the same. Some dictionaries cast us asunder, and others intentionally include us in (normative) positive illustrations. Dictionaries can teach you so much about language: how slippery words can be (especially after definition number three). Dictionaries remind you that the alphabet is an organizing principle, that when you put words in order, you alphabetize letter next to letter next to letter. An ever-increasing interiority—of order. Dictionaries offer you far more than the one top-line definition, which is what you will get when you look up a word online. Dictionaries explode your vocabulary because you have to read through dozens of other words in order to find and define the word you're looking for. As I flipped past words I didn't know, looking to define a word I didn't know, I discovered diacritical marks, which I had to then define, of course. I discovered syllabification, proper nouns, etymology, the foundational importance of being able to alphabetize. Dictionaries are less cryptic than they seem at first glance. Sometimes there are illustrations, and sometimes word origins. Always diacritical marks: what syllables should be emphasized, what sounds should be made. I practiced. I wanted to use all these words I was learning were out there.

Who is using all these words? I restated my question, poring over books week after week after week.

You and me, said the books. *You and me*.

READING MORRISON WAS PERFECT FOR a child like me. It taught me to think about our stories and how they fit into the stories of this country. Taught me to notice and value our intellect and mental agility, capabilities that our country has refused to nurture and has historically denied. Taught me to consider language as a tool.

For as long as I have been reading books without pictures, Toni Morrison has been out there with her torch blazing. I, like many others, read book after book, mesmerized by her procession, her precision, her blazing firelight. Hers was a flame you could not help but see. If you had good sense, you joined the parade.

As a child reader, I recognized Morrison's omnisciently delivered Black world as "out there" but also loosely connected to me. Just as I recognized Cholly as out there but also a man I'd seen. The hovering or overarching or hegemonic abuse that kept Morrison's characters poor and marginal and unable to take the lid off their lives—this matched the battery I experienced in life writ large, and in Catholic school. I recognized my life in her work, consistently. Her works revealed the ways in which oppression hovers—with horrible halitosis, mouths made funky by curses and bile. Oppression is old and stale and pointless. Oppressors read as ignorant and do not have friends.

In adulthood, having worked in corporations and academia, having started as a teenager with a job frying fries, I came to view facility with language as a gateway to cash. Communicators rise. You've got to say the right things for your environment, but language is the conduit. You can't communicate your ideas without language. You can't make progress without knowing the language for the task. You can't participate on a team without understanding the language of the assignment. If you can use language, and turn on a dime, then you have a shot at wealth and at success in this corporate American life. If you remain languageless, or are halting in speech, American capitalism will pass you by.

Our system loves to say *no, not you; you come, you go.* Ineptitude or inexperience with the language of commerce gives naysayers easy and immediate reason. I teach Black students; I coach Black students: I have seen the outcomes of languagelessness or language paucity. The horrific disservice America has done by keeping literacy illegal or inaccessible has had an exponential detrimental outcome on our promise and prosperity. This refusal and denial are still resounding now, trapping new generations, immobilizing many fine, and perfectly adequate, minds.

THE SANCTUARY

The very first time I saw Morrison in person was at an event in Boston, at a church, along with hundreds of people. The *Beloved* tour. I attended as a reader, as a Morrison fan. I'd had plenty of reader-only experience with books, but I knew next to nothing formal about writing then. Reading as a writer is a higher calling, and a whole different world. I had no writing tools at the time, though I did have some facility; I loved words—but the tools you need to write stack up and can be complicated. I could identify and define imagination, but I did not know the concepts of setting or drama or scene. I knew that language was critical, but how few words I knew then! I was hungry, eager, reaching—but I was ignorant of exactly what writers needed to know and do.

I was working as a statistician in the social sciences at the time. I consulted with clients who needed numbers turned into measurable questions. We'd create the questions, collect the data, and then turn those numbers back into words. I liked my work sufficiently, but I was a writer in corporate dress.

The Boston church was large, a fairly cavernous sanctuary, and packed. My awed memory estimates eight hundred in attendance. People sat close together, many of them women, with their pictureless copies of *Beloved* clutched in their hands, sometimes held to their hearts. Microphones waited vacantly for Morrison to complete her presentation, invitations at the top of aisles for the coming Q&A. While Morrison read, but for the sanctuary carpet, you could have heard the proverbial pin drop.

Beloved is a difficult read, especially the first time. The novel had not been out long by that evening. This was before it had been widely read, or deeply discussed, or passed from hand to hand, or canonized. Not having yet read it, we were mostly mystified by what the novel laid bare, but mesmerized by the woman who stood before us, who—the reviews of *Beloved* told us—had created yet another powerful, riveting narrative meditation on the depths and pressures of our American experience. From her earlier novels, we knew that Toni Morrison put Black women in novels in gowns and crowns, with lithe flexibility, with the most nuanced and frenetic lives. Morrison wrote about Black women as if we were real, and important, and conflicted, and brainy, and righteous, and determined, and unafraid of running off. *Beloved* flowed from the ascendant to the enraged to the elegiac to the frightening to the rueful to the anticipated to the outraged to the treacherous; from past to future, through the netherworld. The past was Morrison's landscape. Though we lived in the present tense, we were the future of the past. She gave us our history without sugar or disdain, and through her work, we watched ourselves struggle and survive. She did use pretty language, but pretty is not sugar; her words lean—tough, pointed, and sometimes mean. You were caught when you read Morrison. It was impossible to read and look away.

Back there, back then, in Boston, the book I held in my hand in that sanctuary positively shook with mystery. Long before the event, I had loaned my copy to an old friend who also attended that day; she had wanted to read the book right away. Because I knew I needed the time and space to work with the novel, I had agreed, but I insisted that she not wreck my copy, especially not the dust jacket. A clean, intact dust jacket gives a hardcover value over time. My silly friend took the dust jacket off to protect the dust jacket—per my instructions, she said—and then sullied the actual cloth cover of the book with lipstick and cereal, both unhealthy substances for books. My friend was alarmed by my alarm. "You said the dust jacket needed to be clean!" she said. "I kept the dust jacket clean!"

In time, in life, you learn that you have to be specific, explicit, sometimes almost stupidly blunt. Or, you have to not lend people books. I lend books. I want people to read. My library is a thousand books deep. Too much power there to be selfish and grabby. However, to be clear, the dust jacket is important to a hardcover book's value over time. A hardcover without a dust jacket may as well be an airport paperback. That said, the book under the dust jacket should be kept clean, too. Liquids and lipstick are bad for books. I hold esteem for books.

MORRISON READ FROM THE NOVEL with her husky voice and Black woman's authority. She was an author among us, a higher-up, a guiding light. Many of us in attendance had read her other books; that was how I knew I was going to need time with this one. The passage she read from *Beloved* that day did not disabuse me of that notion. Even if we've never read a book in our lives, every one of us has a read on slavery. Morrison's manner of spearing history with her sharpened pencil in previous books made me know I'd likely be slayed by *Beloved* and that the time for that would need to be carefully arranged. I was in no rush.

During the Q&A, one young woman made her way to the microphone to ask one of the earliest questions. She might have been the first in line, with the first question. In my memory, she rushed her speech; she may have been breathlessly waiting. She described her interest in writing, her aspirations, and her failure to accomplish the fiction she aimed for. She described her struggle with making her stories "just right." Likely trying to be succinct and yet communicate directly with the greatest of writers, she sounded hurried, even as she sought direction. She then joined the rest of us in silence, to hear what Morrison advised.

"Well, it sounds like you don't know what you're doing," Morrison began.

Quiet in the sanctuary. I drew in my breath. The huge audience almost gasped in unison. I remember the hiccup of my own heartbeat; the whole scene went instantly wavy before my eyes.

My anxiety pounded in my ears, which made hearing hard. My embarrassment for her echoed and bounced around the chambers of my mind.

I empathized: I understood not knowing what to do. But I would not have asked the great Ms. Morrison such a question—so nakedly personal, and too particular to be answerable, really. Especially over the heads of hundreds. And in front of God and everybody. And in such a public space. And when the great writer was expecting to be asked about her own masterful novel—just published, just read from, the whole reason for the tour.

Narcissism can cause mistakes. What could Toni Morrison possibly know about that woman's struggles with her own blank page? Not knowing the definition of complete self-absorption can make you foolish in the context of community. The young woman might have obtained a different or better response if she had asked a writing question about the author's work. She could have asked about her own writing under cover:

Ms. Morrison, how do you make the impossible believable?

Ms. Morrison, how do you get your characters so tied to the invented place?

Ms. Morrison, what are the best strategies for research?

Or, even, *What writing suggestions do you have for an aspiring writer, for a dreamer like me?*

I slid down, trying to hide, mortified and wanting to be invisible for the young woman who had asked the ill-considered question. The spirit in me, the spunkette, the woman who wanted to know what Toni Morrison did and thought, harbored a hungry curiosity over how this would turn out, but I couldn't help but dream of a hole opening up to swallow the awkwardness.

You don't know what you're doing. Morrison did say this aloud.

I don't, I thought to myself, as if this were my conversation. *You're right. I have no idea what I'm doing. What am I even thinking?*

Who did that reaching aspiring writer think she was? To be so personal, publicly? Showing all she didn't know? And now likely having to slink back to her seat in that crowded church, having been told off or, more benevolently, told to practice and learn—*and by Toni Morrison.* This was a public event, so, relatively quickly, the line for the microphone shifted. The aspiring writer left the mic; I could not see the exit well. Maybe the questioner walked straight out the sanctuary doors. That is what I might have done.

I, too, worried about whether I understood the terms of writing. I had not yet begun to write seriously or in form. I had pages of words, observations of my little travels, my tiny thoughts. Occasional poems. But books and long stories need shape and scaffolding. It takes knowledge, experience, study, apprenticeship. It takes architecture.

This young woman needed the basics. Morrison continued, pointing her, and us, toward some fundamentals:

You need to study what writing requires. And:

Writing has rules, conventions, requirements. There is form. And:

Writing is more than your thoughts about characters. Drama has structure. You can learn.

That nameless young woman who had scurried to be first at the mic prepared me for what I did not know my future would bring: stinging quips and side-eye admonishment from the greatest living writer. All these years, Morrison's first spoken sentence (from the first time I remember seeing her), her whip of a reply, has stayed with me. In that huge sanctuary, I felt personally stung, even if only empathetically.

You don't know what you're doing. Yes, this is true.

Yowzah and ouch!

For myself, I decided to heed Toni Morrison's advice and start learning. Structure. Form. Convention. Drama. Precision. Characters. Insight. Vocabulary. Magic. Surprise. Scene. Dramatic weight. Heft. Resonance. Naming. The grammar of storytelling. The architecture of narrative. Research. Imagination. Reach.

Morrison's assertion, way back then, introduced me to the formal demands of writing. Morrison's posture and response also prepared me for her tough talk, her blunt speech, her whip snappishness. A kind of crackling was in the air that night in Boston. And when that crackling, that whip speech, showed up in my future, I could not pretend I hadn't been warned. Time will warn you, if you listen. Matters of time can be about ideas and not just about the clock.

In *Paradise*, my favorite of her books, Morrison sends an old man walking to town, across St. Mark's Street—fully suited, to the tie, wearing neither shoes nor socks. He is not imbalanced, but he feels challenged by sin—thus, the bare feet. He is not asking for formula forgiveness; he orchestrates atonement on his own. For all to witness. Morrison allows a midlife woman, newly acquainted with insomnia, to walk down a quiet road alone in the middle of the night. Allows the woman to enjoy the season, the summer night, to meet a safe community, even in the dark. Allows this singular night wanderer to hear a baby crying; she knows her neighbors; she goes right up to the porch and rocks her neighbor's child. Let the mother rest. Out meandering in the wee hours, this walking neighbor could be helpful. Different era. Black town. Fiction that seemed true.

In a dozen years from that sanctuary moment, Toni Morrison and I will be up close and personal. (Thank the fates I took that time to work and work some more.) We will discuss *Paradise* like TV episodes. Through the quirky lens of my questions, we will parse and parry. I had all sorts of queries from all sorts of angles. I learned to learn about writing from asking about Morrison's strategies. I'd remark about the book from a writing standpoint and then let her elucidate and, thereby, teach me. After one of our conversations, she asked me, "So, is it my best book?"

I remember thinking: *She is asking me if* Paradise *is better than* Beloved? I answered that, yes, I thought it was. (I was blown by the question, too, so, my mind was racing.) It's not every day that Toni Morrison asks your opinion of her work, and in such a pointed way. My enthusiasm for *Paradise*, I should admit, was then and is now practically boundless. Morrison does everything in that novel. There's not a scrap of life you can't find. And its storyline, its chronology, covers pretty close to a full century. Masterful. No argument.

On an otherwise unremarkable afternoon, early in my new writing practice, I slept in the sanctuary of my apartment in leafy, green Jamaica Plain. Taking an afternoon nap. Because I had embraced the burden of what I needed to learn, I had become obsessed with getting up before light. Often, that meant I needed a nap, especially if there were plans for the evening or night. Without a nap, I would lose the following morning. This would be worse. To watch yourself lose tomorrow today is grim and worth avoiding. There was a knock at the door. Bright green leaves of late summer waved outside the front windows. The trees were classically dappled in the sunlight, and I felt soothed by the nature the windows framed.

I rose from the bed and opened the door. Safer days, calmer times. I felt fine swinging my second-floor door wide open that dizzying afternoon. Huddled onto my narrow landing were Virginia Woolf, Langston Hughes, and James Baldwin. Almost instinctively, I smoothed the clothes I had been napping in, reached up to test the situation with my hair. I expressed both surprise and honor that they'd come. "You're not even from the same era!" I exclaimed.

I remembered my manners, I invited them in. My humble digs could not possibly adequately accommodate the triumvirate who stood before me. With all the welcome I could muster, I swung the door open genially and stood aside to allow the three to pass through into my apartment. Woolf was the tallest; Baldwin was smallest. Both he and Langston were sartorially splendid, each dapper and dandy. I can still see them all three—Langston, Jimmy, and Virginia, wearing shades of oat and heather. The dapper men in their calm taupe, Langston with cuffs, and Jimmy showing a slice of sheerish nylon sock above his loafers. Both men in white shirts, though only one was crisp. All three of them wore black shoes. Langston wore laced shoes, near brogans. Jimmy wore loafer-style shoes you could slip on while standing. Virginia wore ankle boots with laces, their tops a little roomy on her narrow leg. Woolf was dressed in understated, near-monochromatic clothes. She dressed like a Quaker having passed through a fashion center: Milan or Paris or Abidjan or London. I heard myself chattering: "I'm so surprised to see the three of you in person. And together."

The sound of my voice shocked me awake. I opened my eyes to late-afternoon light. Startled, I sat up and took stock of conditions in real time.

Well, if there was ever a sign, I thought to myself as I padded into the kitchen for a bracing cold glass of water. Passing by, I peeked into the living room. Nobody present but the five o'clock sun.

I have never lost sight or feeling of that dream. I tend to marvel that Morrison wasn't there, though I am certain the dream was catalyzed by the unrest she caused—with hundreds flocking to hear her read, by her zinging answer to that first question of that sanctuary night, by the masterful, incredible, earth-rattling release of her fifth novel, *Beloved.*

Morrison was not at the door of the visitation I dreamed for good reason. Even given the language of spirits and dreams and magic, she could not have been there without violating principles of breath and blood and gravity. You can't be in the otherworld and still be on this planet. You cannot visit folks, and populate their dream state, and still occupy this geography. Morrison was still here then—writing and thinking, changing the face and the history of literature.

The main character in *Beloved*, for whom the book is named, a teenage ghost in the story, was murdered (in the real life of the fiction) as an infant. Her mother murdered her and tried to kill another child at the same time. The mother's goal was to protect her children, from lives of chattel slavery— which was brutal and ubiquitous and soul crushing. Soul murder, really, as the historian Nell Painter has so elegantly argued.

The infant survived. Only the toddler died, and she re-emerged as a living ghost, a decade and change later, during the years she would have been an adolescent. As if the child had been maturing in the netherworld. The teenager has come back to reckon with her mother, to wreak havoc, to reinject her-self into the family drama and family history. Other than being dead, Beloved is just like any other teenager—newly willful and determined, angry, and wildly impressed by her own power.

But Can You Read?

During my long years as a teenage reader, the search for narratives that treated African American girls as human beings with feelings and thoughts and intentions could be exhausting and sometimes fruitless. Few books presented us as the people we knew we were. Living in our own skin, we were not confused about our stories. But books in print were few.

When we found Toni Morrison, we understood that someone understood. We had found an author who could see us. In Morrison's ninth novel, *A Mercy*, the narrative journey has barely started when one girl demands of the other girl, "But can you read?" The interrogator wants to know whether the other girl has observation skills—an ability to "read" that can be deployed on the landscape of their lives. *Can you read signs? Seasons? Can you read the night sky? Its stars? The moon? Can you read faces of strangers, unknown women and men? Can you read the compass from moss? Do you know what we should pay attention to? What way does the ground tilt today? Can you tell the future from the information at hand? How should we know what steps to take next if we launch from here together? Can you read in any way that will provide us protection, or offer us some cover at least?*

Morrison's novels are full of teenage girls showcasing or dramatizing the discoveries, the misdirections, and the assaults that implode and plague their lives. Even as decades pass for the characters, and they mature into parents and grandparents and exhausted observers, still, the novels spotlight teenage girls.

Morrison trained her eye on us girls. Our educational development, our intellectual development so subtly and not so subtly deprioritized where we lived and around the world. Morrison's works topped our developing minds with whipped cream, or cherries, or chocolate—whatever your pleasure. There is baseline facility, and then there are refinements, grace notes, embellishments. Most of us still work on building our base intelligence, even though we are treated as if we have accomplished all we need, as if our intellectual needs were somehow covered—when most of us know they are not.

Few young people who read Morrison in the 1970s and '80s were children on the brink. (This has changed over time. More tentative and at-risk students are exposed to Morrison's great works now.) In order to follow Morrison, you have to really be able to read. Multiple capabilities are required for a young person to manage Morrison well: comfort with silence, experience with dictionaries, access to insight, the ability to sit still.

I read Morrison from the time I was able to read single-spaced narratives. My responses to her work have been quirky, writerly—I finally realized. My interest in her novels crisscrossed with the language I'd been trying to locate. Her imagining and her stories and my imagining intersected like roads mapped toward the center of town.

READING IS GOOD AND IMPORTANT. Reading is life-changing. Reading is a gift to those who own and strengthen this ability. Reading books helps with the lives we expect, and are expected, to lead. Reading strengthens the human mind and contributes to personal and public safety. Reading includes words and books and texts, but reading exists beyond the letter. All reading is helpful to a productive life. Read books. Read cereal boxes. Read the room. All of us read—faces, posture, weather, the heaviness of rain. Many of us read the emotion or drama in the house. Some of us are sensitive. Some of us are literate. Would be best if we were all both.

Most knowledge depends on letters, ink, the record. What the world has preserved has been reserved for those who read.

Reading is not static. If tended, reading grows: there are skills, there are curiosities, there are hungers, there are books and libraries. Reading skills increase as long as you read. Even antidementia exercises focus on words.

Read President Obama's favorite of Morrison's novels, *Song of Solomon*. That was her breakthrough book. About a young man called Milkman, almost launched into a state of ruination by his mother and then, again, almost destroyed by his father's schemes. Then, finally, his friend comes for him. You would think this was a story of a man besieged.

Milkman's is a journey story—a boy on the path to manhood who has to wrestle with so much: his wealth; his Blackness; both his parents; his ornery, unmarried sisters; his magical aunt Pilate; his sexual proclivities; his best friend, who grows brash and vengeful; his brutish country of birth; a woman who is obsessed with him. *Song of Solomon* will teach you. You get through its dense references, its wild women; you follow Milkman on his befuddled way.

Or, read Morrison's tighter, blunter early work, *The Bluest Eye*, which tells a story about how children (especially girls) are mishandled, about how men are led by wanton impulse, and about the ruthless and unsettling and unreasonable demand that white be beauty.

In Raoul Peck's film on Jimmy Baldwin, *I Am Not Your Negro*, several sequences show with ghastly and ghoulish precision the elevation of white beauty and ease—white idolatry in motion, on film. Not all that rare, but so garishly presented in *I Am Not Your Negro* that you can't help but feel shock watching a frolicking fiction of whiteness on parade. White women are blonde and wear pink. The men, I believe, are more neutrally clad; that said, the men seem pinkish, too. Beauty and ease are synonymous with pasted smiles, thin physiques, bouncing hair, and pinkish skin, called "white." The white people leap and cavort; their images seem to represent purity and joy; they are supposed to look happy, but to us, they look crazy. These scenes are visual brilliance, and are shocking in their dissonance from the lives we daily lead. Morrison flatly rejected all the white silliness. Morrison cut to the chase.

When you read Morrison, what you catch you catch. Whatever you catch will stretch you intellectually, and you can safely leave the rest for later. (Her works will be around for you to return to. Her works are firm in their permanence. Discussions of her works will be ongoing, conversations you can enter if you read and you so choose.) Reading Morrison will make your mind reach. Reading Morrison will bring elasticity to your brain. Stretching is good.

BECAUSE: CHICAGO

When I was going to college myself, I did not have words for the snooty sensibility that admission to Princeton or to Harvard embraced—the hauteur observable. These admissions were treated as a huge, important door that a person should unquestionably and happily walk through. When I was accepted,

Harvard sent a certificate ($8^1/_2$-by-11 heavy paper, embossed) admitting me to the class of my graduating year, in what was, to me, a far future. Princeton sent a certificate (heavy paper, embossed, half-page size) admitting me to a class graduating the same year, equally far away. Though the year was easy enough to sum to, I had not, when making applications, been thinking of my college graduation year. Perhaps the graduating year is something all students from educated families knew to think of. My mother graduated college while I was in graduate school, and so we realized you could graduate anytime. We did not approach college with that kind of regimented certainty, though I can proudly report that I finished the College at the University of Chicago in the four standard years.

In advance of attending college, with Ma Howell already gone and silent to our college efforts, the certificates embossed with Princeton and Harvard insignias dissuaded me with their haughty, blaring focus on prestige. These certificates of admission to tony white communities unnerved rather than appealed to me. I went to the University of Chicago in large part because Chicago. My classes, however, were 99.8 percent white—as they would have been at Harvard or Princeton. But in Chicago, there was Chicago.

No denying that city, and its Black history, and its South Side. I didn't want to leave the whole sight line of my culture behind, even if I went to a white college. I wanted to be able to access a Black community, to be able to see Black people without boarding a jet or taking a train to other climes. I wanted to hear Black people play live music within a distance that could be traveled in an evening.

While an undergraduate, I attended Jeremiah Wright's church, Trinity, which was on the South Side and accessible. Rev. Wright was a well-known theologian, in the Black Baptist community. When you went to Chicago, "to find a new church home," Rev. Wright's church was number one on your visitation list. I took the bus on Sundays to hear Jeremiah Wright preach in the tradition of Charles Adams of Hartford Avenue Baptist Church, in Detroit; and Henry C. Gregory, of Shiloh Baptist Church, in Washington, DC. Both these men were present in my childhood and instrumental in helping me build a perspective of faith in a higher power and Christian charity as a way of life. Both of them were role models, spiritual pillars of my youth, and both counseled me when I called, crying, that U of C was too hard.

Jeremiah Wright was instrumental to my college years; he preached a tradition I recognized. He called for transformation in the name of an omnipotent God. Referred to by some as liberation theology, Rev. Wright's preaching was part and parcel of my Chicago experience: his biblical and theoretical teachings I associated with my school, with my past, and with the life of the mind. Jeremiah Wright helped me bridge U of C and my history. He could have done me no greater favor.

By choosing the University of Chicago, I was able to stave off risk and fear of total Oreocity. By matriculating into an isolated and reified swirl of white values, white intellectualism, white materialism, white preference, I worried I might lose myself. I understood how formative an experience college would be. My first years on my own. I did not trust the joyful whiteness of the manicured, glorified Ivy League school. The adult I wanted to make of myself needed to be not too far away from the grit and growl of urban America. The future is the flower of the past, and I did not want to seed my independence in the white sands of leisure and exceptionalism. One of the many major truths I learned from my phalanx of grandmothers is: *It behooves you to remember where you come from.*

My INTENTION FOR COLLEGE WAS to learn to speak of our history and accomplishments and affinities and preferences and perceptions with an array of new words. After undergraduate, I stayed in Chicago and studied for a master's in applied statistics. So, I was there when the South Side Black community beckoned in a historic way by welcoming the great and legendary Nina Simone to present a concert, as the first event after the revitalization of the South Shore Country Club. A singular, historic venue, the reopened South Shore Country Club billed a singular, historic event. I could not believe I was going to see Nina Simone, and all I would have to do was take one bus. I was already a graduate student; I was educated some. I knew my preferences; I knew my heroes. That one Nina Simone performance made Chicago wholly worth the seven years I'd spent there. Nina Simone was a powerhouse and a treasure, and I was at that reopened country club early and with bells on.

I grew up on Nina Simone. I could sing Nina Simone before I'd ever heard of Toni Morrison—especially "Cherish," "Consummation," and "I Wish I Knew How It Would Feel to Be Free." Singing comes easily to children and certainly precedes being able to handle whopping books of literature, like Morrison's. Nina Simone and Nancy Wilson were two of my mother's favorite singers, and so we owned and played their actual LP albums, 33⅓ rpm, in our household. Those records are what we/I played when listening to music. While writing *The Good Negress*, my first novel, I came to understand that we all know our parents' favorite music as the first real music we know.

Before I learned of the expatriate as a concept, as a choice, I was mystified to learn that Nina Simone had moved to France. I developed a fantasy that I would also move to France: Josephine, Jimmy, Nina, me. When I met Nina Simone in Chicago, I realized already that my adulthood would not likely move me to France. In order to commit to an expatriate life, I would need to commit to artistry and to abandonment of these "united" states. At the time, I did not see artistry in my future. I had been convinced to be more pragmatic.

Further, my mother and I had already had a brouhaha over my leaving my own country. *Why would you abandon the country your grandparents bled to build?!* My mother has a fine vocabulary, but when she starts slinging it, you'd better get a catcher's mitt, or remove yourself from the arena. You might get hurt. It was no secret that "getting away" meant getting away from venomous and unrelenting American racism. My mother's position: This country is your home. You have been here for *generations*. You have the right to be here; this land is soaked with our blood.

I respect my mother's wisdom and point of view. I know my grandparents believed themselves righteous as Americans. They believed themselves making a freer future for us.

Morrison also admired Nina Simone. Alicia Keys (singer, songwriter, megastar, Black woman, pianist) expressed the same deep respect for Nina. When Keys explains her views on Simone's significance, she quotes Morrison, who said, "Nina Simone saved our lives."

Not everyone knows of Nina, her music, her activism, her life story, her importance to our culture. But you pass a certain test if you do know. Nina Simone brought fury and fierce musicality and instructions for revolution to the stage. If you know her catalogue, huge extra credit. Her significance and resonance and stature are inarguable; she made vast contributions to our struggle and our progress in her lifetime. If you know of Nina Simone's work and pressures, her voice and her power, you know an encapsulated story of Black America. You have an overview of how Black genius cracks the concrete of racism. You might agree with Morrison that Nina saved our lives.

I went to the concert alone. None of the few Black students at Chicago at the time were people who recognized or wanted to pursue a sighting of Nina Simone. Not a problem, I'm a loner, and I was fine not to have my Nina Simone experience interfered with, in any way. My experience was perfect as it was. Nina was still in fine form then. Because I knew her catalogue almost intimately, I could recognize her improvisations. After a powerful piano solo, I clapped loudly—as jazz decorum demands. I found myself clapping almost alone, but—oh well, I was willing. I was among squares. While my singular hand claps rang out, Nina belted into the mic, "I need that applause, I need that applause." Other people then joined in.

At the end of that concert, I waited at the backstage entrance and was eventually invited into Nina Simone's dressing room. Of course, I told her I was the lone one clapping. I believe

I had flowers, just in case I got to meet her directly. And so, there I was, standing within three feet of the illustrious Nina Simone. A driven musician and composer whose work predated my awareness, full stop. Nina had a little-known a cappella song called "Consummation," about a little girl who wants to befriend another little girl, and the mother says no. You can guess why. One girl is white and the other Black, and so this house visiting is just not done. This little playdate story is a sleeper alongside Nina's bellowing ballads. In the song "Consummation," the little brown girl—*She's as old as me*—looks like chocolate. They are both in first grade, but I was in second grade learning this song. I could sing the whole song then, and I can sing the whole song now.

NINA SIMONE'S DEPTH, COMPLEXITY, AND seriousness were nakedly observable. You walked into her mighty power like you'd passed through an invisible wall. You could pass through, but then you were *inside* a universe where Nina Simone took up all the space. There was no option but to watch her, listen, attend. Her propensities could not be ignored. You gave her a piano, or a cause, or an anthem she'd composed, and she might go full nuclear. Blow the whole place open. You had words to deal with, percussive piano to deal with, heavy harmonics to hear, real complaints, real thralls, real torrents, real documents of history. Decades of classical music study and practice retired to white history, to background.

GAINING THIS AUDIENCE WITH THE great Nina Simone had taken either all the time I'd spent in Chicago or my whole lifetime up to that point. For me, that experience, that meeting, recast the entire Chicago project into a journey that was meant to be. Sometimes life plays a long game. I would not have been in graduate school had I not gone to Chicago in the first place. I will always be a Chicago Maroon, but I will also always be forever grateful for my concert and those twenty minutes with Nina Simone. I emerged forever changed.

In the dressing room mirror, her gaze angled down. There: that profile, that shapely head. Incredible, strong arms; muscular hands, fingers stretching wide as skillets. Skin brown as tree bark. She commanded the room no matter what angle she took, no matter that a moment went silent or demure. Nina Simone was such an amazing package, such a force, such a voice. Punching high with Black logic battling decades of belligerent white debasements.

At the South Shore Country Club, I verified that, yes, she lived in France. (My planned questions unfurled.) "Is your French amazing?" I asked, probably too cheerfully. I fantasized that her musicality granted her mellifluous French.

"I speak street French," Nina Simone answered, almost desultorily, looking directly at me in the mirror, and then away. I only realized that we were making eye contact through the mirror when she looked away. We stood in basically three different postures in her dressing room that night: I could not have been there more than fifteen or twenty minutes, if that long. But the time seemed much longer, a monumental hour squeezed into a moment. This was my first experience ever in any backstage.

I understood "street French" immediately; made perfect

sense. Here again: an artist speaking volumes in few words. She had words in French that she could line up together to make herself understood. Perhaps she'd also learned profanity. Now, looking back, I see I could have asked so much more. But I was just twenty-five. I had not yet left the country. I had only so much, and flowers, to bring.

Pretty quickly, during a pause in my run of pre-planned questions, Nina turned to her man/manager/gentleman sentinel and said, "Find out what she wants."

Of course, I stood up. Time to go. I smiled but did not laugh aloud. The gentleman turned and asked what I wanted, what I'd come for.

I answered that I'd just come to see Ms. Simone to thank her for the music, to tell her how much I appreciated her. To tell her that her songs had coursed through my whole life. I was no longer talking to Nina, but I stood talking to him. She was so funny, how she handed me off. She looked at him and said this whole inside thing: *I don't know this kid. What is she doing here?* "Find out what she wants."

The man said, "We have a concert in London at the end of next month. Would you like to come?"

I smiled and did not roll my eyes. I had bus money, not London money. And what kind of invitation was he offering, anyway? Was I to make flight reservations, book a hotel, fly over to London, and go to a named theater on a specified date? Take a black cab? Stop in at will call for tickets left in my name?

He asked me to write my name down, phone number. Back then, those were the coordinates. I wrote down my information, I thanked them for inviting me to London. I told them I was a graduate student and that I wouldn't be coming to London next month.

"If you change your mind," he started to answer, but I had turned.

"Thank you so much, Miss Simone," I said. I left the small room changed, charmed, elated.

As an undergraduate, I went to a big auditorium downtown and saw Sarah Vaughan live. Another monumental musical evening—creating the contours of my adulthood. I discovered my preference for live music only once I left home. Arthur Jafa, filmmaker, is someone I came to know, in New York. He and I talked about musicians and how keeping up with the musicians, emulating the musicians, responding to music, seemed necessary for our (different) arts. Music leads revolution. So history shows. Once I discovered how much live music inspired me, I started writing without pressure. I started working with music in the background, accomplishing so much by maintaining a rhythm, listening to their methods, letting the pencil cross the page with Eric Dolphy on the horn, or Monk on keys, or Sarah crooning, her lyrics sailing, soothing.

Sarah Vaughan helped me understand how music can carry you, how our musical history can fuel our newer arts. Seeing Sarah Vaughan helped me realize there is no barrier in the hungry air between legend and reach. If you angle your attention toward your passion, knowledge, heroes, sheroes—you can close any gap. You can join the party. You can look, see, watch, even dance. You can also imagine—this chocolate lady with the velvet voice—innovating, singing, sliding. Making music.

Making history. Making money. Making change. Making me understand life as oyster.

I was thrilled and overwhelmed to see the legendary Sassy, never considered that seeing her live was a thing that would happen in my life. That concert was a touchstone, a superpowerful experience resonating backward and also tugging me forward. My daughter's favorite bedtime music was from Sarah Vaughan's live album, *At Mister Kelly's*. Because that's the music we liked and the music we had. Because Sarah Vaughan had been out there, with her dark skin and huge talent. Because: Chicago.

THE GOOD NEGRESS

When I was twenty-nine, still years before I'd written a novel or met Morrison, I had a watershed moment: I'd done what my parents asked. My parents viewed writing, and the arts in general, as a ticket to starvation. Choose a more solid, stable profession, they urged. You will need something to fall back on. I did ask the obvious question: What if I don't fall back? But my parents were vociferous about their concern; they wanted me to be practical. So, I studied political science, intending to go to law school. The American Bar Association was headquartered in Chicago, so I was fortunate to be able to work there. Many of the lawyers I met in my job had half-finished novels in their desk drawers. I quietly and immediately committed to not becoming an attorney with a novel packed away.

Law and writing develop and depend on top-notch thinking skills. As an alternative to law school, I worked on a master's in statistics in the social sciences and launched a career as a numbers cruncher. I was making a fine living—which satisfied my parents and me—so, why not test my dream and see what happened? I wanted to know whether I had potential as a writer. Writing had been what I'd wanted to do since . . . well, since learning that somebody wrote everything I was reading.

I DECIDED TO WRITE (or, more precisely, draft) a novel. Easier decided than done.

Other people had written novels, so the task could not be impossible. Countless others before me had learned and polished and published. The effort demanded loads of work and lots of study, both of which I freely gave.

I went straightaway to homework: making myself reading and practice assignments, given that I had not been an English major. Writers who led me to the word were my first course of self-study: Alice Walker (archaeologic storytelling), Barbara Kingsolver (strong-hinge verbs), Toni Morrison (lyrical, risky, deeply imaginative storytelling), Maya Angelou (narrative nonfiction), June Jordan (philosophy and architectural poetics), Willa Cather (capacious, landed women in constricted times), Gayl Jones (literary horror), James Baldwin (classic structure, shouting Black). The writers I cut my teeth on were assembled in my first workrooms and lay open as textbooks. Reading books when you already know the dramatic arc educates much more efficiently. I had a plan: reread, analyze, count scenes, study surprise. I created a study strategy for learning how writing actually worked. Once I started studying scenes, my whole world changed. Getting to the point where I could recognize the unit of dramatic construc-tion was a watershed moment in my career as a writer. Took me too long, but I arrived.

There were no straight lines from reading me to writer me. No clear trajectory. No specific directions. I had to do my homework and find my way. When you write, you have to motivate yourself. Nobody knows what you're doing. Nobody cares until the work is done. Nobody can enjoy a half-finished work. Not that many people can advise you. Not that many people think the choice to write is wise. My blunt decision to give myself a test yielded *The Good Negress*. The project took three times the time I projected.

I MODELED MY WRITING PRACTICE after what I knew of Morrison. Not what I knew of her work, but what I knew of her practice. Daily, early in the mornings, I called forth both the strategy and the confidence Morrison so bluntly spoke of and modeled. *Get up early and start. Don't worry about starting late.*

Of course, "get up early" means get up; rise when you wake, instead of turning over and calling yourself back to sleep. And "starting late" does not mean late in the day, but late in life. Writ-ing benefits from wisdom, and wisdom comes with age.

I learned how to put the cusp of sleep in service. Before the day takes over, I am dreamier, more imaginative, more steeped in wild belief. Let the day dawn over your efforts. Your mind just might reach deep into the murky maw of creativity and surprise you. Morrison spoke bluntly of drinking her coffee in the dark. Morrison famously felt she was smarter before dawn.

Morrison was not one to offer a lot of detailed advice. She

thought you should decide for you. Particularity, specificity—of vision, of thought, of activity—is where the action is, where the uniqueness lives, where your imagination shows its plumes and colors. Or so Morrison contended. Specificity, uniqueness of vision, and expression—these are the approaches that reign. We artists learn to allow our particular vision to rain down on us, to drench us, to wash us awake. We stand in place to receive, maybe with our arms thrown wide.

IN THE GOOD NEGRESS, I attempted to write a story of a "negro-nobody" family and to show that fine-tuned and complex lives are led, and faced, and finessed, by the very same families and young people our society routinely treats as detritus.

The first time I heard this word spoken aloud, *detritus*, I was listening to Morrison. She was giving a public lecture, and I realized instantly that I would have pronounced the word incorrectly. I recognized the spelling, and the Latin, and the meaning. I'm sure there was a pronunciation guide in the dictionary, informing not just of Latin etymology, but also of the spoken emphasis on "trite." *Deh-TRITE-us*, listening to Morrison taught me. The word was not new to me as written, but I had never tried to speak it aloud. When people know a word but mispronounce it, you know they've learned the word from reading. Learning from reading is to be encouraged, to be celebrated, without exception. The meaning of *detritus* is basically "trash"; material (or people, if you are ruthless or racist or unconscious) that can be dispensed with, or disposed of, to no consequence. That was bad-assery, on Morrison's part—to bring *detritus* into currency, into fluency, into everyday speech. Precision, to so aptly define how routinely and caustically and inhumanely our lives are preemptively devalued, our futures trampled in advance, our options erased as we are kicked to the curb.

Living Under Limits

Most every Black child born is subjected to racist practices often aimed at shutting down Black potential at or near birth. Racist practices shunt Black people off into arenas of inattention or, worse, states of surveillance, cages, relentless negative attention, banishment to Povertyland. From now backward into history: Shooting Blacks in the street, duly recorded and replayed round the world. Underfunding schools. Limiting work to physical or service jobs. Limiting access to education. Removing possibilities for professionalism. Creating and enforcing rigid residential constraints. Maintaining real estate exclusion laws and practices. Depressing salaries, where there is pay. Cheating. Beating. Burning down whole towns. Lynching boys (just babies) and men (breadwinners, husbands, somebody's brother, somebody's man, somebody's inspiration, some lady's son). Offering only sharecropping. Outlawing learning to count. Punishing learning to read. Whipping at will. Normalizing and practicing routinized disrespect. Yanking Black names and changing them. Forbidding nonwhite languages. Separating families. "Selling" people, or selling "people." Listing Negroes as property when listing and counting assets. Standing people up at market, having them inspected, moving them in the interest of owner-class financial gain. Destroying Black individualism, coercing Black energies and claiming the fruits—for white personal wealth, white family wealth, regional, state, and national wealth. Using market antics and presumptions that swell the "seller's" wealth. Corrosively dehumanizing people, making of them market wares. Creating a dispensable class of people, controlling them, shunning them, shuffling them around. Keeping them poor, barely clothed, disallowed. Pretending they are not people. Fostering callous unconcern about their demise or murder. And then, at the end, the laborers have nothing.

Racist violence and abuse is evil, and evil clings. History has proven that racism can neither quash the mind, divinely made, nor silence the soul, divinely held. Full stop.

Morrison's landscapes and episodes contained these people and their sorrows and their indefatigable human song. You can withdraw humanity from your consciousness and your actions; you can make a devil of yourself. You can fashion yourself a trickster and a thief. But the humanity of the despised will not disappear, no matter what actions are taken.

TONI MORRISON WROTE ABOUT Black triumph and Black dehumanizing, inventing character and imagining place. Her eleven novels put greed into a burlap sack and hung it up there where a light fixture might be, a mounted symbol of

95

avarice and misery, an isolated emblem of how money drives men—one woman's calm, intentional preservation.

In Lorain, Morrison was spared a youth of virulent segregation. Morrison's grandparents fled the vicious South to Lorain, Ohio. Multicultural, industrial, a haven for her parents—Lorain enveloped Chloe and her curiosities, did not bar her from the library, did not shoo her away from school. Had she been worse off and been born in 1931 in the Alabama her grandparents escaped, she would not have been allowed to read. When you cannot read, you cannot write. Those menacing forces that hobble literacy and therefore kneecap life are still alive in America. There are laissez-faire forms of hindering literacy; there is also direct and active malignancy, reaching into the future from times that should have gone by.

Not until matriculating at Howard, engaging with her peers on the Hilltop (Howard's nickname), did Morrison directly encounter the "stand off" racism, the "get back" admonishments, the "you are inferior" mythology in the form of infrastructure separation. Her parents and her elders certainly knew the truth of white violence; Morrison was not secretive about the trauma that drove her family from the mean, whipping South to the grinding, industrial North. Black people struggled to survive in both imagined "two parts" of our nation. Morrison's work shines a spotlight on history, both nurturing and malign. Morrison asserted that we all write in search of our ancestors. At best and most benign, mean shenanigans work hard to make nobodies of Negroes and to continue the manufacture of life under limits. At worst or most malign, our lives don't matter, and neither do our deaths. Like the construct of race, the making of a nobody results from invention and malintent combined, woven together, devilishly admired. Limits create an oppressively low sky.

FOR FOUR CENTURIES AND COUNTING, our country has lied and pretended that we somehow "naturally" have a whole swathe of "Negro nobodies." Enormous, relentless, resounding falsehood leading to an explosive (and expansive and expensive) waste of minds. Perfectly good brains going to seed. Year after year. Generation after generation. The manufacture of inferiority is necessary for the white mirage of superiority.

Morrison simultaneously observed and dismissed this nobody-ness idea. Morrison eliminated this falsehood from the daily lives of those who bore the weight. Her characters certainly have confrontations with oppressors and with oppression, but beyond confrontation, we were presented with agency over our lives. Human beings are born this way—to be agents on their own behalf. The limits imposed on us were present in her fiction, but not omnipresent.

MORRISON PARTICIPATED IN MANY RECORDED interviews, television interviews, movies. Morrison will forever be all over "the interwebs." Of her many remarks preserved on film, I have two favorites. In one interview, Morrison merely says, in answer to some question about our history, "After all we've been through."

In five words, Morrison raises the whole scourge and triumph of our past; she also manages to level an accusation in that short line.

After all we've been through, you should know . . .

After all we've been through, you should see . . .

After all we've been through, you should respect . . .

After all we've been through, you should invest in . . .

After all we've been through, you should repair . . .

After all we've been through, you should not be asking the same asinine questions, decade after decade, century after century.

Examine the source of the problem, buddy; the source of the problem is you.

In another important clip, in an interview with Charlie Rose, Morrison makes possibly her most important recorded remark ever: "If you can only be tall because somebody else is on their knees, then you have a serious problem. And my feeling is, white people have a serious problem." Morrison brings to the table forthright reality: "feeling" tall because you've forced someone else to half their height is ludicrous and deceptive, damn near diabolical. Morrison wielded such a strong mind; she used her ideas like archery. *Where's the target? Move out of the way. Quiet, please.*

In this interview, Morrison calmly rails against the construct we call race. She defines racism as "a corruption, a distortion and a waste." A profound neurosis, she continues, "that nobody is willing to examine for what it is." Brevity and philosophy brilliantly torquing round each other, the axis being the clear though unstated challenge: *Question where you are in this scenario.*

My mother, a student of philosophy herself, also rallied for this clarity. To my sisters and me, all three researchers, she has all our lives insisted, "You all are studying the wrong issues." Why ask why Black people are poor? Why ask why Black people do not finish the schools that contain them? Why not ask about or at least acknowledge the dangerous pathologies of rampant racism, excessive aggression, violent tendencies, unrelenting greed, repeated practices of inhumanity? Be clear where the problems lie. Investigate the real problems; do not be distracted investigating scapegoats. Consider who is brutal; consider who demeans; consider who steals opportunity, and futures, and peace.

Racism keeps you from expecting, from anticipating, from pursuing, from interrogating, from investing in your own waiting talents; racism keeps you from believing in your own real personhood. Victims of racism, in our country, are held responsible for the racism inflicted against them.

You can't make progress because of racism? Why not?

You can't buy a house because of racism? Yet and still, why are you poor?

You can't find success in college, or in employment, because of long-term literacy laws and problematic school preparation? You really should be better able to compete.

You have no financial legacy to leave to your children? You really should learn how money works. You never bought a house? Why not?

A translation of this cyclical conundrum (or catastrophe), in far more words than Morrison might use, could be this: Some people, racially specified, must spend their lives or their talents on their knees or kneecapped. Simultaneously, other people, also racially specified, armed with weapons (a whip, a branch, a pistol, a law, a mansion, ease, good health, low stress), stride around insisting, *I am better, I am most deserving, I am endowed.*

Constructing her novels, Morrison leaned into our heated, jostled, labyrinthine, often exuberant and accomplished Black lives. Morrison's protagonists tend to be wildly inventive and sometimes brutally determined to accomplish their goals, tend to their motives, even given the attenuated and sparse resources available to them. Success takes many forms in fiction and in life; malignant treatment over whole lifetimes turns basic survival into success. There is no scarcity of Black success in the real world, either. Nor is there any scarcity of Black intrigue. Complicated people live in Morrison's stories, and most of them are Black. Offstage, but fully present, brutality continues to try to beat Black thriving to death.

Any of us could become anything. If we can see it, we can be it. History on top of history piles on, blinding us, trying to keep us from seeing life, from seeing possibility, seeing art, seeing beauty, seeing ourselves fully. History and the present tense together prove that Black genius is observable and not a rarity. This was Morrison's position. There's no scarcity of Black genius. If you believe there is, you don't have eyes.

Morrison, of course, was an outsize model of Black genius and Black success. As was Louis Armstrong, whose spirit and talent and wailing trumpet rose as the inciting incident in *Playing in the Dark*.

Birth of a Writer

To introduce *The Good Negress*, or to celebrate finishing, I made my own little circulating copy, with a yellow card stock title page and a plastic protective cover. I got twenty-five copies spiral bound, so anyone who wanted to read could carry the manuscript—outside, on the train, from room to room. This was a prepublication marketing stroke: I distributed the twenty-five copies only to people who knew me, and loved me, and were connected to publishing. I was unknown and unconnected then, and I started by checking out where those manuscript copies might land.

One of my graduate school professors, Tom McDonough (kind man and Oscar winner), sent a copy of *The Good Negress* to the Center for Documentary Studies at Duke. People at the center sent the book to Algonquin, and Algonquin acquired the book. They sent me a contract. So, I wrote a query letter, referencing the contract, which I sent, unreferred, to Toni Morrison's agent, Lynn Nesbit, and to Alice Walker's agent, Wendy Weil. I faxed both letters in, and Wendy Weil gave me a call. After we talked, she agreed to represent me. And there I was, with a manuscript that I had rewritten dozens of times, a generous and proactive teacher, a contract that was small but actual, an agent of the highest order, and a promise: publication.

THE EDITORIAL PROCESS IS A PROCESS. It takes time; there are many steps. In my case, things were rocky (enormous understatement). The publishing process was more dramatic and argumentative than I'd anticipated.

Because *The Good Negress* was my first time out of the gate, I didn't know what to expect, so I just tried to roll with the shenanigans, headed toward the goal. My first editor launched our engagement beautifully; she was lovely, almost legendary, and had worked in publishing for years. She was quintessentially literate—from one of the finest literature educations in the South; she seemed to want or to need to discuss everything, from typo to theory. In the beginning, I loved the particularities of editorial considerations. When she sent the manuscript back to me, she cautioned me not to become overwhelmed. You only have to pay attention to the pages with the sticky notes, she said. I opened the package she sent with excitement and anticipation and delight. Of the two-hundred-something pages I'd submitted, there were maybe thirty that did not have sticky notes on them. I was stunned though not dejected. I had been warned. I was curious about what all this commentary could be. There were small matters, and some good suggestions, but mainly there was a building and brewing argument that I'd been wrong about how I chose to handle what was to the editor a chasm between how Black people think versus how Black people speak. The exchange we had about Black people's consciousness versus Black people's spoken word grew from discussion to disagreement. The editor vehemently believed what she described to me in this way: Just because Black people speak in dialect does not mean they *think* in dialect. No matter how people speak, they think they're speaking the King's English. She argued that all the main character's thoughts should be *written* in the King's English, even if the character primarily *speaks* dialect.

Her logic was neither logical nor supportable, to me.

The argument eventually became a brutal brouhaha. The editor shifted in my mind from "my editor" to "the editor," after she insisted that I did not understand the distinction between my main character's mental process and her spoken word. I chafed at being told how Black people think versus speak by a white woman intimately familiar with neither. After an extended hullabaloo (weeks long), the editor volunteered to release me from my contract. That would of course be a terrible ending to the process—no debut novel for me. We tussled intellectually. Our distance in cultural understanding and intellectual positioning morphed into dissonance and friction.

I wrote a long, explanatory editorial memo, taking pains to outline the evolutionary theory behind the main character's progressive dialect in the narrative. Three levels of dialect speech in the novel:

1. deep/rural, encoded intimate—early childhood speech;
2. transitional, toward public facing—the age of social and personal awareness;
3. mature and reaching for worldly—ambition becomes a locus of control.

Eventually, this editorial memo turned into a promotional essay that Algonquin published and also gifted; it was titled "All Lined Up and Smiling." As an artifact of this long argument, and of the tussle over my first novel, the essay felt like a gift of an outcome. (Years ahead of all this, when the road ahead for my cowboy novel starts to seem impassable, I expect that in the end, all will be well. I may have been incorrect about this, or, I may not yet have reached the end.)

The Good Negress moves on emotional time. The novel begins at the highest point of drama in a young girl's childhood, but you are informed immediately that the narrator has matured, has survived, and, based on her diction, perception, articulation, and sense of humor, has managed (finally) to thrive. The language fluency of the main character evolves, which matches language development in real life. Reading Morrison had already freed me from the boring drone of chronology, which represented huge, enormous liberation. Especially in a writing career. I suppose I could have learned how to rework chronology from other writers, but I learned from her. There is no need to go from Tuesday to Friday just because the calendar says so. When you write, you go from important to important, from significant to significant, from resonant to revolutionary. You don't marry your story to any unexamined march of dates.

In my twenties, I discovered the Latin roots of the names of the months of our calendar. You can see the forced divergence if you consider the latter part of the year. September has a root word, *seven*; and October has a root word, *eight*. Similarly, November matches *nine*, and December matches *ten*. So, why are we two months off? Because Roman dictator Julius Caesar and the first Roman emperor, Caesar Augustus, wanted to be represented as the world counts time. So, they inserted themselves. September would have been where July now lives, and October would have been the eighth month, as planned.

My outrage related less to *that* they'd done this than to that I hadn't known. At the time, I hadn't a clue about these cats. I was outdone to have had my calendar shifted with such alacrity. The ways in which "people" upended things to suit themselves just jarred me. This is a perfect example of hegemonic power. Desire for this level of power apparently courses through the souls of (white?) men.

The calendar has been imperialized in other ways, too. I was born on April 1. Ribbed all my life for being born on the joke day of the year. After my mother delivered me, at 5:30 on a weekday, they called my father to let him know I'd been born. He thought his brother was joking and didn't get to the hospital until 9 p.m., when my mother's not showing up at home convinced him.

I later learned that April, because of planting season, had been the start of the year in the agrarian age. Someone thought the New Year would be better following the birth of Christ, so the New Year moved, hegemonically, to January. Farmers were up in arms. Some of them refused to participate. The New Year in the middle of the cold? Why? Moving the New Year? What for? Many farmers refused, rejected this logic, rejected this edict, this imperialist nonsense. They maintained April 1 as the New Year. In order to "persuade," the imperialists branded the resistant farmers, and their antique New Year, as April Fools. They gave the New Year to January and ridiculed the holdouts. Made a joke of what had become the farmers' day of resistance. This calmed me about my birthday. I have always applauded resistance, since so much of what I need to save my life and live my truth requires that I resist hegemony, supremacy, invisibility. I was twelve or thirteen when I started to imagine that I could have been born on New Year's Day. More than the antique New Year, it's the resistance that I love.

I'm not sure the editor expected me to invoke a theory of language development. Eventually, I worked my way through a couple of other editors at Algonquin, and eventually the book was reconsidered for consistency, polished for syntax, defended for emotional chronology, and then, finally, was done.

After all the editing hoopla had been resolved, I thought *The Good Negress* would be smoothly on her way to market. It's hilarious that at this point I cannot remember the penultimate title, but we didn't have a title we could agree on. I will never forget that I was at Algonquin's offices in New York City; it was nine o'clock at night. We had just finished one of a million things, and we needed a title yesterday.

ELISABETH SCHARLATT, PUBLISHER AT ALGONQUIN, had engaged with me, and she encouraged me once the novel shenanigans turned catastrophic. Elisabeth brought *The Good Negress* across the finish line. One night, late in the publishing process, she sat on the edge of her chair across from me. The place had emptied, and her office was dim. I remember it being close to 9 p.m., which is when I like to head toward bed, since I mostly get up at 4:30.

Elisabeth stared at me resolutely; she looked at the time. Tell me the story again, she commanded, and I replayed the short version:

The novel is about the differences in how we raise boys and girls. The main character, Denise—who is a smart cookie, even though she has not been educated well—returns to Detroit from deep rural Virginia and tries to renegotiate a place for herself in her family. She does the same at school, and then she does the same when she finds she can get a job. Meanwhile, her schoolteacher has decided to mentor her and doesn't want Denise accepting the menial, rag-waving work she's being offered. Her teacher wants her to be a teacher or a nurse. She wants to convince Denise to study rather than wipe and clean and sweep. The teacher pleads with Denise: "You are a smart girl. You can do more. Those people at that department store are just trying to make you a good little negress, and that does not have to be our lot anymore . . ."

The phrase "a good little negress" just rolled off my tongue, but Elisabeth's eyes widened, and I followed suit. This wasn't the first time I'd said this, but at this last minute, the words seemed like the title, and a gift.

My agent, Wendy, said, "You can't call your book that. It's like saying 'a good Jewess.' No one says that."

Of course, I was too outside, too unfamiliar to know whether *Jewess* was an okay term to use, as it was not a term I used. Wendy checked with her people to find out if *Jewess* was acceptable usage, which I paid little mind to because *Negress* had been my word.

Negress as a word had fallen out of favor—like *negro*, and *Negro*, and all the curses and slights that preceded these. In its original, common usage, *negress* was not considered a polite term, which was what Wendy was referencing. My project involved how language affects us: oppresses us, diminishes us, violates us, means one thing at one time and something different years later or before.

Wendy asked, rather irritably, "Is that phrase in the book? Do you actually use the words 'good little negress' in the novel? If you're going to use that as your title, you damn well better have those words in the book. Otherwise . . ."

The title pressure was pretty extreme. I had been coached: A title is a marketing decision. No one knows your name. You have to depend on the title to get people to pick up the book. The title has to grab people. It's okay if it alarms people. But it can't be flat. It can't be easily ignored.

We were down to the wire.

Wendy repeated, "It has to be in the book."

Elisabeth said, "You have forty characters and three days."

"What do you mean?" I asked.

"You can change any forty characters. Not forty-one. You have three days to figure out where you're going to situate the title in the book."

These were high jinks.

"Characters," in publishing parlance, refers to the combinations of letters and spaces that an insertion or deletion makes up. The book was already typeset, which meant it was ready for galley production. The pagination could not be disrupted—and so, Elisabeth's "forty characters." I could use only that many characters and not affect the pagination. It was a curious exercise, but I followed her directions, and the whole title madness finally calmed down.

Finding a place for the title somewhere in the book, in the mouth of one of my characters, enabled me to revisit my intent in writing the novel: to reach into recent history and try to draw out our complexities, including our linguistic land mines and booby traps. I found a place in the main text for my title, which permitted us to settle the cover, and permitted Algonquin to (finally) send the manuscript file to the press for printing.

I then turned my attention to my book party. I wanted to have a lovely teatime shindig. I had a vision of our being assembled at the magic hour, when the sun started to wane over Manhattan. Light withdraws from every day, from every date. And the sun was setting on my life as an unpublished author.

ONCE *THE GOOD NEGRESS* WAS titled and tufted into galleys, Algonquin designed a beautiful ivory-and-deep-brown galley cover and sent the book out as the publisher's Christmas gift that year. The galley cover loosely emulated a woodblock print and, so, was visually compelling—good for gifts. The Center for Documentary Studies applauded again. Wayne Ponds, a director of public programs at the National Humanities Center, read the galley and asked for another copy; he forwarded the second Christmas galley to Morrison, who was on the center's board then.

Wayne Ponds for years ran a public radio show called *Soundings*, based at the National Humanities Center in Raleigh-Durham. He invited me to come there to record a show, which was where he told me the story of sending the galley of my book to Morrison, of receiving a note from her, of her thanking him, of his treasuring the note, and of him faxing Morrison's handwritten response to Algonquin.

Morrison remarked that she found *The Good Negress* truly extraordinary. Elisabeth Scharlatt verified the note and asked

Morrison for permission to use her commendation as a blurb. Of course, I was elated, but I was nervous that we were overstepping. Elisabeth bluntly declared that Morrison knew what she was setting in motion. "She was an editor," Elisabeth reminded me, "she knows how this works. You just watch, honey," she teased. She might even have winked.

Within a few days, Morrison gave her permission, and then—pandemonium. People behaved as if I had won a prize. I was already at Hedgebrook, a beautiful, peaceful, enriching women's writing colony in Puget Sound, busy drafting my second book, my cowboy story. There, the fax machine started beeping. (A different technological age.) This was my first writing retreat ever, where I lived in Owl House and daily walked the soft turf. I feasted my eyes on awe-striking northwestern trees. Nothing like the northeastern trees, which looked young and scrawny by comparison. Several weeks into a previously unseen quiet, I became only the fifth or sixth person Morrison had blurbed in her career. By this ink and generosity, and by this back-and-forth, my career and my life changed all at once.

I SCHEDULED MY RELEASE PARTY for late afternoon/early evening, figuring people could go have a New York City night on the town afterward. Older people, like my mother, could come to my party and still be seated for the nightly news. The door closing on the day is treated romantically in our culture. So, the book party was from four thirty-ish until sunset. An easy hour to love.

My beautiful book party was held in Rose Hall, at Lincoln Center. Big windows, facing west. Tenth floor. We invited good friends and jazz people, the folks I'd been hanging out with during my few years in the city. My partner then was deputy director of Jazz at Lincoln Center. She got the room for me and helped me shape an invitation list across the literary and jazz scenes. Because it was an elevator building, and because this was New York City, the party was also supremely accessible, so even my disabled friend from college, Beth Sutter, could get there. She came from Philadelphia, struggling in on her silver crutches, and was able to share a highlight of my life. I was enormously happy to see her. She was determined to make this event and had been building strength for the trip all the while I was working and editing and arguing with my editor(s). She was able to come up in the elevator and walk unimpeded into the room. I'd had to investigate all the travel paths in advance. That task was one among many on my very long checklist. The moment, I think, was a highlight of Beth's life—and mine. For me, I was publishing; for her, she was having a shared experience in a faraway place. We able-bodied people don't think enough about accessibility.

Elisabeth Scharlatt also deserved to invite people to the party, so I raised the question of how many she might invite from publishing. She was busy, as always, and seemed to listen with only one ear. I went on to explain about the time, the location. I offered her card stock invitations, in case she wanted to hand them out. She turned to face me, as she had done so many times as we wound the novel down from manuscript to bound book.

"Wait, what?" she said.

Elisabeth Scharlatt was a wunderkind in publishing. I

cannot catalogue how much energizing she could accomplish, how many moving parts she could manage. I explained again how the party was shaping up, where the party would be, who all had been invited.

Elisabeth always had several channels running at once, but she repeated the names she knew: newsman Ed Bradley; impresario George Wein and his wife, Joyce; trumpeter Wynton Marsalis; bassist Lonnie Plaxico; jazz vocalist Cassandra Wilson.

"I don't know if they'll all come," I said. "Depends on if they're in town on the date." March 31, 1995—the eve of my birthday, and the birthday of my first book. A heady time. An antique New Year's Eve. I could finally plan a celebratory moment.

Elisabeth took out a notepad, seeming to change the subject. I wasn't watching what she was writing. I thought we'd lost the plot. But no, she was shifting gears.

"Oh, honey," she said. "I'm glad we had this conversation. We're going to have to get you better hors d'oeuvres. And flowers. We need flowers."

The party was better than fabulous. Elegant. Very New York. The sunset performed its gorgeous routine over the Hudson. The view did not disappoint. There was just one center table, an eight-foot round, in the middle of that gorgeous room. An abundance of hefty flowers splayed out from the heart of the table, surrounded by finger food laid out in concentric circles. The book had finally arrived.

I wore a white boatneck dress I'd found at Barneys, ankle-length with ballet flats. A slim shift decorated with understated lace. Seemed that everybody I loved was there. I read aloud some; I mingled. It was a gorgeous night; a beautiful, serene, and celebratory end to a tumultuous editorial experience. Retrospect casts a soft light of beautiful.

Jon Pareles, jazz writer, sweetly and memorably remarked, "So many people dream of this, to write a book and see it come alive. Nobody will ever be able to take this away from you, A.J. Finishing a novel is a very big deal."

Eons ago, and I remember his perspective: the novel is the lawyer's dream, the novel is the dream of the writer who has yet to learn to write. The novel is the novelist's dream. For some people—geniuses with language or story or discipline or imagination (or all of the above)—perhaps the novel is the métier.

ONCE THE BOOK HIT THE streets, I was thrilled and surprised at its reception. It was a finalist for the *Los Angeles Times* Book Award for First Fiction, for the PEN/Faulkner Award, and for the IMPAC Dublin Literary Award. The American Academy of Arts and Letters awarded me a commendation for Distinguished Prose Fiction; Maya Lin won the prize for architecture that year. I met big-gun white writers for the first time in my life. I chatted with both John Updike and Kurt Vonnegut at the awards ceremony. Vonnegut was affable and dapper in his striped bow tie. I sat with William Styron at the lunch. I absolutely loved meeting Rose Styron, who wore a pale pink suit, jacket and skirt. I told John Updike that I felt like a raisin in a bowl of rice pudding at that event; he laughed, a little uncomfortably, though he said he could see my point.

All the finalist prizes had money awards attached, which was a new experience for me. In the first year, between the hardcover and paperback publication, I also kept track of reviews. I made a list; I don't know why. Now I know the uselessness of such list making. However, back then, I used a spreadsheet. *The Good Negress* garnered more than 150 reviews, and that seemed like a big deal at the time. When I got to 150 on my spreadsheet, I stopped. Nice round number.

Jane Tompkins, whose work I'd read and whose scholarship interests me, reviewed my book for the *Charlotte Observer*. Her review began, "I've never used the word genius in a book review before . . ." That was my favorite of the reviews. Especially coming from Jane Tompkins, who was an author I'd admired.

Ultimately, however, *The Good Negress* brought me to Toni Morrison. I didn't know her then, to invite her to my elegant launch party, but in certain ways, Morrison became my ultimate literary prize.

What About the Women?

I was selected for a Bunting Fellowship at Harvard in 1996, the year after the novel was released. The fellowship, which supported forty women each year, was founded by microbiologist Dr. Mary Bunting, who became the fifth president of Radcliffe in 1960. As president, Dr. Bunting advocated at the highest levels for women's standing in our country, by both her accomplishments and her reach. Mary Bunting wanted women to be drawn into the upper echelons, and she supported research to enable women to do their best work. In November 1961, because of her thought leadership and her pioneering work in starting to integrate the sexes at Harvard and Radcliffe, Bunting appeared on the cover of *Time* magazine. She was concerned then about women rising to their own best performances. What could women do, she asked, if supported and allowed? Like Morrison (and likely other geniuses and deep thinkers), Dr. Bunting began her work with a question. She answered that question by founding the Bunting Institute, which I benefited from in its fiftieth year.

Unforgettably, Mary Bunting came to speak to our cohort during 1997, my fellowship year. Mary Ingraham Bunting was in her eighties and somewhat frail when she sat down at the conference table where we were gathered. Her voice was thin, and her hair Grace Paley white (though not as risen), but her mind raised no queries. When it was time for her to speak, she stood and explained her thought process behind founding the Bunting Fellowship at Radcliffe. In what turned out to be only months before her death, she recounted how she had thought to establish the fellowship after the Soviet Union beat the United States to space by launching *Sputnik*. A whole world of research changed because of *Sputnik*, Dr. Bunting said; opportunities in science changed mightily—*for men*. What are we doing for the women? she remembered asking. And so, she planned what became the Bunting Institute.

Perhaps training your thoughts in pursuit of a question is genius behavior. I am reminded of the very famous Zora Neale Hurston quote: "There are years that ask questions and years that answer." Genius.

A few Bunting Fellows each year are artists, and there are scholars in all disciplines. Women chosen for the fellowship received a year of uninterrupted time, office space, and a salary, all to pursue innovation and excellence, to continue promising work.

I remember sitting back in my chair to listen to Dr. Bunting relate the Institute origin story. This pioneering woman, in the twilight of her life, was aligning us with *Sputnik*. She was telling us something we did not know. The microbiologist and college president who had designed a response to an infusion of investment in men had begun a program that now benefited me directly. What novelist would ever imagine that her work would one day be referenced in conjunction with *Sputnik*, with the space race? My sense of mission grew.

In 1964, Mary Bunting was sworn in as the first woman member to the Atomic Energy Commission. In his remarks at her appointment, President Lyndon Johnson repeatedly emphasized Mary Bunting as a mother and a wife and, almost secondarily, as a distinguished scientist, educator, and national leader. Johnson referred to her by only one name in his not-so-brief remarks: "Mrs. Bunting." That was his chosen form of address. Comical and enraging, from this distance.

With her words that day, Dr. Bunting brought us encouragement, expectation, and the background of our placement. Within a year, in January 1998, she too would leave the planet. Dr. Bunting's last years have been described as a sad story of frailty and memory loss, but when she spoke to us, her mind didn't appear to wander, though we had to sit perfectly still to be able to hear her thinning voice. What a grace, and a near miss. To have seen her, met her, to have heard her explain her thinking, to have had a moment to think of myself, of where she had placed me, all of us. Her contribution to our understanding—not to mention the time to work—felt like a great favor. Mary Bunting's visit was mind-expanding, and I felt lucky, especially given how soon after it she was gone.

Invited into the same cohort of Bunting Fellows, Farah Jasmine Griffin and I met that year. We spent our year at the Bunting working hard on new projects. Farah was working on her Billie Holiday book then, as I remember. I was roughing out my Black cowboys. The intellectual and social intimacy of that year carries the two of us along today.

Florence Ladd was the director of the Bunting Institute when we were there. Florence, who is African American and also a Howard graduate, studied with Toni Morrison in the English Department when they were undergraduates. Wofford (Toni) and Cawthorne (Florence) were in a poetry class together with a third student, a young, Howard man. Florence and Miss Chloe remembered their august teacher almost reverently, literary founding father Sterling Brown. They were studying on the Hilltop, which was the place to be; there are stories, particularly about their struggles there to *really* study Black.

Florence has been half-expat for as long as I've known her, living between Cambridge, Massachusetts, and a stone village in Burgundy, France. Chloe Wofford became Toni Morrison, literary luminary, and Florence became an exemplar and a champion in education administration. Ultimately, Florence did publish two novels. Florence's son, poet and musician Mike Ladd, is based in Paris, with his wife and two teenage children. Florence is an expat in part because her grandchildren are French.

Florence and I bonded over knowing Morrison, each at opposite ends of her life. In time, we developed a pattern: I brought Florence news of Miss Chloe from the States, and Florence brought me news of Morrison from France. I learned most of what I knew of Morrison's heralded 2006 residency at the Louvre from Florence. Later, I heard from novelist Edwidge Danticat about the Louvre experience. Edwidge is Haitian American and a French speaker, which helps with a residency in France. Edwidge had two small children then. Morrison arranged for an apartment and for Edwidge to bring both her daughters, and her mother to help care for them. Morrison had been writing when she was the mother of two small children herself. She knew what the days demanded. Edwidge reported that for her mother, visiting Paris had been a lifelong dream. Morrison made Paris happen for three generations of women in the Danticat family.

WE ALL KNOW MORRISON'S STORIES now. The stories she wrote. We know how she laid bare the travesties of our time and our before-times. We know how her mastery of language and mastery of literary form strengthened and complexified our presence in the literature, and strengthened and reflected our spirits. We are accustomed to the enormity of her insight. We need, and needed, her books. We know she wrote for African Americans—or Black folk, or Black people, or Negroes/negroes, or coloreds (to keep collecting the terms of Morrison's era)—and others were welcome to read and enjoy. African Americans, or Black folk, have been both foundational in America and canonical in American art and literature. As to literature, Morrison stands in boldface type. Her narratives frame our participation in *the full length* of American life. *They brought us here to get this country started,* our history and her narratives shout. The work seems almost inestimable, but the evidence is irrefutable. Her work is done and catalogued. Her record of accomplishment can neither be diminished or erased.

CALL ME GRAND.

Toni Morrison had many names; I called her Miss Chloe. This was a moniker she seemed to appreciate and which, I realize, was unique. Calling her Miss Chloe was efficient: I could identify myself and greet her at once. As an address, as a phrase, "Miss Chloe" was cryptic, abbreviated, brief yet robust. I referred to her as Morrison, but I addressed her as Miss Chloe. To be able, and be allowed, to call her Miss Chloe was a privilege and was special and was *inside*. Ultimately, I could see that she liked being called the name she'd pointedly left behind. I'm not sure whether she applauded my nerve, but she answered seamlessly and pleasantly.

Eight years older than my mother, Miss Chloe was a generation ahead of me. The convention of using "Miss" with your first name was a familiar mode of address for both of us. It signified respect, familiarity; greater intimacy than strangers, than people thrown together. It suggested you knew somebody—often from back in the day. "Miss" was an honorific, a statement of considered, cultivated, well-trained deference—to age, to wisdom, to significance. You called Black women elders Miss because they knew more than you, were ahead of you, were leading you, were allowing you to follow them. They did not dismiss you. They might deign to tell you what's what. But you were expected to observe them take slings and arrows in the interest of protecting your future, while you lagged behind, while you tried to grow up, while you contemplated skirts. That's why you called them Miss.

Note that the honorific "Miss" makes absolutely no reference to a state of being wed or unwed. The state of marriage was not enfolded in this expression of cross-generational intimacy and esteem. The naming convention was "Miss + First Name." To use this convention was to say you understood both the conventions of the community and the community itself.

All my years at Princeton, people referred to Morrison respectfully, sometimes demurely: *Miss Morrison, Miss Morrison.* Her audience called her Miss Morrison. Her assistant, Rene Boatman, very precisely referred to her as Ms., pronounced *Miz* Morrison. People close to her called her Toni. White people called her Toni. All those irritating interviewing white men called her Toni. Gloria Baldwin, Jimmy Baldwin's surviving sister, reports that she was introduced to Toni Morrison as Chloe, and that is what Gloria has always called her—Chloe. Gloria has known Morrison for decades. I can only imagine being peer enough to legit engage with "Chloe Toni Morrison." A different era, a different baseline. To think that James Baldwin called Toni Morrison Chloe is another wonder. Did she introduce herself that way? Did he reach back into her past, as I did? Was she not using Toni then, or not for him? Though we did have the gift of a friendship, I got all the backstory late and on the q.t. Miss Chloe and I had no history, though we would make one. But at that moment, I was a newbie: I rose to her sight line from the literati next gen.

By calling Toni Morrison Miss Chloe, I was acknowledging the power of naming, and reaching back to a fictive past. (Engaging with a herstory I did not live and could only reimagine.) A past that, in Toni Morrison's case, could never have occurred. "Miss First Name" is a convention from the neighborhood. Young people and children called older women from around the block Miss Pat, Miss Elaine, Miss Joanne.

Miss Chloe flew the coop early, and so was not around the block. By the time she would have been Miss Chloe, Toni had already risen up and taken over. The children and young people who might have called her Miss Chloe were growing up in a neighborhood in Ohio where she did not live. And children who might have called her Miss Somebody where she did live would have had to call her Miss Toni.

She and I were both aware that I was uncovering a name that had had no purchase. There was nobody to enact the convention until . . . there I was. Motivated by convention and by linguistic history, I found a name that would announce me, that would be affectionate, but that would carry an important layer of respect. As a form of address, the name "Toni" never once crossed my lips. I. Just. Was. Not. There.

I tested the name "Miss Chloe" first. She was wearing her trademark gray that day. We'd had a visit and had come to departure time. Although I considered bluntly announcing, *I've decided to call you Miss Chloe*—I didn't. Early on, we had a conversation about how early in my youth I had learned that her birth name was "Chloe," and how I thought that was so avant-garde a name for her era. I contextualized my discovery, reporting also how feminized the town name "Lorain" seemed to me, but acknowledged that that was because of Lorraine (different spelling) Hansberry.

She laughed and said, "There's nothing avant-garde about 'Chloe.' It's in the Bible."

"Well, 'Chloe' is a name that's gorgeous and rare," I said.

With Morrison's cross-novel focus on the Black folkway of naming children with "a finger placed" on a biblical name, I might have presumed that Morrison was named that way herself. The practice developed as a measure of half-literacy. You look for a raised letter, and that would be a capital, and therefore a fine choice of name. Morrison was very serious about displaying this folk tradition, especially in her two most biblical books, *Song of Solomon* and *Paradise*. This preliteracy strategy did not always work out. See Pilate. See First Corinthians.

"Chloe" appears only once in the Bible, in First Corinthians (1:11). We get no backstory from this verse. Though Chloe is mentioned, she remains undefined.

When I left her that day, I did stand up and, by way of goodbye, did say grandly, sweepingly, "See you next time, Miss Chloe. As usual, visiting you has been so much fun." Silly for me to use such a childish word, *fun*, but I was focused on a different word then. I was looking directly at her, and I carefully watched her register this brand-new reference. *Miss Chloe*. I gambled that she would not openly object, and she didn't. I called her Miss Chloe forever after that, but it began on a nondescript afternoon. It felt like a personal victory, to claim that special name. Reaching into her history for nomenclature was bold, but not out of bounds. If history had been different, a real Miss Chloe could have lived. But as it was, Chloe became Ms. Morrison, who became editor, who became writer, who became the late, great Toni Morrison. "Miss Chloe" in my mouth was a term of endearment, and it was thrilling to be correctly interpreted, to be allowed.

The Wildest Kind of Chosen

After years of reading Morrison (and scores of other writers), I wrote a book, which she read and "blurbed," and then she called me. That is the short version of how our story began. After our first visit, years of engagement followed. Rememory carries her voice, her wit, her laughter, her communicated wisdom, her snappishness, her timbre, her daring, her willingness and ability to wrestle with the mysteries of the past.

While I was not clearing paths as she was, I shared her barely contained disdain for society's disregard. We agreed that even in our late era, Black people were still denied intellect and/or emotion. In fiction and in real life, our human qualities were consistently erased across the broad culture. Our erasure has been intentional and multidisciplinary. Attempts to erase us continue, as if we are not here watching. Morrison and I could comfortably move forward in our assessments of our country, though she brought her truth to the page, and I still just carried mine along. Baggage. Weight. The unwritten past is its own wild chaos. Unwieldy and a drag on the spirit. Toni Morrison took to said chaos with her writing hand as machete. *Get out the way.*

IN LATE SPRING OF 1997, at the end of my Bunting year, Rene Boatman reached me on my cell phone; I was in New Orleans, where we spent part of the year and where I had a house. A yellow house with chartreuse trim, in the French Quarter. Between Rampart and Burgundy. Very near Louis Armstrong Park and Congo Square. Rene, whose voice and phone number I soon came to recognize, was unknown to me then. After she introduced herself, she said, "Toni Morrison would like to see you."

In my mind, I reached for a chair's back or a bookshelf, something to steady me. Maybe I thought I might faint. Really, I wasn't quite that dramatic, but I could have been. I didn't ask the silly question no doubt bouncing in my brain: *For real? You serious?* I'm sure I took a seat, as an investment in sounding calm and collected.

"Ms. Morrison would like for you to come meet with her. Would that be possible? Sometime later this summer?"

I'm sure I tried to reply in a reasonable register. *Yes. Yes. Of course. When? August? Yes. Yes. Where?* I am redundant when I'm enervated.

The answer to "where" was New York City, and the answer to "when" was TBD. Rene indicated that we'd resolve the details later, that in the next week we'd settle on a date and time that worked for both of us. I suggested that later in August would be better for me, as I would be coming northeast at that time. Of course, I would have traveled to see Morrison whenever she chose. I was not yet a mother then; I had clients but no daily workplace constraints.

Visiting Toni Morrison at her home in New York took on the character of a major life event. I was very preoccupied about this upcoming date. So huge a surprise sailing into my life. I urged myself to be nimble, humble, receptive, to use my worried energy for forethought. I plotted my strategy for the date, once announced: JetBlue direct from New Orleans to the fam in DC; then Amtrak, DC to NYC; then the A Train from Penn Station to Canal. *This is a pilgrimage*, I said to self, on the train.

After my long journey, I felt triumphant. I had kept my clothes clean. Prior pilgrimages included six countries overland in Africa (Togo, Senegal, Benin, Nigeria, Burkina Faso, Gambia); France, England, Canada, Mexico; umpteen united states. But compared with my prior pilgrimages, this visit to see Toni Morrison ranked high on the list. Taking that very first train ride to Morrison loomed as a huge adventure, an apex, a summons I responded to with anticipation. Wonderment had been idling in me since the first of the many steps toward this meeting was taken, nearly all the way back in spring.

That August afternoon in Lower Manhattan, I arrived early. Unusual for me. I did not have an iPhone then, did not have GPS then. Besides, I didn't know how long each leg of the trip would take. And further, I was apprehensive, though mostly in a good way. So, I had to be early, to get my bearings, to be in place by the appointed hour. I walked past the address a couple of times, to be sure I knew where to find the buzzer I needed to use.

I did buzz exactly on time. She buzzed me in, and I elevated up. At the door on her floor, I met a woman whose eyes sparkled. She was not a tall woman, which was sweet to notice. She could have been a giant, and I would have been unsurprised. She invited me in, asked me to sit down, and we talked for two hours. Toni Morrison presented as warm, curious, and engaged, full of good humor and blunt questions. She was in no way frightening.

Before this visit was scheduled, I had not even tried to imagine Morrison up close and personal. But I knew I needed to plan what I would say. How, again, would I express my great appreciation: for her invitation, for her taking an interest in my work and in me, for blurbing my book without being asked (which I had thanked her for already). I also prepared and held in mind a few questions—in case conversation lagged, in case silence threatened, in case so few others were there that I had to converse with her directly and hold my own.

We were having a private meeting, it turned out, visiting only with each other. When I had learned that this visit was social, I presumed I would be among others. In retrospect, I hoped I wasn't too open-mouthed, too visibly amazed. You can't go visit somebody at their house and gawk. To be present and personable, to be conversational and affable and adept—those were my goals. The years I'd spent round musicians taking to the stage had taught me how to be engaging on demand, to raise issues the person I was talking to might care about, to listen to what they might say.

During my years in New York City and New Orleans, I bopped around the jazz community. My partner then was a concert producer, and we spent much time around genius musicians and producers. Her world was full of luminaries like Abbey Lincoln, Wynton Marsalis, James Brown, Ed Bradley, George and Joyce Wein, Regina Carter, Akua Dixon, Susan L. Taylor (of *Essence* fame). Abbey had the same brevity, and expressive eye light, that Morrison had. They both could be snappish, and oh so real. They both could shut a situation down with a look. Abbey Lincoln was in her wisdom years the whole time I knew her, too. I believe Abbey is one of the greatest philosophers our culture has produced. Her original lyrics—especially from her later years—are like a guidebook to life, including the spiritual part of life. Abbey Lincoln lived a Black woman genius story, too. I often wished that Morrison and Abbey had known each other. They were so alike. Both powerhouses. Both geniuses. Both completely full of disregard for any silliness or illogic or stupidity. Like Morrison, Abbey lived a long and powerful life, and in the arena she inhabited, Abbey, too, was a queen. A philosopher-queen, if you ask me.

In Morrison's loft, alone with her, I had to remind myself that who I was had brought me there. That the diva had called, and I had arrived. The windows were large, the ceilings were high. Her furnishings were white, and she was genial.

As there were only two of us, I could not be a wallflower. I breathed deep to calm my nerves, urging myself to be myself. All went well while we sat in her stunning apartment and talked. Seeing her in person and up close was invigorating and amusing and more than memorable—honestly, more than I thought my life might contain.

Morrison's Tribeca apartment must have been somewhat new when I visited. Spare and vast were its primary characteristics. Not just huge for Manhattan, but enormous for anyone, for any set of people. Her rooms were a series of well-lit, breezy, airy white boxes. The white furniture was pristine. The walls, curiously unadorned. I asked no blunt questions, like *Is this a new place? How long have you been*

131

here? How big is this crib? I refused to embarrass myself, though scoping out real estate is a regular and accepted behavior in NYC. I hope I didn't seem disinterested; it was hard to know what was best to do.

Shortly after Morrison passed, the Tribeca apartment showed up on the real estate market. By then, it was lavish, saturated with the appointments of a world-class author and celebrated intellectual. Bookshelves built in corner to corner, a rail ladder installed to make high shelves accessible. Every space holding books; shelves spanning wall to wall. I looked closely at the realty pictures for signs of the place I had been, but the white-box rooms had been replaced with literature, decoration, and reward. The place was suffused with interior design and Morrison's particular appointments. The listing showed a place that was all about Morrison; when I visited her in 1997, the place was mostly blank and all new, though all about Morrison for me.

I spent our first afternoon together sitting on a huge, wide, expensive-looking white ottoman. She sat on a white sofa across from me. In a figurative way, I sat at her feet. I remember thinking, writing in my mind, *This is the wildest kind of chosen. This is my audience with the queen.*

AROUND A QUEEN, ALL IS ordered. There is decorum. Fine clothes and sparkling jewels. High language and measured conversation revolving around the interests of the queen. The real estate is stunning. The experience forever memorable. You present a deferential posture.

Toni Morrison was a powerful and unique incarnation on

132

this planet. Experiencing her was big and grand and somewhat confrontational. Seeing her was like standing before a thirty-foot flag. There was no avoiding the display or the honored colors. You had to stop and acknowledge the purpose and the ceremony of your moment. You couldn't see around Morrison; she was totally preoccupying. You knew to pay attention to the billow in the wind.

While I was sitting there, observing her, trying to stay present and be on my game, the significance of the moment squealed like a siren: *This is really happening. Here we are.*

There was no guarantee she would like me, enjoy my perspectives, be able to tolerate my company. I wondered myself if I could keep up. Our first encounter could have been a one-off. Instead, this two-hour meeting, for which I'd traveled more than thirteen hundred miles, was the beginning of years of engagement. We spent time together many times, alone. We also saw each other in many of her crowded, sometimes crushing, public situations. Everywhere I saw her when we were not alone, she was being honored. There were thrones.

For the next couple of decades, Morrison invited me to visit, or to lunch, or to dinner, or to her condo, or to her Hudson house, or to her office. To many events in her honor. The Tribeca loft visit was first; there, we began a rhythm and an expectation. We could talk to each other freely, about language mostly, but also about events in her books, which covered Black people and Black women and Black history and the ways we plotted and planned and managed to press forward. I loved being able to talk about language. We could rely on each other to use and hear words in their fullness.

I lost my favorite scarf that very first time I met Morrison, just the two of us together. We were leaving what had been for me a magisterial meeting. We came down in the elevator together. Toni Morrison's longtime friend Eileen Ahearn had arrived at the end of our visit; the two of them were going to a movie. Eileen Ahearn is herself quietly legendary in the literary community, having first worked in New York as Toni Morrison's assistant and then, ultimately, being engaged with the Baldwin literary estate. Eileen Ahearn knows Morrison like Fran Lebowitz knows Morrison: alone-together friends. Knew each other for decades. Supported each other so long that defining life changes were part of their experience. These are Morrison's travel-to-Stockholm friends— meaning they accompanied her when she received the Nobel.

Miss Chloe introduced me to Eileen in the lobby. So, I met them both on the same day. I had come down the front lobby stairs. Morrison stood at the top of the short staircase, holding on to the banister; she looked indecisive and then announced that she was cold. She stared baldly at the scarf I was wearing, which I had wrapped around my neck now that I was departing. The scarf was easy to wash, quick to iron, oversize. Easy to see on a train seat or in your bag. It worked well to combat freezing air-conditioning.

I remember reaching up to be sure what exactly she was staring at. She said nothing, but continued staring.

"Do you want me to go back up and get a jacket for you?" I asked.

Of course, there was no point to that question. I was stalling, and she kept glaring.

After an extended silence for a social situation, I asked, "Do you want to borrow my scarf?"

"Yes," she said immediately.

I tried again: "Are you sure you don't want to get a jacket or wrap from upstairs? I'll get it for you if you want." I was just being stubborn, repeating myself. I knew she wouldn't send me back up to her digs. "Maybe Eileen could go?" I recall looking over at Eileen, who was apparently not watching this heist unfold. She was looking away, and I was on my own.

I did not want to give up my wardrobe staple, but I did hand it over. "This is my favorite scarf; promise not to lose it," I urged. "I'll get it back from you at Princeton, this fall," I said, forcing optimism onto a scene I was not liking at all.

I never saw my scarf again. It was a cotton-blend scarf with fringe, made square. A base of black with splashes of red and magenta, lilac and purple. Totally my color palette. Changed plain black, or plain black and white, into an outfit complete with a festive finesse of black fringe. Toni Morrison was wearing black and white that evening, so my cherished scarf served her the same way it served me: dressed her plain black and white right up.

Took me a long time to get over the sting: I dressed up for her, and she absconded with my favorite drape.

I remember being cold riding Amtrak back to Washington. Usually, I'd open my scarf fully, fold it in triangle halves, and add another layer of heat, an added barrier. Keeping the shivers away.

Without speaking a word, she had disassembled my

dress-up, my New York City clothes. *You handed it over,* I reminded myself, pulling my linen jacket closer around me against the blasting cold Amtrak air. I revisited the reality that she had just stared, had not spoken a word on the subject, and yet I'd offered her my scarf. These could be two people starting a rhythm, one demanding, the other acquiescing. Could be far less dramatic, just a transaction. This could be a test. This could be but one exchange in a future multivalent with exchanges. In fiction or in film, this abdication would function to sear the moment, to show who was boss, to highlight wordless commands. Fiction allows for myriad opportunities for what this could be, but life is not fiction. Viewing real life as fiction will skew both your thinking and your writing, the instructor says, standing in front of the class, gesturing with the story, which is rolled up like a diploma in her hand.

Over time, I came to view this event and Morrison's other silent communiqués as basically a test of trust.

Can I depend on you?
Will you watch me for cues?
Will you be sure I'm situated, protected?
Will you keep the clamoring public at bay?
Can I trust you on the sidewalk?
Among the hundreds?
Can I rely on you to ascertain a message in my eyes?
Will you make me call your name out loud?

After years of orbiting round Miss Chloe, in multiple eras and multiple venues, I can tell you her silent treatment, her indirect demands, were not all that rare. There were bodyguard aspects to moving with Morrison. I imagine bodyguards will shiver to keep the principal warm.

Mother Sonia Sanchez—poet, activist, elder, and close friend to Toni Morrison—told the story of Toni admiring *her* mudcloth hat when Mother Sanchez saw Morrison for the last time, in the hospital, near the end. The documentary filmmaker Louis Massiah showed me a photo of the three of them, and Morrison's oxygen tubes, around which Morrison complimented Mother Sonia's mudcloth hat. Mother Sanchez took the hat off and placed it on Morrison's head. If you know Mother Sonia, you know she is protective; she wears her hair covered for definite reasons. When Mother Sonia told me this story, she said, "You know when Toni admires what you're wearing, that means you take it off and give it to her." The mudcloth hat story came at the end of Morrison's life, more than twenty years after my first visit with her. The year of her (or my) silent scarf shakedown, I was just learning. I didn't know. There are many of us who would have given her anything we had or were wearing. Not just me.

Not yet in the thick of things, I was not totally silent in response to the loss of my favorite scarf. One or two times, when we were together at Princeton, I bemoaned not having gotten my scarf back. She was coy once and then twice, and so I just stopped. I was making myself angry. *Is she wearing it?* I wondered. *Did she leave it somewhere? Is she just refusing?*

Years into the future, Morrison will return from Paris and she will bring me a scarf that she seems delighted to give. It is embroidered and light wool. The base is orange, and the woven foliage is deep greens and blendy browns. The fringe is barely noticeable, a short brown suggestion. The scarf is long and narrow, like standard. Like an ascot made for women. Like an Isadora Duncan special. It's perfect for fall or winter and for wearing with a trench or winter coat. Ultimately, I came to appreciate that Morrison and I both had fondness for France. We did not experience France or Paris together, but we told each other Paris stories. The orange scarf was one of her Paris stories, and I expressed appreciation for the gift.

I think that the scarf—upstairs in my bureau—is the one physical gift Morrison ever gave me. That doesn't matter, of course; she gifted me with her interest, her engagement, her wit, her time, her glaring stares, her presence, her blurb, her continuing invitations. Her books—gifted to me and to everybody else. I hold the orange scarf dear because she offered it. Of course, it's not my color palette, and it doesn't go with black or white. It's fitting, in a way, that I don't wear the scarf she gave me. I keep it. It's an artifact. On her birthday, in February, it's cold enough to warrant wearing it. And so, once a year, I take it out.

MORRISON'S PUBLIC ARMOR INCLUDED WHAT I affectionately referred to as her silent treatment. Morrison could and would communicate flatly, fully, and in the imperative—without saying a single relevant word. She would not hesitate to angle toward or tap into your basic intelligence and "make demands" without deigning to speak. We could reference this as "Black girl telepathy," but we could also just accept that Morrison needed to be able to claim space in the rush of reaching that characterized her life around her public. In order to roll with Toni Morrison, you had to respond if she needed you to—hold up, stand back, back off, block. She wanted to ask things of you without having to call you, raise her voice, or speak abruptly—or speak at all. She wanted to be able to look your way and you'd come. Her silent communiqués often started with some level of side-eye. (Is side-eye a thing outside the inside of our communities? I'm not sure.)

Every once in a while, I'd get worried. I didn't want her to think I was up for being a beck-and-call girl. That wasn't going to happen. I was a writer, and a new mother, and a partner, and a daughter, and a sister, and a college professor, and an ex-statistician. Fortunately, my two sisters are my best friends, so I did not have a huge social network to maintain. But the beck-and-call specter kept me slightly recessed. I did not want to (seem to) promise more than I could deliver; I did not want to offer what I could not consistently give.

WHEN I READ TO CELEBRATE Morrison at the Schomburg Center the November after she transitioned, there was a young curator presenting; she told a story, not too different from the stories I tell, of trying to *plan* what you might say to a rock star if you met them. This young woman read at the memorial about Morrison and art; she told me about having once gone to a Morrison event in NYC. She had prepared what she wanted to say to Morrison if they ended up face-to-face. Later, she was washing her hands at the sink in the restroom when Morrison emerged from a stall. The curator looked up, and her eyes met Morrison's in the mirror. The curator reported that Morrison's eyes basically communicated the following: *Don't you dare speak to me under these circumstances.* Full sentence, full stop, according to the curator's report.

The curator told the story as a hilarious anecdote. I could, of course, have started in on Morrison's demand for my favorite bohemian scarf, or Morrison's "request" for Mother Sonia's mudcloth hat. But I just laughed. The curator was very demonstrative about her anxiety while in Morrison's sight line; she waved her hands, describing how she rushed to rinse them of soap and hurried out of the restroom, to leave Morrison to herself. Her encounter with Morrison amounted to just that—eyes meeting in a mirror, the august author "insisting" that no chatting would happen in that space. The curator's planned remarks went the way of mist or steam—evaporated.

SINGING MY NAME

One random, at-first-insignificant afternoon, I was in the Creative Writing building, where all the creative writers at Princeton had our offices, walking through the sunshine of its wide halls. As I came back down the hall toward my office, still around the corner, out of view of it, my attention was arrested by the sound of Miss Chloe's voice. I had left my office door pulled to, resting on the doorjamb, but it was not fully closed. Miss Chloe had apparently stopped by my office and encountered my "open door." I had thought I heard her calling me, but a visit from her there would have been a first, and I initially doubted that I had actually heard what I thought I'd heard.

But I *did* hear her, almost singing, *Aay. Jay. Aaay Jaayy.*

I thought what I imagine anyone would have thought: *What?! Is that Toni Morrison calling me? Singing my name out loud?* Hearing her cause my name to echo in that wide school-house hallway.

Ours was a building with ginormous tall windows and broad staircases. The building was a former district school building. Halls wide as classrooms. Old and solid, the building was perpetually drenched in daylight. Designed and erected midcentury (twentieth century), the school was built to accommodate hundreds of adolescents, to be pounded by oxfords and loafers and sneakers, to have space enough on the stairs for classrooms funneling out. Princeton student groups were sparse there compared to the crowds for whom the building was originally intended. We faculty often walked the halls alone, or with one student, momentarily engaged. Students visited our offices for conferences, which they almost craved.

I hurried round the corner, answering, "Yes, yes, here I am!" by way of hello.

In the sunlight from the high windows, there she was. She asked if I wanted to have lunch. I had actually just gone to wash my hands, and I was planning to eat the lunch I'd packed and brought to the office. I looked at my watch.

"Do you have time?" she asked.

"I have a class at one," I said.

"We have time, then."

We don't really have time, I thought. And then restated to myself: I *don't really have time.*

"Well," I ventured, "I brought tuna and crackers. I have it in the office. I'll share it with you."

"I saw it," she said. "I tasted it. I didn't like it."

Again, I second-guessed my hearing. I'm sure I asked the question with my eyes: *What?*

We stood for a second, suspended in place. She was smiling; her eyes were sparkling. She giggled, and eventually, I halfheartedly joined in. I wasn't sure exactly what was happening, but I had to move on from the moment, because she moved forward with her objective, the reason she had set my name ringing in the air.

We went out to lunch in her dark-green Jaguar. She made me choose where we should go, which caught me off guard. She blamed it on my having to get back for class, so I should choose a place I liked that wouldn't take forever. Of course, I'd run in to see the secretary and asked to have a note posted for my class. I gave myself two hours to get back, which would put me forty-five minutes late for a two-hour class. I was a little nervous, a little agitated, but I was also hungry, and I needed to eat.

I directed us to a local Indian restaurant. Not too far from campus, but not high end, either. No one there recognized her—or, I should say, no one interrupted her in any way. And so, we had a talkative, engaging lunch. She wanted to know what I usually ordered. We arranged a little plan: what we should order and that we could share. But then we didn't share. We ate individually, and talked about Princeton, and India, and strip malls, and how geography registered in the mind. I mentioned Lorain. Couldn't hold my interest in Lorain a secret. We talked about the politics that encases you when you grow up, as I did, in DC. As huge as this moment was for me, I realized as it was happening that no one else would know the significance of that day. Even with the tension of the timing, I was brimming with delight. Thrilled with the serendipity of the lunch date. I left the lunch that day believing she was joking about tasting the tuna. But I did not return to the subject as we ate. I did not confirm. I did not ask what I was thinking: *Did you really taste the tuna? Did you really eat my food?*

I felt like I was playing hooky at that lunch, though I was back in place by the forty-five-minute grace period I had given myself. We went to that restaurant only once. She interrupted my class schedule only that once. She did not like fennel.

The schoolhouse hallway part of that afternoon was most meaningful, surreal in noon light. Hearing Morrison's husky voice sing my name, and the sound bouncing off those thick midcentury stone walls, was exhilarating and wholly new. The campus and Princeton were new to me, too. But in my novel *The Good Negress* (which was the overall reason I had been invited to lunch), I had written about a big, inspiring schoolhouse, almost like the Creative Writing building we occupied at 185 Nassau. The model for the school in *The Good Negress* was Monroe Elementary, in DC, where I went to preschool and had graham crackers and apple juice. The first inside of a school I ever saw. An early, baby memory. The building and the snack—that's all I remember about preschool: I see peachy light, I think because the walls were painted some strange shade of nearly nectarine.

The Good Negress contains a setting that I inhabited in preschool and at Princeton. That old school building at 185 Nassau was a monument to the municipality called "school." In the wide halls of my fiction, the protagonist of the novel comes to understand that *there is a world*, as she would have said; she learns this in that school building. She discovers knowledge of the world all written down in books.

Toni Morrison sang my name that afternoon, in exactly the kind of hallway I hallowed in the novel.

If the mind can call things to you, I could have called that school building at 185 Nassau. If you believe you can call a person to you, then you could argue that I called Toni Morrison to me, too. I knew nothing formal about manifesting during those young years. But my Lonts came from her Cholly. And for me, Morrison was the inventor of emotional chronology. She freed me from Julius Caesar's July, followed by his adopted nephew Augustus's August. The original order was itself rearranged, so reconsider chronology altogether. Don't let the calendar batter your projects; invent the days and dates you need. That's what Morrison's books said to me. Separate from how I studied her masterful writing, meeting and getting to know her was like magic happened. Although she was my hero, Toni Morrison and I eventually sat face-to-face, scoping each other out, inventing ways to play badminton with words. We were careful not to draw attention, not to flail our arms.

OVER TIME, WE GREW CLOSE in our own way. Our relationship developed and stayed steady, though writing remained the invitation, and the basis for our knowledge of each other. We developed a flat-footed friendship—which is very hard to say aloud and which I think we both registered as surprise.

We were two of many women in the world's wide history who built a friendship across generations. One of us had lived more widely, more comprehensively, and longer. One of us was heralded, and tended to enjoy the smallness of our gatherings when we were just us two. One of us followed the elder's lead and honored the request for just duets. The younger loved how the elder relayed or replayed knowledge the younger could not have gathered. The accomplished one modeled poetic brevity, especially in speech: compress, consider, compress. The younger listened, acknowledging the grace of being there.

We became faster friends than I think either one of us expected. We enjoyed each other; we laughed; we played with and talked about language with abandon. When we had time and were proximal, we met up and, often, made impromptu plans, though she had a penchant for making a specific suggestion and then making me choose the final lap. Usually we got together, got food, and went to where she lived. I planned questions in case she wasn't talking. And I listened to what she said when she spoke. When the other was no longer nearby, we talked on the phone, which reminded me so much of talking to my grandmothers—comically, as if I had not aged. When big events happened for her, especially near me on her road trips, she often said, *I'll be at such and such a place. You should come.* Our relationship was never impersonal or distant, until it was. Our tests and requests of each other ducked and dodged, leaped and flew, sailed like kite tails over us.

Sometimes kites plummet into trees.

To Write by Hand

Morrison and I sat in her Princeton office one afternoon talking about teaching. She said she could tell the difference between students who wrote by hand and students who wrote on a keyboard. I asked her how she knew, and she repeated that she could tell from the work. Completely curious, back in my own office, I looked at my roster of students and wrote *c* (computer written) or *h* (handwritten) in the lightest pencil at the top of their story submissions, as my guess about their stories. After I checked with my students, I found that only one of my guesses was incorrect. Fascinating even to consider that I, too, could tell. Of course, I had not asked them the question. Another attribute of genius: learn to ask questions. Morrison famously seeded all her work in questions.

I write my drafts by hand. I revise my typed drafts by hand. The pen and the hand, and the resulting penmanship, are tied to the mind directly, in different and more robust ways than QWERTY can muster. Our hands and our handwriting are part of the process of creation. The work of the hand can be key to creativity, unlocking its flow, loosing its wells, delivering up bucketsful of dreaming.

As an aspiring and developing novelist, writing in the dark, I dedicated a couple of years to studying creativity and intuition. Figuring out what matters to engaging the mind. Brenda Ueland, Dorothea Brande, Kenneth Atchity, Mihaly Csikszentmihalyi, Kenneth Kempton, even William Zinsser's formulations about routine, which can be the opposite of creativity—old-school writers, mostly; experts from a prior era. Sometimes, when what you read is distant from the reality you know, you can interpret what's being said more clearly.

Morrison was responding to perceived differences in creativity from observing whether a student story had been once written by hand. She wouldn't elaborate, so I had to create the questions I could answer, to help me predict. First, does the story delve into itself, or does it flit? Second, does the story have detail that shows any staring or hesitation or pause? Third, do the characters say or do what is predictable, or has the writer considered speech and action more deeply, more particularly? Fourth, does the story seem thorough in its dramatic moments or rushed, glossed over?

So often, Morrison raises a truth you already know but never thought to name. She renders sweeping observations concisely and crisply. When you listen to Toni Morrison, you listen to the sound of clarity. Maybe you nod your head. You definitely experiment with writing by hand. You test the waters so that you know about the power or density of your own work emerging from keystrokes or rising up from ink or lead.

Years forward into the future, much of the work I do with the page, the pencil, with words, and with my students is influenced by how Morrison worked, the nuances she articulated, the innovations in the classroom I had a chance to discuss with her. Her pedagogy is not as well known as her novels and nonfiction, but her teaching methods had significance, I am here to attest.

WITNESSES

Our friendship was several years deep when Miss Chloe mentioned that she was Catholic. I was almost aghast. I almost recoiled. I almost backed away.

My personal experience with Catholicism was mostly horrible: nine years in Catholic school. I could not separate their race prejudice from their religion. And so, I emerged from their tutelage battered and bruised. Miss Chloe listened to my recollection (complaint, rant) and behaved as if she were not surprised. She agreed that, often, Catholic schools are "little" schools, neighborhood schools, parish schools. Village education. We joked about the primitive connotation of the word *village*, when there are actually villages everywhere. Not all provincial. Some sophisticated, like Greenwich. We nodded to Jimmy Baldwin, who wrote about being outside said Village, or outside *a* village. We all know about being outside. Morrison has written about the terror of being outside. And then there is the village you need. The village of people rather than place.

From reading her work, I would not have guessed. In one conversation, I had referenced the catechism, which suggests inside knowledge of Catholicism. She asked if I was Catholic, and I answered no (pretty vociferously). Morrison considered herself righteously Catholic and reported that she'd been Catholic all her life. The nuns who assimilated the Arapaho girls, and who poached Consolata, making her a little slave child—these behaviors comported with my direct, though modernized, experience.

In *Paradise*, the Catholic Church is presented in a way that fits the organization I saw and experienced in Catholic school: aggressive, mean, prejudiced, and duplicitous. There are more adjectives I could use. The biblical thundering that happens all through Morrison's work seems Protestant, if not all the way Baptist. When Jesmyn Ward memorialized Morrison at St. John

148

the Divine, this "argument" Morrison and I had (about her work being biblical, contrasting with my notion of Catholic practice), came rushing back to mind. Jesmyn Ward meticulously arranged a eulogy that echoed both testaments, treating Morrison as leader, as Moses almost. Ward's words about Morrison guiding us from the wilderness actively referenced Morrison's power, her inventiveness, and the definitive association in Morrison's work between our cultural past, our historical beliefs, and the centrality of the Holy Book. To me, Catholicism associates not with the Bible, but with its dully Socratic catechism, which has none of the biblical range or order, nomenclature or rhythm, or acknowledged authorship. Besides, Catholics create and canonize their own saints, and then congregants pray to the saints the Church has chosen. Once you learn the concept of monotheism, then you have to wonder about this. Or, I did. Granted, I was still a child. But the way the schools treated me was so hurtful that, by adulthood, my interest in Catholicism had burned to a crisp. There was nothing there to be salvaged or rehydrated, only the dry ash of bad memories.

The catechism (v. Bible) and canonization—those were the two most startling aspects of Catholicism, for me. The idea that confession and apology on the deathbed can wipe out a lifetime of sin also mystifies me. The practice of confessing sin and then routinely asking for forgiveness, receiving a "prayer recipe" for atonement, shocked and dismayed me. Seemed like an odd kind of pass, always available—ostensibly to Catholics only. No matter what you do, no matter how you misbehave, forgiveness and a rosary await.

I wanted her to say why she was Catholic, but I did not

ask. What kind of question is that? *Why are you Catholic?* A childish question. A question that came out of all the memories of Catholicism that her announcement brought rushing back. Doused me like cold water.

My experience in Catholic school was *so so so so* racist. As a young'un, I conflated the bald racism I experienced with Catholic religious practices. I blamed the nuns and fathers and laypeople associated with my Catholic schools. These were people who actually snarled at "colored me." Ugly stuff. How the Catholic adults in my school treated children. I say "colored" with intention, because I'm convinced that's how they thought of us. In backward ways. I was not the only colored child, but I had more words than all the kids in my little "village" school. *Colored, white,* and *disappeared.* More words than the sum of some of those children. *Catechism* was a new word, once, a word that seemed strange, rare, and spelled curiously. I could never keep straight whether it should be capitalized.

Catechism is how Catholicism is taught to children, based on repetition of questions and answers. Not sure whether the catechism is used for adults. The child's job is to memorize both the questions and the answers. From the catechism you learn the answers to countless questions you may never have asked. You learn that as long as you confess your sins (to a priest), and then say your assigned number of prayers (using a rosary), you will be forgiven (in the name of the Father, the Son, and the Holy Spirit, Amen). Instant forgiveness via counting "Hail Marys" may be Catholicism's most bizarre strangeness, but there were other oddities, too. For example: Authorship. The names of the men are recorded, the authors of most books of the Bible. Authorship of the catechism remains an unanswered question.

Perhaps it is obvious I never converted to Catholicism. I consider myself a child witness to their misuse of me, and their fawning over others, and their consistent preference for white skin. I was a student integrating a formerly white Catholic school. A young person interrogating a catechistic faith. I can say quite honestly that my major difference from the other students was not really race. My main diversity was language. I had words enough for a pocket dictionary. Left to study language, I could probably have written rings around Jupiter, in impressive form. Unfortunately, I was not encouraged to study anything, not independently, not special, not in groups. If I finished the assigned work early—which most often, I did—they didn't care what I did, as long as I shut up.

THE DIFFERENCE BETWEEN EXCLUSION BY RACE and exclusion by religion was not discernible to me then. In my school life, both these excisings were happening daily, in spades. *Serpentine, these Catholic arguments*, I thought—at age twelve, fifteen, seventeen. *Freedom!* I thought when I graduated. I had no complaints about Catholic *values*, as stated, but the difference between stated moral principles and administrative or daily practice—well, the latter called the former into question.

Morrison had not attended Catholic school. So, I concluded that she did not understand the experience that stunted and attacked me as a child. White students in my classrooms were neither hassled nor ignored; Catholic students were also encouraged and fawned over. I considered whether I was wrong to associate Catholic school with the Catholic religion. The answer, of course, is no.

So, Miss Chloe and I had a religion disagreement. We accepted this, talked around it from time to time, and managed to survive the difference in heat between my strident vehemence and her quiet belief. I tried not to suck my teeth about Catholicism, tried not to mention that while they were selecting and canonizing, they were silent about Black saints, as if none had ever been chosen. They did not acknowledge or foreground any Blackness in the religion. I was not the only Black child in my class; but no effort was made to include or inspire us. To me, we seemed unimportant as dust mites to them.

Miss Chloe seemed, after a while, to refrain from raising the subject between us—which I appreciated. I am so far beyond my schooling now; I'm in my third act. But I remain stung by my wicked Catholic "education." I'm still pissed. I wouldn't send a child of mine anywhere near a Catholic school. I carry my sword and lift my shield.

MY YOUTHFUL EXPERIENCE WITH CATHOLICS and their magical thinking, their canonizing, their prejudice and routinely practiced aggressions, all conflicted with the Bible and with my self-made impression of Morrison, the author. In part because of her big biblical book, *Paradise*, and her biblically named breakthrough narrative, *Song of Solomon*, and her incorporation of Bible-based folkways in her work—I maintain that her biblical exposure from childhood kept "ahold" of her. *Black Bible religion* preens all through her novels! Her characters deal with reverends; priests are few, if extant at all. Miss Chloe, though, carried Catholicism personally. Like DNA. As unquestioned as flat feet or long hair or arched eyebrows.

IN COLLEGE, I CAREFULLY AND deliberately retired catechism, Catholicism, and all its exclusions. I put all those memories in the bank of my unchosen past. Goodbye, man-made deities, fodder for genuflection! Goodbye, incense; goodbye, confessionals; goodbye, vestments; goodbye, mean people! I should have thought to purge myself of what they thought of me. But I did not think of that then. Years would pass before I thought to separate what I heard them say or felt them do from what I knew would have nurtured me. It's powerful to try to backdate your nurturing, because then you have to revisit and recast each past event. You have to acknowledge the damage and decide why you carry it along. You have to look straight back at faces full of malice. You have to think, *Yes, malice, and toward a child!* But that was in a future beyond the initial purge I'm describing, trying to take Catholicism from inculcation to flat knowledge. Nothing about Catholicism could stay a minute in my soul after the age of my emancipation—until I met Morrison. Her announcement called my fury forth, all fresh again. Our tone shifted. Morrison could hear; so could I. I can honestly say I was wordless, yet, *still*. She could hear me arguing—*most Black people are Baptist*—by my tone of voice, even as I was saying other words.

Her Catholicism created a spiritual distance between us that, once we observed this, we allowed to go unmentioned, to trail away. The smoke was always in the air, but we did not suffer or speak of what we both witnessed. Our silence reduced the potential for sudden friction, or prevented us from diving into a deep crevasse. But yes, the smoke was in the air.

While I did not wrestle with my knowledge of or resistance to Catholicism again—I'd had enough experience not to waver—there was, however, the Morrison effect, or the Morrison respect. I was stunned to find myself, every once in a while, wondering what it was that I didn't understand. What about Catholicism engaged her or sustained her? The rituals. The incense. The bells. The saints. Maybe even the vestments. Maybe the rising smoke. Maybe people move only minimally away from their source religion. Maybe Catholicism was simply not presented to her the way it was to me.

LATER, OUR RELIGION PLOT THICKENED. Another sect entered our little religion stage. We had moved the props to the wings, but quietly, tenuously, empathetically. We rebuilt a place for religion and kept the sound down. In one of our long conversations, before our long hiatus, Morrison reported that her sister, Lois, had become a Jehovah's Witness. When we had this conversation, I had no idea whether this "becoming" a Jehovah's Witness was a new situation or a long-term conundrum. I did not ask, "When?" I wanted to listen to what Miss Chloe wanted to report, but I did not want to appear to be collecting facts. Eventually, I deduced that this affiliation was not new. Like always with Miss Chloe, I listened, quietly and actively, connecting what she told me with what she had told me before or with what I knew about the subject at hand. This is how you learn, connecting new knowledge to what you already know. In reading and rhetoric, we refer to this as *schema*, the body of knowledge we all carry in our minds. Schema is what a church aims for when they educate you; they will ultimately depend on you to live out the tenets of the religion. My schema about Jehovah's Witnesses had also been intact since childhood, and news of Miss Lois was really all the fresh information I got about Witnesses, in all my adult life. I won a church baby contest (for recitation) when I was a mere three years old. My little dress was a monument to crinoline. I could sing "Jesus loves me, this I know" before I knew the word *tune*, and likely before I knew what the words of that song even meant. We attended an African Methodist Episcopal Zion Church then: Trinity. My memories of Catholicism, of Jehovah's Witnesses, of my own Baptist youth choir tradition, arise from my earliest years, all the way back to wordless years. Amazing how religion burrows down like roots.

MISS NOLTON LIVED DOWN THE block from Ma Howell, maybe three houses away. We knew Miss Nolton's children, Maxine and David. Because they were Jehovah's Witnesses, Maxine and David could not celebrate birthdays. Their religion taught that a birthday was excess, that personal celebration was excess. *Each day the Lord's day, equally.* The birthday erasure shocked us, especially because Ma Howell approached birthdays with singular focus and a grandmother's purposefulness.

When one of us had a birthday, Ma Howell made sure all of us had a birthday. All three of us got presents for each of our birthdays. We might even have invited Maxine and David to a party once, but just once. A religious refusal does not invite persistence. The religious refusal is bigger than the individual with whom you speak.

Michael Jackson and his family were Jehovah's Witnesses. I know because I researched them carefully, at the age of ten, in advance of donning my pink (polyester) pantsuit to wear to my first live concert ever. The Jackson 5 at the Baltimore Civic Center. Michael Jackson was a little boy then, wearing fringe suede vests. He was, as my nine-year-old nephew said, "still Black." Going to the Civic Center to see Michael and *Marlon* (who, dancer boy, was the love of my life), I was a little girl, wearing what my mother bought. All three of us got new outfits. I don't think I knew the word *research* yet, but I had read—maybe in *Ebony* or *Jet*—all I could find about the Jackson 5. The Jehovah's Witness information was *public knowledge*—another term I did not yet know.

Witnesses set up pamphlet stands and spend the day out-doors; the women wear long skirts. Sometimes Witnesses go door-to-door. They check to see if you might be ready to hear the Good News, to take a pamphlet from all the many printed, distributed, kept so miraculously clean. Though they stand on the street, or climb up and down steps, their paper wares show neither soot nor grime, nor any other lack of holiness. I remember wondering who was paying for all that print. Not the people standing on the street corner.

Prince was a Witness, too, but I learned that only after his stunning demise. Michael Jackson and Prince—both famous Jehovah's Witnesses. Rockstar Jehovah's Witnesses. Both so similarly, tragically gone so abruptly.

Miss Chloe whined about her sister choosing to witness when she visited. Lois visited but did not visit really, according to Miss Chloe. When Lois came to visit Miss Chloe at her upstate house on the Hudson, Lois did not stay around. "Lois is one of the Jehovah's Witnesses," Miss Chloe almost confessed. She sounded hurt, or sad, or something. Maybe by Lois's "going out" when visiting. Or maybe by Lois's rejection of the religion Miss Chloe maintained? I did not ask. I listened to Morrison's meandering reportage, that she was just wanting Lois's company and not understanding why she couldn't have it. "She goes out in the morning with the Jehovah's Witnesses," Morrison said, "and stays all day. To places I don't even know." To stand outside with one another and their materials. "She spends more time with them than with me."

I can understand how Miss Chloe would have been discomfited by her sister's coming to visit and not really hanging around— at her beautiful upstate home, with its grand views. Sometimes life is inexplicable.

"She comes back in the evening?" I ask.

"Yes, but that's no way to visit."

CATHOLIC ALL HER LIFE, MORRISON was confirmed—which is like a little wedding. I can't remember what the boys wear, but the girls wear white formal dress; they look like little brides. (Maybe that is part of the appeal.) The children are about fourteen. I can't recall whether the young people are joining with Christ or joining with their Church. I think the former, but I was not confirmed. The catechism, which I studied—because: grades—does not address confirmation explicitly. There are confirmation classes, to which non-Catholics are not invited, so I don't have the least idea what in the classes happens.

I was not and will never be Catholic. I was there when all

this happened for the girls surrounding me. Some of us were brutally excluded, not just me. When you are confirmed, you take your saint's name. I can only back-imagine that young Chloe, with Toni Morrison fluttering within her, found choosing a new name for herself thrilling and monumental. Choose a saint whose attributes appeal; choose someone you will want to pray to, the catechism or the Church or the confirmation training suggests. Your chosen saint will watch out for you forevermore, you are told.

Choosing a name is a gift and a grace, and a big responsibility. We know young Chloe turned Toni would have been fascinated by naming; perhaps she was already. Young Chloe also read prodigiously, so she had likely read all the biographies of all the saints she had to choose from. She may not yet have known that she was going to lean on what Saint Anthony's nickname might have been had he lived in our time, before he was coronated saint. Young Chloe chose a saint who holds a book. Saint Anthony is also the patron saint of lost and stolen things. I daresay Chloe Anthony Morrison took her saint name seriously and used her genius and her life for uncovery. Reenvisioning our lost and stolen history. Finding our humanity in our pummeled past. Retrospective imaginary. Writing it all down.

THE BAPTIST CHURCH I GREW up in believed that you prayed only to the omnipotent—as in one believed-to-be-all-powerful God. You did not pray to angels or saints made or named by men. Catholicism splits everything. Even the "monotheistic trinity"—Father, Son, Holy Spirit—is spoken in its separate forms, every prayer, every day (because of the sign of the cross). The writer in me applauds specificity, but the believer in me questions all this fracturing and votes, splitting omnipotence and canonizing saints.

I went to Catholic school for far too long. My parents engaged with Catholic school as affordable private education. They paid for Catholic school believing in the value of religious compassion and the benefit of fewer students overall. My parents thought we'd be safer. There would be fewer fights. In the strict, almost tactile sense of these ideals and expectations there is truth. But Catholic, or parochial, school did not notice or acknowledge (or support) civil rights when the movement was upon us. The authorities at my school ensured that only the docile could be rewarded and, also, that the answer to the colored child is *no*.

I have never been docile, and I have always been colored. Within cloistered Catholic walls, school days were full of sequestered, dusty, suffocating prejudice; of nuns who knew no check, or witness, on their power over children. Some of those old girls were stone-cold racist under those habits; some of those same girls considered themselves moral as their Jesus, white as their fabled snow.

By fourth grade, even little-girl me could see: our school meted out education like crumbs. We were given a French language workbook when I was nine. During that year, we went over a half chapter or so a month. The French workbook—which seemed worldly to me, and more engaging than most of our curriculum—brought news of other words and other parts of the world. I learned to conjugate verbs from studying French. The workbooks were collected at the end of the year, but I conveniently and permanently forgot mine at home. Fodder for a long summer. In careful script—in pencil, mostly—I finished the workbook the summer between fourth and fifth grade. I brought it back to school with me in September, proud both of my new knowledge of French and of the care I'd taken with the workbook. I had managed to snag a summer with my French book, unnoticed. They would have disciplined me had they realized. Thereafter, from fifth to eighth grade, we did a few more of the chapters in the workbook each year, until—ta-da!—before we graduated eighth grade, we completed all the chapters (over five academic *years*). And so, for the last four years of Catholic grade school, I looked at my careful nine-year-old handwriting in the French workbook I had completed hungrily and carefully, in a prior age. From my assigned desk near the rear of the room, I watched the little white girls get noticed and encouraged and engaged. Not so for the colored kids in the class. No one noticed my completed French work but me. My teachers tried their best not to notice me at all. This was a struggle, given that I was neither diminutive nor invisible, and you could usually catch my eye because my work was already done.

After grade school came Catholic high school, where the racism was equally relentless. My favorite and least favorite example of this was the Science Fair, eleventh grade. After years of "How many days does it take to mold bread?" kind of science projects, I committed in eleventh grade to take the Science Fair seriously. I spent months working on a left brain/right brain project. My hypothesis: right brain–dominant association with creativity can be proven by creativity and linearity tests basic enough to be administered by a layperson (i.e., me). My mother had a Styrofoam wig head in the house, although I'd never seen it sport a wig. I begged her to let me cut it up to diagram the hemispheres of the brain. I was sheltered, and not a shopper. I didn't know how cheap and mass-produced Styrofoam was. I thought the wig head was something special, since it sat around solo, untouched. I thought untouched was for reasons of preservation. Untouched can also mean near discarded.

In my Science Fair division, Psychology, the school science fair judges decided to give two second places and no first. In no other Science Fair category were there two second places. Again, I was plain pissed. The first-place prize winner for each discipline went forward to compete at the next level, aiming toward the county- and state-level fairs. But because my category had no first place, nobody went forward from Psychology. I can remember complaining, and being admonished. Second place is good, I was told, as if stupid. Second is the highest award in that category, I was told. So, you got the highest award.

ALTHOUGH, OBVIOUSLY, I MADE MY way in the world, I have thought furiously back to that Science Fair moment as the culmination of a lot of raggedy and reprehensible behavior. If those people could have, they would have reduced me to rubble. I remember learning the word *impervious*, and saying under my breath, like a mantra, "I am impervious to you."

But what if I had been a budding scientist? What if I had wanted to go into STEM? Could they have robbed me of an important opportunity, could they have drawn up the bridge at an important crossing? Absolutely. Yes.

My feelings about my Catholic education have been terribly negative and have not softened in the scores of years since. Recently, our high school had its final "closing ceremony," because now they are tearing the old girl (the building) down. At the date of the last hurrah, the "school closing" event in 2021, I met a woman who was one of twelve Black girls in her class. She graduated in the late 1960s, a dozen years before I arrived. We got into a conversation, and I mentioned that my experience of the school was terribly racist. She got animated. "Oh yes, they were," she agreed. "I just found out," she told me, "just in preparation for today, that our class had a whole class trip and they didn't tell us. They didn't tell us Black girls about the trip at all."

"Wait, what? What are you saying?" I requested details.

"They brought out their pictures to show here today," she said, "from their class trip to New York City. Not one of us knew about that trip. All these years. Not until now."

The woman went on to name the "Sisters" (meaning nuns) who had suggested and agreed to exclude the Black girls from the class trip. Junne was the graduate who told me this story, and she was hot under the collar to learn this, fifty years after her graduation.

My grave will probably welcome me, and I still won't have forgiven or forgotten the horrors of Catholic school. They robbed me of experience and exposure and of positive self-regard.

When Morrison announced herself so oddly Black and Catholic, I determined that I'd have to be on guard not to rail. I determined not to show the prejudice I'd developed.

In Washington, DC, there is an Association of Black Catholics. They were my one saving grace. They worked at the

Archdiocese level—which meant that multiple schools and churches, within regions, were considered "under their umbrella." When I was seventeen, the Association of Black Catholics gave me its annual youth award. My mother shopped for a floor-length dress for me, for the awards dinner. I felt like I was dressed for prom. I worked hard, for weeks, on my very short acceptance speech. The first line I still remember: "My parents practice what I euphemistically call forceful encouragement."

I had only during that academic year learned the word *euphemism*. I found it a hilarious word. A word to explain that you're saying something different from what you're saying, in the very sentence where you are saying what you're qualifying. Amazing.

In my youth, I thought adverbs were fancier language. For weeks in advance, I practiced saying euphemistically: *yoo-fuh-MIST-ick-ly*. Turned out it wasn't that hard. Brushing my teeth, washing the dishes, walking to school—I practiced. *Euphemistically*. When I made the speech, the word rolled off my tongue. Of course, at that time, the issue was not the word. Who is this kid, using this language?

People in the audience at the Archdiocese dinner tittered; I was watching them from the lectern, where I stood in my "prom dress." Parren Mitchell, congressman, was there and on the dais, in my line of sight. He laughed; the congressman got my joke.

I ended up resolutely anti-Catholic, mostly because I was so horrified by how they treated me and stifled me. I kept this anti-Catholicism mostly a secret, but over time, I've let the hiding go. People don't like for people to talk about religion, but I see myself talking about racism in the Catholic

Church anyway. Is racism that is cloaked in vestments racism or religion? Somebody needs to decide. What child has an answer to that? I thought both—maybe because I was a child, or maybe because it *was* both. Maybe I had the correct answer. If the Catholic teachers had been less racist, I would not have become anti-Catholic. But as it was, they were paragons of snarling and derision.

And so, when Morrison said she was Catholic, my soul jumped back, and not in wonder. We were years in when this divergence emerged, so we had some history already. My spirit felt, *This is the stuff of your torture . . .* and so there was some backing away.

Once—I think I was in seventh grade—I was in trouble for identifying a misspelled word on the board. The teacher had put only one *s* in *misspell*. That is not how to spell misspell, I said. Maybe I laughed, hearing myself.

I was told to stay in at recess. I was told to sit in the front row. All accomplished. I had a paperback copy of *Manchild in the Promised Land*, which I took to the front desk and sat reading.

I heard the principal as she came pounding down the hall. She was a nun; she wore flat shoes and had wide legs. Her pounding stride was loud and notorious. I don't know that I'd listened so closely before, but her feet sounded furious. She came into the classroom like a torrent, her veil and her scapular rising behind.

Once inside the classroom door, she slapped me hard across the face. I dropped my book, accidentally. I was big enough to

164

sock her back and cause some damage, but I forced myself to be controlled. Her slap had hurt. I felt tears spring to my eyes, and so I narrowed them. I would rather look like I was cursing her than let her see that she'd made me cry.

This was not our first altercation. It was almost our last. It was definitely the first (and only) slap. By that point in my education there, I had already recessed, my nose in my books. And after that, I became even more withdrawn. It wasn't very effective, because my work was so above grade level, and my fury would not be contained. So, even though I tried to hide, there I was, all advanced and beyond myself. Beyond their little school. I am *decades* beyond their bullshit racism. And: I'm. Still. Pissed.

At the time, I learned something about them: they had a perspective, and they never turned the page. Day after day, they began from the same perspective: *We are here to make good citizens and good Catholics of white children. Everybody else can go to hell.* I did not have those words at that time, but I had the idea. It is amazing to see people choose to despise and deny you while you watch. Many people of color in this country live lives like this. It's tragic. Despicable. Tawdry. Ill-informed. Snarling. Disgraceful. Even if you don't yet have the words to describe what you see, you see.

I stopped expecting anything different. I stopped looking to them for approval. I stopped responding to what was on the blackboard. I started counting down days. I remember multiplying and subtracting and adding; I constructed an elaborate math problem. The number of years left in that school times the number of weeks in a year (minus the number of weeks in the summer times the number of summers left), times five days per week, equaled the grand total of the days I still had to deal. From that big number, I'd subtract one every day, or five at the end of the week. When I got really bored, and couldn't read a different book in class, I might start looking at the holidays and holy days we got off from school and subtract those paltry numbers from the grand total, too.

My parents were happy that we could walk to school. They were glad we weren't in public school, where too little learning and too much acrimony were going on. *Acrimony*, I thought to myself. *I know what acrimony means.* While I understood my parents' motivations, and I responded to their efforts, the Catholic nuns and priests and teachers—they were acrimony in holy clothes.

OTHER THAN THE SHINING-EYE WAY that she spoke of and traveled with Saint Anthony, I didn't see much that seemed Catholic in Morrison, or in her characters. In other words, nothing prepared me for her religion announcement, after she questioned my use of that inside word, *catechism*. To my mind, her work was biblical. Full stop. Except for the old nun in the *Paradise* Convent, Morrison's characters seemed to me to be either Black Baptist or field religion. The girls who lived in the Convent I remember as mostly wild. No Catholicism involved.

I realized eventually that I was conflating racism and Catholicism, but then, they seemed entwined to me, and both seemed mean and callous and mental. The Catholic schools I went to actually made me anti-Catholic. Year after year, I was disabused of any notion I had, any gumption, bluntly discouraged from seeking intellectual advancement. I was vehemently discouraged from getting too far ahead. Their racism was sneering and vicious—on their very faces, looking meanly at me. They made me ask the question: Can racists see gifts in Black kids? Maybe they can't see, maybe they see and choose to quash.

While Morrison was inviting and accepting and kind and Black and Catholic, I remained suspicious and silent on the subject of religion because of the abrasive experience I'd had and the scars I carried. Miss Chloe and I lived out the adage not to discuss religion. If I could have praised Catholicism . . . oh, the talks we might have had.

HAIR STORY: HALO LOCKS.

For me, for us Black women, the headwrap is sometimes protection, sometimes crown. Can be both at once. A self-loving layer between us and exposure: to critique, to peering, to fetishes, to unwanted touch, to looking as crazy as we felt before we covered our crown with cloth. During the years I knew her, Miss Chloe often tied up her silvering hair.

Her headwraps sent a queenly message. A tiara, a covering, a symbol of survival. Back in the brutal times, a Black woman in a headwrap had a sliver of control. I can remember days Morrison seemed to be resonating: *Don't be scared / to cover your head.* In her husky voice and with her ear for cadence, it sounded like a rhyming couplet.

Don't be scared
to cover your head.

Morrison started her dreads while we were friends. Once she started locking, her whole hair project grew big and thick and ropy around her face and canny gaze. She inquired about my approach to locks, as I was on my third set. Promptly, as if a button had been pushed, I quoted ingredients: "Aloe vera, coconut oil, essential oils—lavender, usually, but peppermint is good, too, especially if your mind needs cooling off. Mixed into paste with chopsticks and stored in reused plum jelly jars." Part ritual, part chemistry, part hair story. Dreads need hydrating; dreads need care. Dreads are not low-maintenance hair; they are a drape of stored memory, and they bespeak a certain beauty sense, a declaration of freedom from emulating hair hanging flat. Ours grows sunflower style. Dreadlocks—like Afros, like cornrows, like headwraps—are a physical manifestation of rejecting the white gaze. Locks argue vehemently against "prettiness expectations" based in concepts of beauty tied to white attributes. Locks are the antithesis of flyaway hair.

Toni Morrison's locks grew out wide first, an Afro halo round her face. From that Afro ring, that circle round, her dreadlocks dripped, and dropped, and signified.

INVITATION. BECK AND CALL.

One spring season in a nondescript year deep in the thick middle of our friendship, Miss Chloe asked me to come visit her at her Hudson house. We talked about a plan. She said she wanted me to wash her hair. We'd had hair conversations, but none had covered service, or tending, or intimacy this deep.

I considered what exactly she was asking. She wanted me to wash and oil and probably twist or separate her locks. The way I knew how.

Almost immediately I began imagining which handmade hair oil I should concoct. Which essential oil might be best for her wholly wild hair. Orange is calming. Lavender: calming and innocuous. Peppermint and eucalyptus open the pores. Geranium lingers and makes you feel giddy. Bergamot makes you happy, almost high. I felt a latent eagerness to introduce Miss Chloe to clary sage, but clary sage, like lapis stone, is not for the head, which means not for the hair. Probably I'd carry a few essential oils and let her help me choose.

Naturally, and also almost instantly, I envisioned the scene: the preparations, finding the dates, arranging the drive, my homemade supplies, the long trip; my readiness; guarding against fatigue; the logistics of a hair wash in her home. I saw my coffee-brown arms burrowing deep in her explosion of then-oat-heather-gone-stainless-steel hair. I wondered about the ratio of sable to wire. In my vision, I stood over her, her face up, her eyes closed, her hair weighed down and drinking water. We had set ourselves up in her downstairs kitchen. She was not chattering; we were comfortable with the silence, both of us listening to the rubbing, scrubbing.

In my imagining, I dove into the assignment as if it were ordinary, the assignment being washing Miss Chloe's hair. After a few minutes' scrubbing—or, more accurately, rubbing—I removed my hands from her wild gray cloud, expecting my hands and fingers to be covered and cumulous with soap. Instead, I drew back nubs. My fingers had been singed off, had disappeared, lost in her wet wild wisdom hair. The stubs—where my fingers had been—were smoking. Digits charred and swallowed by her billowing crown.

That sequential imagining was astonishing and a mystery. Its own little instant movie.

We continued talking, ostensibly uninterrupted by my smoking vision, which I did not disclose. I decided not to mention or explain. For sure, I got the message: like Morrison (maybe even learned from Morrison), I tend to privilege my vision. I genuflect before imagination.

And so, I did not follow through on washing Morrison's hair.

Imagine the request turning to an "air kiss"—another oh-so-New-York behavior: You reach for the person you are fond of, you align your cheek with theirs, and the two of you barely touch at all. It's rather a pantomime. It's the leaning toward each other that's a PDA, even though your reach means something to the both of you: affection that is both real and not physical. The hair wash idea was like an air kiss in action.

Yes, Miss Chloe. Sometime, Miss Chloe. I'll mix the aloe and the oils and bring them, Miss Chloe. Truth in the infinite; but only an *air* of promise now.

This air kiss means something to the two of us. Planning is participation.

IN ANOTHER SEASON, AFTER TIME had safely passed, I returned to the subject of lock care. I asked Miss Chloe about her locks, how they were getting washed, who was caring for them. She told me the housekeeper, whom I spoke to sometimes when I called.

"Cool," I answered, and I mentioned the housekeeper's

name. *Jeez-lenn* was how I pronounced it, mimicking Miss Chloe's pronunciation, without knowing the name's origin language or how it might be spelled. I never asked, never worried; I did not think I would ever need to write her name. But then, years later, like a light bulb, I recognized that, yes, her name was "Ghislaine," pronounced *Jeez-lenn*. I knew the housekeeper was Haitian, but only years later did the accurate spelling dawn amid tawdry revelations about unchecked power and predation. We sometimes learn in the most circuitous of ways.

As an icon, as a rock star, Morrison attracted the cameras of countless photographers and has also been the subject of visual artists' vigorous viewpoints, their trained eyes. For visual artists, Morrison's hair has been a fixation; a preoccupation; a repository, in frame, of twinkles and highlights and plain light positioned as holy. Artists trail her hair behind her like a veil, like a garment, like a curtain over history—that is, presuming that what is behind you equals past. Most works of art that render or memorialize Miss Chloe make much of her robust, rising, flowing hair. A gray Afro halo, locks radiating out, longer than rulers, sometimes curled. Her hair figures prominently, sometimes abstractly, like a mystical morass the artist could not resist or unsee. Visually, there is impressionistic possibility; perhaps, as with Rapunzel, you might put to some use the ropy ladder of her hair.

When I first met Ms. Morrison, I had similar hair— simpatico, though not yet gray, not then. I sat across from her so many times, me with my young dark dreads, and she with her wisdom hair, accentuated and increasingly graced by her time and work on earth. When you let go of the dominant culture's views of you—when you abandon *their gaze*, as Morrison so weightily and consistently modeled—one of the first things you become is quietly more au naturel. You stop being willing to straighten or fry or yank yourself bald. You start to appreciate other women who sport Afro halos of their own. You applaud women who crown themselves in wrapped fabric. You realize all of what you are releasing yourself from, and when you look three feet in front of you, you see that she has hair like yours. When the rock star and the works of art tell the story you are in, you feel your choices corroborated.

Whether her locks were loose or wrapped, Miss Chloe's crown was regal; her hair a symbol of resistance; her headwrap a symbol of *all we've been through.* Toni Morrison accepted her coronation gracefully. She honored her public by embodying regal bearing. She generously showered her admirers with jewels of her own creation: shimmering novels, shattering stories, glittering speeches, incisive nonfiction, impressive insights, capacious ideas, biting humor, and the lifestyle of an idol. She earned the veneration bestowed.

PARIS

My daughter, Ailey, was born to a dreadhead mother, which made her partial to free hair. Of course, my daughter wanted to dread, once she could reason. My daughter pestered me for months and months for you-don't-yank-it-every-day hair. I explained to her—she was seven—that dreads were a long-term commitment. That once her dreads locked, I was not going to cut her hair or take them out. That she'd have dreads in high school, if we started them now. I urged her to wait, but kids don't know from waiting—and how much nagging can a mother take? Especially when the child is speaking good sense and reason, there's no reason to stubbornly say no. I used an upcoming Paris trip to help the lock-starting seem momentous. Dreads you start in Paris should stay with you as you grow.

We traveled to Paris for our birthdays in 2008. My daughter's birthday is one day after mine. There in the City of Light (and sweet bridges), I washed and oiled and twisted in her new locks. My main goals for our Paris trip: to introduce my daughter to her first foreign clime and to start my daughter's dreads.

Starting locks takes hours and hours. First, you have to wash and squeaky-rinse the hair. Rosewater is a great launching rinse. Starting locks the first time demands freshly washed hair. Locks should be twisted only while wet.

We surfed television channels during the lock-starting hours. I found Morrison being interviewed on CNN International. I was delighted and astonished by the serendipity, but also not surprised to see her on television in France. She had already rocked the Louvre—having conducted a whole series of well-covered events there, as an invited diva, a rockstar curator, a guest from the highest echelons of American culture and thought. She invited young brown poets from the Paris streets. They were living, and reciting, and were elevating their art. There were news reports of rap in the Louvre. The headlines carried question marks.

Morrison's 2006 stint at the Louvre encompassed a whole

month's worth of curated events on dislocation, on foreign-ness. Florence Ladd lives in France, and she reported that the tickets to the Louvre event were the hottest tickets in Paris at the time. So, to watch Morrison interviewed from a Paris hotel room was normative, reasonable. I imagined I was watching a repeat on television, though not a replay for me.

We were on a high-ish floor in our boutique hotel. There was a Juliette balcony, views: cascading Paris rooftops, angling and peaked and dropping into one another, ultimately merging into indistinction and then disappearing into the sky over Europe. On that balcony, on that trip, my daughter took her first camera portrait of her mother. When you get dreads, you get bold. The two of us walked out for *pain et de café* every morning; *chocolat chaud* for the kid. I encouraged her to handle and count euros. Breakfast was calm and routine and sunny. My daughter was unaware that she was living a legendary lyric: Paris in the springtime.

It was afternoon when the hair wash was done, the soap doubly and triply rinsed, the oil conditioner and shower cap applied, the waiting, the rinsing, then parting and twisting with aloe, basting with coconut oil, and listening to Morrison, who was speaking English—which means she may as well have been talking directly to me.

The interviewer—white man with accent—asked Morrison how she had accomplished the fine writing she produced.

How? Wow. How banal, I was thinking.

Morrison answered, "I take out every extra 'the.'"

My hands glistened with aloe and oil. Circular tendrils of my daughter's hair clung to my nails and knuckles. Perhaps I made a gasping sound. Perhaps a hoot or a *whoo*. Morrison's precision and brevity always astounded me. My daughter could see me as she sat still, gazing at "the process"—two of us in the hotel mirror, which spanned the length of the closet door. My daughter dressed herself for the occasion: cool black tee, black Converse high-tops, jeans. She didn't have to turn her head to query me. Our whole afternoon was on display, and doubled by the mirror.

Six words. In six words, Morrison had proffered a real directive. The six-word craft book, like the six-word story, like the six-word autobiography. I know what Morrison means. No excess allowed. Commit to compression. Choose and deliver words that deliver. Don't be lazy; don't just point. Lose any words doing insufficient work.

My daughter sat poised at the gate of hair freedom. She was aloft, so happy the styling did not hurt. Proud of her success with persuasion, she coolly and expectantly watched her hair change form. In the mirror, I could see her real delight. With an example in her mother, she knew exactly how this project would turn out. Considering outcomes ranks high as a factor in good decision making. The lore of locks argues that your hair carries knowledge, contains memory. Dreads do not support ignorance; all you've done has been watched by, and wound in, your hair.

My daughter was a girl child, turning all of eight in Paris. Basking in the reality that if you can reason, you can win. There I sat, caretaking, all buttered in glisten and shine, basking in Morrison's international reputation, her brief, almost hilarious advice.

When Miss Chloe first informed me that her sister, Lois, had died, I sympathized, and felt alarm. Miss Chloe expressed anger—irrational though understandable—that her sister was gone. Miss Chloe was upset that her sister had predeceased her. I do not know whether her sister's death was sudden. I do know Miss Lois was a little older than Miss Chloe, although when you hear any of the parts of their story as sisters, you can see that, at least as children, they were almost simultaneous.

Death blows a hole in the sonic vibration of life, whatever the other rips and tears and regrets. *You will never hear that voice again. You will never. Hear that voice again.* The first of the postmortem tussles involves accepting the truth of the brand-new absence, accepting the absence as forever, accepting the voice as forever silenced. This is a very hard part of grief.

Grieving is all about deciding where you will stand given that death has changed your life. Will you stand beside your sadness? Will you hold it in your arms? Will you rail and retch and wail? Or will you go to photos, to rememory, and possibly smile?

There is also a timing question: How long will you stand there, where the hole has blown open? How long will you be sentinel, standing at the gate of goodbye?

Miss Chloe referenced her sister in each of our last conversations.

Lois is gone, and I miss her every day.

Lois is gone and I want her to come back, so I can slap her for leaving me.

Lois is gone. Lois is gone.

I told you my sister died?

Listening to Miss Chloe after Lois passed made it unsurprising when, in just months, Miss Chloe followed to the next plane. Her tone was tinnier than usual; her speech was rather quick. I was quiet, only interjecting a word here and there, and so, she meandered along mentioning memories and intentions, logical or not. When, after a while, there was a lull, I did ask whether she talked to her sister every day. There was something in the air, in the tone, in the acuteness of her injury that made it seem like she'd been robbed of a mighty routine.

"Yes," she answered. "Every day."

Any younger sibling identifies their close-by older sibling as a fixture in their lives. Morrison's earliest victory, learning to read early, came because of Lois. Major transitions in her life were defined by Lois's company, encouragement, accompaniment, advice, example. From learning language, to the library, to Howard, to her first publishing job—Lois had been present to her sister, Chloe, to aid and counsel, to help her get where she was going.

This one person has been both a witness and a catalyst to your entire life. They have known you longer than you have—a powerful understanding that continues to plow forward without a constant need for explication or permission. Morrison would sometimes tell the language joke that she thought, in the beginning, that *Loisandchloe* was one word. The Loisandchloe nomenclature has hints of that kind of trained unison. What comes after the combined one word?

These directives, to the unit, begin the training of the unit and plant the unit's recognition of itself. So many of Miss Chloe's stories involved Lois helping her, paving the way for her next break. Being alongside.

My older sister, Brenda, is three years ahead of me. When she learned to read, I learned to read. I can almost see her small finger moving under each word. Naming each word for me. I had been reading for nearly two years when I started kindergarten. I could read without my sister by five. Morrison read before she started school, too. We both harbored enduring reverence for our big sisters—marching ahead of us, advancing us into our futures, teaching us to read. We followed them.

My sisters and I have a rare kind of sibling unison, and I attribute that in part to Ma Howell's birthday celebrations. This slant toward unison had other practices in our childhood. The pressure to consider and act collectively had a huge effect on our ability to collaborate and think communally. My two sisters and I were summoned, often, as *Brendangienoonie*, as if the three of us were one cheer to be raised, one task to be assigned, one step away, moving forward all together. When my older sister learned to drive, my father bought *us* a car. We went everywhere together, which sometimes didn't make sense. My father did not want my sister driving alone, so we three went where she had to go. And if my younger sister or I needed to be taken anywhere, my father expected us three to pile in and be present. Sideways witnessing? Sideways accountability? At the time, it was strange, but two score and ten years later, we remain an active team. We work together.

We make stuff happen. Who wouldn't understand the painful end of simultaneity? I offered Miss Chloe all the sympathy.

Lois and Chloe were two survivors of a complement of four children, the girls barely two years apart. "The girls" likely operated as a unit, which fit the gender-driven expectations of their era. Miss Chloe's two brothers may have been a separate unit of their own. For the two sisters, for many years, both the brothers had been gone. Their parents were gone. Only the two of them left to testify to their past. And then Miss Chloe—of her generation—remained all alone.

Because: life.

MISS CHLOE AND I ENJOYED each other's company, and that showed up in our plans. We egged each other on with our suggestions or additions. We weren't trying to outdo each other, but we tried to respond to each other in some way that doubly referenced: language and a thing, a today thing and a yesterday thing, a folkway in educated language, a folkway in fictive language, a point made by a point made in her books. Consistent praise was offered for the tautly imagined. I think she would have loved the story of the shampoo and smoking fingers; I didn't tell that story; I could have only if the story had not been about her and me.

Our conversations were content-predictable, though the angle either one of us took could be anything on any day. That's where our spontaneity came to rest. We talked around and about subjects in which we were both keenly interested—life and language and Black people. Our point of origin, or of reference, was Black womanhood. Our Black women's reality was our living, breathing frame. We talked about all kinds of things that mattered to us, from the police (a subject she raised), to maternity (my concern). A whole continuum of conversations hummed in between.

For example, we both referenced and apprehended the bottomless disregard for Black children in this caustic society. What folk will do, what we have done, to protect our children from haters. Morrison's two sons had been grown for years, and yet she talked about how she tried to protect them from the police. This conversation was easy to have—about her sons, or any, as we were all on guard post–Trayvon Martin, post–Tamir Rice, and post–all the resurging white supremacy craziness Morrison and I (and all of us) have lived through. We both lived the daily life of watching our young people, especially boys and men, treated like straight-up waste.

Our concerns for our culture and for our children and for our future were predictable and simpatico, even though our conversations were free-ranging—lively, unpredictable, sometimes humming with shared objections, sometimes twinkling with surprise.

PREDICTING WHAT MORRISON MIGHT SAY was near impossible. You could rest assured that her chosen words would be lean and cleanly delivered. Her brevity often brought whip and snap to her language. But how you felt or how you responded was up to you, and she would not give that much thought (your job). We were both sensitive to language hurled at our colors and cultures; we both recognized that language often encodes disdain, contains heaping, steaming malice aforethought. We were against those usages.

Morrison took her machete to the weeds blocking our history from view. Clearing, so we could all better see what was going on. Miss Chloe and I often nodded to the past when we spoke. We encoded eras in language when we talked. The conversation we once had about the word *haint* placed it in the nineteenth century mostly, only trailing into the twentieth, possibly on the apron strings of superstitious people. Maybe negroes who cooked, who worked in kitchens. There, where the aprons (and apron strings) were and where the conversation did not have to hide. We mulled over *haunt* and its possible or probable relation to *haint*. I believe *haint* is used in *Beloved*.

The Good Negress probably prepared her for this interest of mine, but what a surprise to discover this in conversation. Using *The Good Negress* as a title dragged a term from a far past. Morrison noticed. No surprise to me. You could always expect that what you said would pass through her finely developed ear for language. When we were together, she and I eyed each other, making language references; the toss of words between us, between us. Sometimes, other people would be there and would either miss the pitch or look away. We entertained each other with language. Eventually, when we saw each other less and talked on the phone more, I came to miss her query eye, her raised eyebrow, her side-eye reactions, her speechless rebukes and entreaties.

We both were nearly awed by how much words could be made to do. We were both exceedingly willing to play with language—on the page and out loud. In pencil, in ink, in life. Many occasions, I heard her dip and slide, whip and slice, using a shorthand that sometimes seemed inaudible to others. Other times, she winked at me. I dip and slide myself; but whip and slice? Not so much. I can do language shorthand. I can dip and slide and torque. I never learned to wink, sad to say.

MALE COMPANY IN NARRATIVE ARCHITECTURE

Both *Paradise* and *Song of Solomon* appear to me to be novels centering men. *Paradise* even more so than *Song of Solomon*, which is a daring assertion. Morrison's men tend to come in pairs or small crowds—dedicated bands of brothers. As best they can be, of course, in a society bent on their destruction, a reality that Morrison neither softens nor avoids. Singular men are not central to her stories. Solo men are peripheral characters, even if some drama of theirs reverberates throughout. Plum and Shadrack both are examples of big drama from the solo periphery. Nel's husband, Jude, too. Morrison pairs male characters, and then they can effectively reflect each other. Women's opinions or perspectives on men do not matter to who men think they are or to how men think they should behave.

Male company is very normative in our culture. Men and women are oddly yet starkly separated. Emphasizing male company structures male reflections into the narrative—a perfect strategy for reading men on men.

In real life, men often make choices and behave as if they are unobserved. Or, if they have the hubris, they assert that observation of their deeds or misdeeds is of no consequence. Men in pairs replicate this and bolster the narrative structure by keeping male appraisal outside women's point of view (an undoubtedly loaded frame of reference). Women often focus on sensuality and/or possession relative to men: men, absent pairs, could electrocute every male appearance in the novel with the spark of sensuality or sexuality. Morrison set up her male characters to make demands of each other, to engage with each other, to perform for each other, in each other's presence. This male mirror approach strengthened her presentation of men, made them seem more objectively drawn.

My reading and my experience led me to believe that Morrison might be somewhat partial to men or boys. In her era, that was not rare. That's the same influence that made my grandmother "Jim." There is hardly a Black woman alive who doesn't want to save a Black boy from the ruthless and noxious predations of our culture. Yet and still, some women are partial; they prefer boys. Who would question this for Morrison? She raised two sons; she had two brothers. Writing about Morrison post-Morrison, I realize that when I wondered about her pairs of men, my thoughts did tend to gravitate toward her late brothers. Not that her pairs of men were like her brothers, but they were a pair. Think Howard and Buglar, Milkman and Guitar, Ajax and Jude, Deacon and Steward, Coffee and Tea. And then, finally, two pairs of pairs, a quartet: the trio of Pauls and Sixo. That idea came from somewhere—maybe brothers, maybe sons. Maybe the structural demands of narrative architecture.

BLIND TRUST

Morrison's works both celebrated and assailed the language we live with and labor under; her work helped me to understand that the ways language assaulted me were not a misperception. We had this in common, both of us hyperattentive to the way language shakes and ricochets. How words confine and condemn. How expressions elevate you or grind you down. How, without armor or defense or keen understanding, language can limit without your even knowing it. People don't see or interrogate language; we accept language the same way we accept history—as presented.

Morrison maintained a wild, relentless, and sweeping fascination with the unexamined facts of the past. Through all four of our American centuries. Morrison chose to mine the times on which the door had closed. Morrison was not a futurist, although she definitely tagged echoes in the present to their origins in the past. Morrison did not hesitate to reimagine any event, any crisis, any original scream.

THE ARGUS COMPANY, IN THE business of classroom wall décor, produced a poster that used no capital letters and listed words and phrases that showed what I refer to as "cast Black." The poster was called "white lies." Under the guise of motivation, most Argus posters reminded or admonished: *readers are leaders; sometimes you win, sometimes you lose, sometimes you learn; winners don't whine.* I had a fondness for Argus posters as a young student because the messages were broader than my life and also because the messages often played on words. These are the considerations of language I ruminated on while my classmates finished their work.

I know the "white lies" poster was not posted at my own school. I imagine I encountered it at a library. Perhaps the brand-spanking-new Martin Luther King Jr. Memorial central branch of the DC Public Library, on Ninth and G Streets NW, in Washington, DC. Ma Howell dragged us to all the major civic and municipal openings in Washington and nearby: the new King Library, the big white Mormon Temple, the Kennedy Center, premieres at the Tivoli Theatre. The King Library was a whole big new world for me. My first rare books room. Floors of stacks much grander and more curated than at the little community corner library I visited weekly while my mother shopped for groceries.

The "white lies" poster presented "white lies" in large type, accompanied by a hefty list of words that positioned Black as problematic: *blacklist, blackball, black sheep, black eye, black mark, black magic.* There were probably forty or so cast-Black phrases listed.

Sometimes I think I dreamed that poster, as I have not been able to find a version. But it was not a dream. The poster was cut square; the background was a neutral gray. The "white lies" letters were white and placed right of center, above the vertical midpoint. The cast-Black words were different sizes, all around. That poster—not fantasy—changed my life and disabused me of the blind trust we are conditioned to place in our language.

A whole list of black words that fit the cast-Black criteria await us in the dictionary. At first these notions raised my temperature and accosted my language enthusiasm. But then I learned the writer's great power to choose the words we use. Cast-Black phrasing is my linguistic detritus.

Argus poster or no, the dictionary can confirm the cast-Black ruination that language heaps upon this construct we've called "race," this dichotomy we've termed "white and black." Neither black nor white color terms make sense for the visual of human beings. (Any child will tell you people are pink or beige or brown.) Once the dichotomous (good/evil) term is accepted, our language more than cooperates, or co-opts, or contributes to murder collective equality, ambition, and esteem.

Morrison did not accept language whole hog; she did not use the dubious assignments of "black" as evil and "white" as divine. (Nor do I.) Acutely attuned to language, Toni Morrison began the little-noticed work of refusing to assign evil to black and virtue to white. Although mostly only writers and students of language would care about this, every vulnerable person who speaks or reads this language is affected. Whether you are vulnerable or powerful makes no difference; the fix is in the terminology. In our society, language conventions make it so that even engaged writers—those who are uninquisitive

186

and not on the receiving end—constantly commit this sin. The "race problem" is rampant in the lingua franca. Inescapable.

When I was a couple of years out of graduate school, where I had studied statistics in the social sciences, I worked at a bank in downtown Washington, DC. My job involved data, using the bank processing systems, which is backroom work; these activities are not public facing. In my early days there— say, the first four or five weeks—I was in a meeting when the presenters began to talk about "master" files and "slave" files, diagramming the files on their whiteboard.

I asked a question about this use of language. My stomach started to grow sour—the meeting had come to a halt. I waited for an answer to my question, and the white banker boys rolled their eyes. Suits. Insisting I was nothing more than naïve, exhibiting a lack of crucial banking experience. If I were a "real banker," there's no way I would have objected, as if these terms were as basic to banking as the words *debit* and *credit*. These files are so named, according to bankers, because of which files give orders and which files cannot take action until there are orders to execute. Explanations were offered with great effort and exaggerated patience.

I continued to express discomfort with the language, even though I quickly came to understand that these words were so deeply embedded in the banking system that I was balking against history, talking about big, systemic issues at our little, local banking level. My commentary or complaint showed that I had not trained in banking specifically; this was the first airing of those terms around my listening ears. I made a case for why those names were impertinent and problematic and not suited for permanence. The presenter treated me as if I had three heads.

"These are standard terms," he quipped, so condescending, "used all across the industry." These were not terms that were made up or new or questioned, he basically asserted, though I'm paraphrasing.

The terms were above all our pay grades.

Yet an argument of ubiquity does not appease me. I couldn't listen to that language. I couldn't listen to them use that language around me. I did not last there very long, and I can still see that stupid meeting, that offensive "whiteboard," that ghastly fluorescent light and roomful of whites. My departure from the bowels of banking was hastened that day.

Curiously, the phrase "in the black" comes from banking, and is one of the few positive uses of the word *black* in our language. "In the black" means you're not in debt. You're not "in the red." You're positive, you have a surplus—as money goes. I want to live in the black always. I have a dream that color-based language gets retired and, thereby, loses its propensity to diminish or dissuade.

NAMING NAMES

Morrison made a project of naming. She handled character and place names with mystery and musicality and muscle. She did not shy away from a sometimes brutal, sometimes joking, heavy-handed strategy for placing and naming characters throughout the centuries she covered in her fiction. Consider Frank and Cee

Money; notorious, liquid Milkman; Pilate, her name carrying its own rueful irony—alongside the esotery of her belly and fortitude of her character. Names have meaning. Characters, like people, grow into their names. Morrison's labels for her invented towns and her imagined characters represent creativity merged with religiosity merged with folk wisdom—all sprinkled with keen acuity. Naming is one way Morrison preened, displaying rich coloratura, imaginative genius.

I can name you as I will, darling character, and under my pen, my pencil, under the sprawling transcriptions of my visions, you will become my very dream.

Place or person, the names she chose were *chosen*. Eleven novels teeming with people and scenes, locales and interiors. Characters, their towns, their children. All her stories dense as roux with rich, resounding names: Chicken Little (poor baby), Milkman (poor boy), Mavis (poor mother), Macon Dead (poor man). Locales: Doctor Street and Not Doctor Street, Darling Street, The Oven, Sweet Home, 124 Bluestone Road. Intersections: the corner of St. Marks and St. Philip, Cross Mark, Cross David; a live town called Ruby; a ghost town called Haven; the Convent, where wayward women came to live after the gamblers and embezzlers abandoned their palace; can't leave out the Bottom; or the brand-new Medallion Golf Course, neighborhoods plowed over, lives disrupted, people evicted, play space erected where the Negroes used to live. Medallion! Toni Morrison's list of nominatives could be a lullaby: Guitar, First Corinthians, Macon Dead I, II, III. Magdalene called Lena. Denver, Beloved, Sethe. Paul A. Paul F. Paul D. Circe. Ruby. Ruth. Pilate. Deacon. Steward. Coffee. Tea. Pecola, Frieda, Claudia, Sloane, Dovey.

Consolata. Sixo. Thirty Mile Woman. Helene, Hagar, Eva, Hannah, Sula, Nel. Queen, Rain, Booker, and Bride. Sweetness. Louis. Malvonne. Heed the Night. Joe Trace. Violent. Violet. Dorcas. Shadrack. Cholly. Hereboy. True Belle. Golden Gray.

MORRISON'S FASCINATION WITH THE QUASI-LITERATE folk practice of choosing a name from the Bible by finding words that begin with a capital letter shows through in multiple books. The folkway of naming based on biblical choices is explained by Pilate, who, by taking a wise and outsize role in *Song of Solomon*, has gained standing as a known and unique entity in African American literature.

Negroes who lived in the times of Morrison's characters could easily find literacy withheld, outlawed, and out of reach. The knowledge that language fluency would allow was the real target of restrictions and withholding. Worlds open up when you can read. Power becomes available when you can speak, write, argue, compete. Reading was illegal for Negroes for centuries, at least in the South. And so, for this most holy moment, the naming of a new child, Negroes were staggered by illiteracy at a pregnant time. Negroes developed a practice of selecting words from the Holy Book, choosing from among the words that began with "high letters," to find names suitable for their children.

Some of the names Morrison chose were poetic, some were referential, some were jabs. Some morphed from the name into a changed name, what might be called a nickname. Some were just straight-up nicknames. And finally, there was the whole cadre of names that were picked from the Bible, or in the case of *Paradise*, from the church.

The literacy crisis represented by the "Bible picking" names is amazing to see in print, and at first it strikes the reader as hilarious. When Milkman has a sister named First Corinthians, you think, *Wow, so funny*. And then Pilate, you think, *Oh no oh no oh no*. Without saying as much, Morrison makes us conclude the obvious: Illiteracy is seriously no joke. Forced illiteracy is another beast entirely. Morrison leads us to the bracing facts using other words. We think to ourselves, *Funny. Not funny*.

When Pilate's name is chosen, the intelligence of the chooser, her father, is foregrounded, lest we were confused. The midwife in the background steps into the frame. We learn that Pilate's father can reason, and we learn that the midwife can remember and can tell a man what he should do. In a culture of illiteracy and forced religion, Morrison names characters poetically sometimes, and sometimes to highlight this culture of illiteracy and forced religion.

I admired all the names she thought of and deployed and made part of our ensuing culture. Her project of naming gave me the impetus to advance the nomenclature, the term of endearment I managed to get her to accept. I never would have called her Miss Chloe, except that she had made such a mountainous, monumental, and magnificent project of naming. I wanted her to see I'd chosen "Miss Chloe" partly as a nod to her many chosen names—from "Cholly" to "Florens," and all the flower and flotsam between.

WHEN I WAS TWENTY-TWO AND still named Angela Jones, I had to make up a Calculus exam before I could graduate from the University of Chicago. I made an appointment to retake the test, and I met with the Math Department associate chairman, Dr. Meyer, whom I had not met before. I was two months away from earning my bachelor's in political science. I had collected three "incompletes" over four undergraduate years. I finished a quarter early to make time to finish those courses. For Calculus, I took the exam from a higher-up in the department rather than my original instructor, because who knew where my young professor teaching freshman Calculus had landed by those three years later? I finished the exam, and once I finished, I stood, as instructed, waiting, as Dr. Meyer had said he'd grade the test right then. We'll know our outcome immediately, he'd said, sounding more imperious than I was in the mood for. I was not overly nervous. I had prepared.

While I stood in front of his desk, he read aloud from my exam. "Angela Jones. Angela Jones," he said again. "The Joneses were a famous family of Welsh singers," he said, and he looked up at me. "Do you sing?"

I was not prepared for this. I had initially been listening to his deep baritone voice; I might have been moving toward reverie, toward thinking about *him* singing, when I registered the full weight of what he'd said. While he remained seated and I stood, I stared at the top of his balding head, his scalp speckled, or freckled, with hair loss and age. What hair he did have was stone white and half-coiffed; he prettified himself to sit in that office, to lord over complex math, and apparently to make remarks designed to rattle. Back then, if you referred to somebody as racist, those were fighting words. And you had better—even if victim—be able to defend your accusation. I made myself stop gawking before the heat of my ire caused his scalp to fissure or peel.

That afternoon, in that office, Dr. Meyer, deputy chair of the Mathematics Department, ended up being a blunt and final irritant. There is much to unpack in the surname area—from the violation of plantation names to the assignment of men's names to the women they wed. At that moment, I finalized a decision that had long been percolating. I decided to formally, legally, permanently ditch the plantation name. Five more years would pass before I went to court, but I fulfilled my promise to myself.

There was a dictionary of names in an appendix of my trusty red *Merriam-Webster*. Multiple appendices, esoteric glossaries and lists: chemical elements, abbreviations, proofreading symbols. All luscious details if you hungered for knowledge, or if you loved perusing dictionaries, or if you wanted to specialize in words. Or, if you were, as I was, in search of a language not spoken at home.

That the name "Angela" means "messenger" became a little secret blessing that I used to help me convince myself that I would become a wordsmith sometime somewhere; I would grow into my *given name*. I would be happy to become what those who loved me and made me had conferred.

Morrison and I shared the whole name-adjustment impulse. Our lives similarly demarcated who called us what name. No one who calls me A.J. knew me before I started writing. A changed name is a historical marker. Morrison speaks on this subject.

If I had stayed a Jones, *The Good Negress* would have been nestled nearby some other well-known, highly competent writer Joneses: *The Known World*, Edward P. Jones; *American Marriage*, Tayari Jones. The future answered Dr. Meyer in words I could not wield in my youth:

The Black Joneses write, Dr. Meyer.

Literature.

TRUTH BE TOLD, I'VE NEVER missed for an instant the surname "Jones." Reminded me of enslavement on the daily, every time I said or wrote "my" name. That weighty baggage I have left behind, and I do not miss the lugging.

My whip-smart grandmother whom we called Ma Howell was born "Jimmie Verdelle." She became an English teacher. When she married my grandfather, she became a Howell. I became a Verdelle in court in Boston, when I was twenty-seven. As a treat to myself when I started my first job, I paid the fee and got the seal. I have enjoyed the flourish of "Verdelle" all my adult life, and I love keeping my grandmother's name alive. There are two Verdelles in our family now: my daughter and me. I know about the power of naming names, changing names, choosing names—in part from reading Morrison; in part, because Chicago; in large part, because our country continues its long trajectory, committing centuries of sin.

PRINCETON: ON PRIVILEGE. OR, PITY POOR GEORGE.

The invitation to teach at Princeton came as a surprise. I was motivated to accept mostly because of Morrison. To have the opportunity to be around Toni Morrison, to learn from Toni

Morrison, to listen to Toni Morrison—this was an opportunity I could never have refused. I learned eventually that Morrison had had a hand in my hiring, but when I received the invitation and started making my plans, I was unaware. So, I elected to join the Princeton faculty to further my own education. I consider teaching a contribution, a service, an investment in the next generation. Concern for our children's future motivates me to teach. I also enjoy the challenge of trying to put knowledge into language forms. Yet, I went to Princeton for my own education. I went to Princeton to experience the insight and personality of one of my culture's greatest minds.

Once I got there, and began to meet African American professors on the Princeton faculty, I considered them and referred to them as "the glitterati." Cornel West, Nell Painter, Arnold Rampersad, Claudia Tate, Yusef Komunyakaa, Eddie Glaude. Me.

MY TEACHING YEARS AT PRINCETON validated the apprehension I felt when considering Princeton for myself. As a faculty member in that environment, I felt a different and further anxiety. My work at Princeton forced me to ask the question whether teaching this cohort of well-heeled, well-endowed Americans constituted a good use of my Black American time on earth. I thought I should devote myself to students who faced apathy rather than frothing, sumptuous support. Lack of interest and investment in Black children's possibilities is certainly one of our national trademarks. Ultimately, I made my way to teach creative writing and English at Morgan State University, which is a vibrant and thriving Historically Black College (HBCU) in Maryland. On campus, I face and teach students who could not be more important to me. Any of the students in my class could be Trayvon, or Elijah, or Tamir. These are the students who need my energy. Young people who have been routinely refused, whose dreams are pummeled, whose lives are snuffed out—sometimes in a fatal confrontation, sometimes in a suffocating slow fade. Students whose nation shows them unrelenting unconcern. The population of students who need our attention is far vaster than that made up of those who can make their way to our colleges, even to HBCUs. These hundreds of thousands, or millions, of students are important to our country and our GDP. We, as a nation, should really stop wasting their time and their lives. Especially while we lavish Princetonians and Yalies with all the good there is.

What ultimately makes me desperately sad is the bifurcation of resources at our society, on every level. At the posh schools, where I've spent my fair share of time, life is good. Good for the students and good for the faculty. Of course, the students tend not to realize that things are as special as they are.

At regular schools, at HBCUs, the road to hoe is hard. The students have been under-resourced for nearly their entire lives, and the lack they face furthers generations of deprivation.

I read a news report about a European study years ago that controlled for all kinds of factors, included all kinds of students, to test what was the best predictor of success in college. The researchers claimed to have multicultural subjects, so that they could question the effects of socioeconomic standing, race, family size, etc. They found the biggest predictor of college success is whether (or not) there were (at least) fifty books in the home when the child was growing up. Sounds like a proxy for literacy, but it could also reflect socioeconomics, I supposed.

Occasionally, I talk about this study in my classes. I, like many teachers, would almost stand on my head or do somersaults to get my students to read more—more widely, more deeply, more continuously, more multiculturally, more personally.

I tell my students that engagement with books is predictive of promise, potential, progress. They look at me like I have three heads, with horns. At the HBCU where I teach, students hardly have fifty books in their homes now, much less when they were children. I try to make clear the distinction between now and the past. I talk about what they're launching into, and I urge them to start now. *Read fifty books now!* I cajole. *Read one hundred fifty books starting now!* I insist. *Everything you need to know is on a page, somewhere.*

By the time I left Princeton, I was sad. I was wishing for parity. I wished for the grounds, the endowment, the encouragement, the expectation, the quiet space, the sense of promise—all for the students I was destined to spend my time teaching. It's tragic that the students in the fancy schools we celebrate have such different lives, such different prognoses, than what the future seems to hold for the dry-longso American student. It's also tragic that graduates of the fancy schools, who will become future leaders and policy makers and "innovators," have no idea how most Black people (or poor people) live. I often think of the reporter Leanita McClain, who was achieving great heights, publishing as a journalist in Chicago, and who died by suicide, when

I was there studying. McClain experienced the life of impoverished Black people, having grown up in Chicago housing projects, ultimately working up to becoming the youngest and the first African American member of the *Chicago Tribune* editorial board. Her essays—collected in her book *A Foot in Each World*—cover the disturbing duality of which I speak: of straddling two divergent landscapes, of trying to live whole while divided, of trying to succeed while your whole community is forcibly contained.

The imagery of her title is never far from front of mind. You can be driven to madness—indeed, to suicide—by trying to live actively in two contexts. Or, if you take the imagery seriously, you can hang in there and keep working, and eventually get torn in two.

The experience as faculty at an institution like Princeton becomes necessary if you're Toni Morrison. You have to be where your huge platform can be supported; you have to be where you're removed and held dear. The vast majority of students, though—whom a professor like Morrison will never see—need energy and acuity, too. They need the world brought to them.

Drowsy, automatic optimism almost makes you say "one day." However, anyone can see that "one day" vaguely references an indeterminate future, which does none of the people who could use a different experience any good.

THE CREATIVE WRITING DEPARTMENT at Princeton, during my era, was in a building we referred to by its address: 185 Nassau. When I first arrived, I couldn't help but hear the parallel rhythm in "185 Nassau Street" and "124 Bluestone Road." I don't often hear of places referred to by their full street address. The parallel registered in my ear.

I heard a Princeton creative writing alum talk about being crammed into that building, 185. Now there is a new facility, the Lewis Center, which may be palatial compared. The ratio of teachers to students at Princeton while I was there was one to seven—so, nothing seemed cramped to me.

Private attention was the baseline of what Princeton students wanted and received. Resources there were many, and were, in some contexts, monumental—like Morrison. Like Joyce Carol Oates. Russell Banks. Edmund White. And like Yusef Komunyakaa, whose office was next to mine.

Yusef, with his legendary, resonant, poetic baritone, reminds that the poets at Princeton were stellar, too. Besides Komunyakaa, there were C. K. Williams, Chase Twichell, and James Richardson. Our department director had won a Pulitzer, as did Tracy K. Smith—who is African American and has been the leading light in Princeton poetry in recent years. Star power. Smith performed at the Library of Congress when she was U.S. Poet Laureate. I love her reading of *duende*, and I love that she brings that word into the foreground. She came after my time at Princeton, but she joins a trajectory of strong poets there.

When he and his partner first moved to Princeton, Yusef Komunyakaa came by my town house in faculty housing. They wanted to scope out the digs and meet the baby. My daughter was a month or two older than Yusef's son; they were babies together. In fact, my babysitter referred her cousin to take care of Yusef's baby son. When his little boy, Jehan, was alive, he and my daughter played together in Jehan's crib. Yusef, his partner, and Jehan lived in an enormous house in Trenton. We had a little two-family dinner party. Jehan and my daughter talked baby talk, standing in Jehan's crib. Reetika, Jehan's mother, stood in their drafty kitchen, teaching me to cook Indian spices first, before you add the food. I didn't expect that, in a few years, both Reetika and their child would be gone. We were new parents, conveying bottles and diapers and listening for wails. Mired in parenting routines.

We left Princeton when my daughter was three, and so she has no memory of Jehan. Beautiful boy. He died not too far from us, in Washington, DC, where Reetika had been housesitting on the white side of town. At our tired parents' dinner, they were adorable, the two babies, their limbs still uncurling. Later, I worked with and befriended a fine poet, Adrian Metejka. Poet Laureate of Indiana. Adrian and I talked about this very tragic story, this beautiful baby boy. (Amazing how we reach hungrily to people who know our stories and share our grief.) Adrian and I compared notes on our own children, and talked about our experiences of and with the great poet, Yusef. Sitting under carport lights, on a Cambridge summer evening, I realized that Jehan might have grown up to resemble Adrian. (Latte. Strong words. Strong morals. Lithe.) Maybe as a son of poets, Jehan would have grown to be a poet, too.

Like many other admirers of his poetry, I loved listening to Yusef's voice. Up close, you could feel his speech moving the air. His register and cadence are the same in conversation as when he's before an audience. He's got pipes, and vinelike memory. Yusef always seemed to be thinking beyond and around what was before him, even if before him was you. Yusef, to me, is the personification of mystery and complexity wound together. In the past, I might run into him at AWP, the Association of Writers and Writing Programs, or in New York somewhere. He welcomed me warmly: "Well, hello, A.J. Here we are." One little couplet meaning far more than those six tiny words. The timbre in his voice conveys full-throated knowledge of our past.

In adjacent offices, I could hear the recitative baritone and rhythm of Yusef speaking, carrying like a low rumble from his open door through to mine. The sound of his sonorous delivery—of basic, quotidian speech—was part of the soundtrack of my Princeton years.

PRINCETON UNIVERSITY SITS STATELY, SERENELY, as a mostly old place. Greystone buildings. Impeccable lawns between. So much turf and weighty architecture that sounds of conversation are dampened to a hum. Princeton is architecture-dominated. The newest buildings on campus are less memorable if only because they're less rare. You can see new buildings out in the world; you don't see age like the old stone on the Princeton campus unless you go. The quiet, stone-heavy quad; its centuries-old exteriors, august entryways, and elaborate stone arches are stood up and kept up like trophies, like artifacts of an era never to come again. One of those old stone edifices, a 181-year-old building at the heart of the campus that used to be known as West Hall, was renamed in 2017 as Morrison Hall. It is one thing to get a building constructed in your name, but to have a cornerstone building named for you is a differentiated action and an enormous honor.

At Princeton, all manner of conveniences have been retrofitted inside these old stone edifices. The resources, both material and human, are expansive and extensive. When you arrive at Princeton, you have arrived.

Princeton is posh. So different from the schools where my neighbors could go, or where my characters could go. Princeton matriculates about thirteen hundred first-year undergraduates. And for those few students, "next" rolls out before them like a golf green, like a model community, like the stone halls of yesteryear sprinkling fairy dust on their sneakers or boat shoes or Danskos. I already had a verdict on Princeton. I was accepted among the thirteen hundred when I was considering colleges. At eighteen, I found bucolic ivory-tower environments worrying; they portended stifling and a pressure toward whiteness. I was also really worried about white education disrupting or discounting or discrediting my Black life.

The African American Studies Department is rocking at Princeton now, but in the late 1970s, when I was in college, venerating white was still standard practice. The times they were a-changing, but incrementally. Academia was on the cusp of a wider lens and greater inclusion, but that day had not yet dawned. At eighteen, I could not have made the serious decision to elevate my own experience, to celebrate my own intellectual promise, *conjoined with my own history*, in an environment where my history was still mostly invisible and ignored. The pull of whiteness, the unchecked "glory" of Black erasure, was starting to slowly be replaced. In the broader world, we grew increasingly Black and proud.

PRINCETON IS SEQUESTERED AND, IN many ways, terrifically unrealistic. In our department, Creative Writing, all courses were pass/fail. Students' work was to be encouraged and discussed; students were to be challenged; no student was to be burdened with the pesky evaluation of grades.

So much of what we write depends on what we understand. As aspiring creative writers, students need to learn and practice things like dialogue, scene, storyline, surprise. The elements of narrative writing are numerous, almost endless, but the basic elements are not so numerous, and are definite, inarguable. Our students submitted their stories and poems to the class, and we read and discussed. I marked student work with suggestions. Where a student was surprising, or startling, or innovative, or had accomplished a successful revision, I might indicate by a ✓+ or a ✓-. One unremarkable day, the department director asked to see me. The director had been visited by one of my students, named George. The director pointed out to me that I had made marks on the student's story that were evaluative. I was surprised, because George was not the most imaginative writer, so I did not recall marking much on his work. Turns out the story George had brought to the director was not his. He had observed, and had *borrowed*, another student's work to show the director how that student's work had been evaluated more positively than his. George had no marks, no ✓+ or ✓-, on his submission.

So, the director had accepted *another* student's work from George so that I could be admonished. The director argued that a ✓- amounted to an evaluation, that a ✓+ acted as a "stand-in" for a grade. I was amused and almost horrified at once. I imagined that, as director, I would not have accepted someone else's work from a student. I also would not have allowed that a faculty member's pointing out a fine gesture, a clear revision, a joke, or an impressive line equated to their grading a story overall. I did ask the director how students should be encouraged, if not by a stroke on the page. "You can use words," the director said rather impishly, as if he were speaking to a toddler. "You can write a note when they're doing something notable, without evaluating."

I pitied poor George, and I also pitied the director. For these two white men, only their perspectives held weight. My approach to teaching did not matter. Myopia caused them to be unable to see themselves as they were seen in the world. Although I said nothing to George, I did consider what I thought made the most sense. I hardly ever used [check-minus] unless I was faced with a cliché in a student's work—writers need to learn to avoid clichés. Writers invent language that people want to repeat. Language that has been used to death, and has already gone stale, should be left for the unaware. But for George and his classmates, I stopped marking at all. I stopped—for that class, that semester—indicating where they'd done well, or where they'd been particularly inventive. I just let them write on, rudderless. Courtesy of classic, almost cliché, white male angst about being better, about being best.

This little "event" amounts to but one small thread from

the blanket of privilege. Mandatory commendation can really suffocate creativity and energy and uniqueness, especially in a place that glorifies and multiplies (and manufactures, really) money and applause. There is no there here. A little mark blown up through ego into a drama, a kerfuffle, a cost to the students who are uninvolved. White males so often are unhappy unless they feel unjudged. In the real world, life is painful for some people, and for others, like many Princetonians, life must be characterized by ease.

This discussion of whether a student's work should be marked or evaluated almost caused me to combust. So many Black students face major concerns. Books. Boots. Babies. Cash. Comfort. Safety. Sanity. A steady life in their own country.

My agitation made me happy no one had to live inside my head.

AT FIRST, I TRIED TO feel guilty about pursuing my own self-interest at Princeton. But twisting myself into a state did not alter the state of the students. The students were just so flush, so unnervingly swaddled—in money, comfort, expectation. I was guilty again because their comfort levels galled me. Even as teenagers, many of them had more money than I would ever see, and more ease than I might ever experience. Their concomitant blindness was as visible as neon across the bridge. I have always been empathetic, but normal Princeton student concerns, the day-to-day matters of eating clubs and upper-crust-teen snit, just aggravated me. The campus was suffused with wealth and near-delirious expectation. Many of the students were completely insincere. Their experience with Black people seemed sparse, if extant. And I suspected part of my role there was to change that, to help offer the Princeton students exposure to "other kinds of people."

The Princeton campus sported quadrangles, alcoves, archways. Greystone with new buildings where necessary. Many of the old buildings are new inside. The campus green was muted, wickedly manicured, doggedly maintained—seemingly by magic. Perhaps uniformed men mowed lawns at night. The greystone stayed gray and unadulterated. No spray paint, no tagging, no marks of any kind. The New Jersey Transit train that served these wealthy babes was affectionately referred to as the Dinky, and no sense of irony carried. (*Nothing* about Princeton is *dinky*.) The commuter train and Amtrak stop are not on campus, though they are not far. The teeny two-car Dinky shuttles students from campus to trains that are really moving: a commuter to New York, or Amtrak to Boston, or Amtrak to points south.

Most of these students lived physically seamless lives: most of them had proper coats, wet boots *and* warm boots, book money and credit cards. There were certainly students who had fewer resources, but in the main, Princeton students paraded through their college years with ample equipment, copious encouragement, and ubiquitous approval. I heard myself say aloud once, "After the kids finish school here, people come for them with strollers. Graduates are scooped up, strapped in, and delivered to the *Times* or the *Journal* or *The New Yorker*. Once they have arrived, the emissaries release them from their stroller straps, so they can start out at the bottom of the top of the heap."

This pronouncement surprised me. How crisp the critique. I hope I didn't offend whomever I was talking to. This may be caricature, but it's also truth.

Best practices at Princeton involved identifying ways to encourage and advance its students. A fabulous model for building esteem, fostering connection, sharing a positive belief system, and applauding reach, ambition, innovation. The Princeton model is a great approach, but it's rarefied. Students of my color and class face hard knocks elsewhere. But for the thirteen hundred annually who are embraced by the big names, the heavily funded, the endowed, college is pure daybreak. Pouring light onto a future that some kids could not even begin to imagine. Princeton is not alone in this. Our society derides and diminishes millions of students in this nation—annually, repeatedly, without ceasing.

LORE REPORTS THAT THE EARLIEST African American people were brought to the lush garden campus as valets for rich southern boys who had come "up" to be students at Princeton. I say "boys" because Princeton began admitting girls/women only in 1969. Boys only before then. During the historical eras, long years of legalized brutality caused campus chaps to matriculate with enslaved males to attend to them during the academic year, to do all the dirty work: laundry, horses, toting slop jars, likely helping their charges when they were drunk. White Princeton boys, then, could focus exclusively on their well-funded pursuits and enjoyments. Valets were enslaved, but in a Northern place. Unauthorized to read or to earn money, the cadre of Princeton valets represented the source community of African Americans in Princeton now. Started in slavery, just like in the South. This is the story that's told.

PRINCETON HOLDS AN ANNUAL GATHERING called Reunions—alumni descend on the campus and they have a parade. Nicknamed the "P-rade," in it everyone wears some variant of an orange Princeton jacket—a design they have selected and purchased as graduating seniors. Very few present are graduates of color. Possibly, there are very few graduates of color; or possibly, the alumni of color don't come to Reunions. Each year, the jacket design differs. For older alumni, the big question is whether their college jacket still fits. The younger folks are fit enough, and the event is all about gathering, reconnecting, reuniting.

One year, I took my daughter in her stroller to watch the people wear their jackets and march. It was a hot day. At the end, everyone merged into the student center, brand-new then, and named after a huge donation from alumnus Sen. Bill Frist. There was a man there who stared baldly at my kid in her stroller. The smile on his face could have been delightful, could have been leering. Strangers are hard to peg. I was hot from the outdoors, and the man was red-faced from the same heat. I was bristling now, too. His ogling seemed a reach to engage with my undiscerning, very small child. Plumb staring at my baby. I could not see how she engaged with him, but the place was so congested, so deluged, that we were in a temporary logjam. Everyone was just relieved for air-conditioning. I stood behind the stroller, being sure to speak so that my daughter could hear my voice. I watched the staring man's behavior, his lack of self-regard. He did not recognize that staring is considered gauche and inappropriate. Maybe he could not imagine that he looked to me like he was leering. Maybe he could imagine seeming suspect—to me or to anybody else. Eventually, he looked up at me; I might have been glaring by then.

"That's a cute baby you got there," he said.

I offered the barest hint of a smile. *Don't be making my child comfortable engaging with strangers* was the thought burning in my mind. My daughter had already demonstrated that, facing away from me in her stroller, if she heard my voice, she would stay calm. She was always more comfortable if I talked or sang to her. If she heard my voice engaged with someone else, she'd be calm. Sometimes, in silence, she would grow fidgety and either wail or try to turn in the stroller to make sure of who was actually pushing her along. Her comfort level in the larger world was nil. She did not sleep, rolling along. She did not sleep in the car. She did not sleep unless the night was late. Otherwise, she was reaching and looking and watching. If she wondered where her mama was, she would let you know.

The man then began to interrogate me seemingly due to his interest in or engagement with the preverbal child in the stroller. He saw himself as "being nice," and interested, and not aggressively interrogatory, asking me questions rapid-fire, in a row. He asked more questions than seemed polite. I think he told me what class at Princeton he was in, and asked the same of me.

"I teach here," I clarified.

And then he had other questions.

What I taught. Oh. What I wrote. Oh. Joyce Carol Oates. Toni Morrison.

The conversation went dense quickly. He knew of the faculty.

"What's your name?" he asked finally, almost in closing.

"A. J. Verdélle," I answered, not really wanting to say, but after you admit you've published, you can't be silly like that.

"Steve Forbes," he reciprocated.

I DID NOT FEEL PRINCETON students needed my knowledge or my passion or my experience or my energy. I believed Princeton brought me there to model an achieving Black person, to give students access to contemporary talents in the discipline. In the main, Princeton students were there to live out their adolescence and to *get finished*: practice social skills, make connections, write papers, read books, learn to wear orange at least once a year, learn to be good club members, practice having conversations about ideas, learn to keep a schedule, and wait out (enjoy) the last years of adolescence. These students would not lack or be denied any learning or exposure or pathway to their goals.

Most Princeton students believe themselves gifted. And they *are* gifted—they are gifted so much beyond what African American students generally can access. It's shocking. There seemed to be no limits to what could be brought to the quiet quad. Students waited expectantly for what they were to be given, beaks open, capacious options brought wholescale to their tiny nests, and then broken beak size. Gifts proffered to the privileged. Days lavish with supply.

The best use of my energy would be teaching Joneses, Johnsons, Smiths, Washingtons—brown students who sometimes knew gunshot and who often needed more world in their lives, who needed to be taught about pathways or shown that pathways existed, or that channels for progress could be whacked open. Not infrequently, I admired Toni Morrison wielding her magic intellectual machete, whacking down weeds in thickets—with her writing as the cutting tool. The need to clear a path for the regular African American student remains urgent and critical. The Princeton stroll just unnerved me, when so many children from my source, who share my color, have needs that continue, after centuries, to be dismissively ignored. I remember being so ignored in school I just wanted to lean back screaming. Our students need both examples of and synonyms for opportunity; they need a campus as a haven; they need mirrors held up to their gifts; they need modest possibilities to be amplified and multiplied. Students who need me need an active experience of encouragement. Students who need me might need an explanation of the metaphor of a stroller coming to a college like Princeton University to collect the graduates and take them to their next station.

HBCUs are high-contrast environments. Since 1867, Morgan has served students who have been entrapped by white disdain, whose lives depend on what's been meted out, whose experience of lavish could not be more remote. Most of the students who come to Morgan are regular, African American, beloved, and deserving—ordinary Joes and Joannes. HBCU students often don't have a lot of money; they don't have a lot of exposure. They come to college to improve their options, to see if they can find a grown-up place in the world—where they can make a living, where they are not doomed to subsisting, where instead they can build a life. Some HBCU students are comfortable, but learning and living their heritage at HBCUs nourishes the roots of their lives. Regular people, many people of color—people who aspire to jobs and safe dwellings and a route through—are abandoned by our society, prosperity the stuff of dreams.

David Wilson, president at Morgan, mentioned "Xeroxing privilege" at a university talk. *Ding ding ding*, went the bell in my mind. *Yes!* I thought. Wilson was referencing how, nationally, Ivy League and "high-echelon" institutions recruit and graduate the same five thousand students of color nationally. Then national companies or corporations compete for that same small group of graduates, year after year. Wilson goes on to estimate/guesstimate/theorize: African American graduates of Harvard and Princeton and other schools considered elite amount to fifty graduates a year who then get five thousand job offers each. At this rate, Wilson hyperbolically suggests, it will take two thousand years to increase corporate diversity. Our work managing the mechanics of diversifying our society needs to be more intentional, more strategic, more robust. David Wilson, as president of Morgan, is actively engaged with both educating the African American student and contributing to the larger-scale diversification of professional and corporate hires. Dr. Wilson raises issues that dovetail with the imagining I advanced of the post-Princeton baby stroller, which engages with the issue that Morrison raises about how racism creates waste.

Consistent disregard for Black lives has never made good sense. The waste of Black potential and humanity does not get easier to stomach over decades, or centuries. This abusive approach, *which continues as we all watch*, does not get us closer to parity, prosperity, or reasonable opportunity for Black people to live and thrive. Especially Black men, who apparently are hunted. Xeroxing privilege will give you copies and continuity of the status quo, but there are so many originals who need their chance at life.

Princeton recruits and accepts selectively and then graces its students with plenteous gains and advantages, including, in my opinion, minimal consequences for adolescent missteps and transgressions. I read somewhere that privilege is defined as being accustomed to a lack of consequences. Seems like a fruitful definition, and it seemed pretty universal among the students there. Legacy students, small classes, orange jackets, parades—and heaping opportunities for the already well situated. Regular students, students of color, marginalized students, impoverished students, are left to an enduring state of scarcity.

We make no effort as a culture to reduce the number of lives we foreshorten or discard because our society fails to correct its malignancies. Diversifying and equalizing our society will require a great education for the ordinary child, adolescent, college student, citizen. HBCUs offer opportunities to actually change families and alter communities, to open pathways in society that have been blocked or barricaded.

Toni Morrison graduated from an HBCU when they were the main or only option for Black folk—before these colleges were deemed "Historically Black." Our society will take thousands of years to shift minimally toward equality. Channeling attention and resources solely toward the already well resourced is just obnoxious, and in no way supports progress. It reinforces the unchanging status quo, Xeroxes privilege.

Princeton was my first teaching job. I have been "accused" of being a natural teacher all my life, and I have saved more than one student in my family from failing required courses. I tend to be able to find the language to explain almost anything I've already learned, and so teaching has always been what I do. At Princeton, the campus and the student group kept me registering brand-new impressions and wonderment. Some Princeton students were so privileged they were stultifying; many were endowed to the point of being totally out of touch, though not all. Some students were eager and aware and engaged. There are always a few students, in any context, who declare kinship; others who understand and are empathetic that not all lives meet with such fine Princetonian handling.

As with all teaching careers and schools/universities, there are students who are greatly affected by you, who remember you, and who call you from their landing places. Liriel Higa, one of my Princeton students, called from the Opinion section asking me to memorialize Morrison for the *New York Times*. The *Times* wanted an essay from someone who knew her personally. Liriel remembered me.

A Princeton creative writing graduate called from Modern Library Classics to ask me to help reintroduce an early African American novel, *Imperium in Imperio*, originally published in 1899. The publisher wanted introductory essays from me and from Cornel West. The former student called to recruit me and then asked for my help in securing Dr. West. Their letter to him had gone unanswered. And so I was a conduit. Cornel and I were already vaguely friendly, but ultimately, those few months working closely with Cornel West were a gift. Focusing on a work of Black literature published during Reconstruction, alongside one of the finest intellectuals this soil has produced. Cornel West is a walking encyclopedia: knowledge spills out of him as from a natural wonder. Be ready for references to history, to our history, to Greece, to God, to the ground where you stand. Theologians tend to be this way, though. Cornel West is extra. Erudite, amazingly "learn-ed," he is like a rock in his association with Blackness, in his articulation of the moral and biblical imperative of the recognition, uplift and aid to the poor and marginalized. His analyses of oppression are never wanting. Dr. West already knew about the author and theologian Sutton Griggs, who wrote *Imperium*, and who became a doctor of divinity in the decades after slavery, when there were few other paths to intellectual agency and/or latitude. The most ambitious and educated Negro men found a path to full humanity through divinity and religious training, gaining respect in their own communities and from outside groups as well.

Cornel and I grew in esteem for each other. Talking with him about Sutton Griggs, and Reconstruction, and backlash, and skews toward religious training, I learned more about Reconstruction, and Dr. West and I learned more about each other. Cornel talked about his own religious training; we discussed Black rhetoric, and ministers now. *Minister* is a pretty major, pretty mountainous word, considering all its forms.

Cornel's Princeton office was a warren of books stacked and arranged as if balance games were being played. You had to move carefully because books were everywhere, horizontally and vertically placed. I didn't want to disturb his narrow aisles, his spatial intricacies, and so, during my visits, I stayed near the door, or even leaned on the doorjamb, taking notes. During one of our work sessions, Cornel introduced me to Eddie Glaude Jr., who directs African American studies at Princeton now. We were all three so much younger then. Especially Eddie and me. Cornel West has seemed wise as antiquity forever. Dr. West is a world-renowned charismatic prophetic educator. Eddie Glaude is author, commentator, and department chairperson. We are all three now gray. African American studies at Princeton got a lot of attention from all those big minds around there. Cornel wanted me to stay at Princeton, jointly in African American studies and creative writing. I did not have the energy to work that out then. But Cornel West was so encouraging and supportive. He was immensely popular at Princeton; his classes drew hundreds.

A few of my Princeton students already had definite plans to become authors. Nate Sellyn, Rivka Galchen, and Jonathan Safran Foer are three Princeton writers I had in class who have been successfully published and have gained mild-to-wild notoriety. Emma Bloomberg was also in my class and had the most careful, thoughtful penmanship: her conscientious, even, proportioned script made you think of Victorian precision and decorum; I half-expected that from her stories. Another writing student, Ibby Caputo, went on to graduate from the Columbia Journalism School and has won awards in health journalism at turbulent times in health care. Elisa Durrette, a writing student who became a lawyer, won the prize for my favorite Princeton story.

Elisa gravitated toward visiting my office after she took my class. As a young African American woman, she viewed the few African Americans on faculty as people who interrupted the white sea. We brown faculty members tended to, or had to, permit students as satellites. Shining moons, hot planets. The order of the universe, of the university, depended on us, too.

Elisa came to Princeton from Omaha, Nebraska. When she told me this, I looked up at this young African American woman—engaged with me in the same way that I had engaged with Chicago—protectively, for inspiration, for affirmation. "Omaha, Nebraska?" I repeated, just to pass those sounds across my tongue. "You and who else?"

Omaha, I thought. *Warren Buffett, steaks, Elisa Durrette*. I'd had no occasion to say the words *Omaha, Nebraska* before Princeton, before Elisa Durrette extended our acquaintance beyond the classroom. When I asked Elisa how she had gotten from Omaha to Princeton, she answered with a story I've never forgotten and that I've shared many times as a towering example of creative thinking and bold action.

Elisa explained that when she was admitted to Princeton, she was delighted, but she also knew that she and her mom would not be able to afford for her to go. Elisa recounted how she researched every company headquartered in Omaha and located the names of each of their CEOs. She wrote an individual letter to three dozen CEOs, she reported. In her letter, she described her high school experience, her admission to Princeton, and her entrepreneurial ambitions; she said she wanted to be a business mogul, like Oprah. Elisa indicated that she was writing to inquire about potential for scholarship support, because without funding, she would not be able to attend Princeton. I don't know whether the letters she referenced were typed or handwritten. Computers were just starting to become personal tools and desktop equipment at that time; there were no laptops then. We were at the bottom of the curve in the trajectory of personal computing. If the men to whom she wrote encountered Elisa's handwriting, they would have been forced to observe concentration and focus in print. Like Emma Bloomberg, Elisa had distinctive penmanship that was recognizably measured and controlled. Both of them seemed to draw, almost craft, their letters.

Elisa reported that three of the three dozen Omaha CEOs agreed to team up and fund her Princeton college career. Each of them paying for a year and change. This is how Elisa Durrette made her way through Princeton, and this is how she answered my question about how she had gotten to Princeton from Omaha. Elisa was nineteen when she told me this story, the first year I met her. Elisa visited my office frequently during her last three Princeton years. She often brought news of the late Claudia Tate, Black woman scholar and faculty member, who died too young—at the age of fifty-four, in 2002. A literature and African American studies professor and scholar, Claudia Tate is someone I only briefly met, but like me, Dr. Tate was a faculty mentor to Elisa, contributing to her further development at Princeton—and to her continued innovation in life.

Elisa is inspiring and impressive. Watching her act on her curiosity as a student reminded you why you taught. When I gave a talk in the writing workshop about avoiding clichés, Elisa voluntarily put together a list for me of one hundred clichés. I used this list as "punishment" for years: if students continued to write with clichés, they'd be assigned to rewrite a number of clichés on the list. Ten for a first offense. Very time-consuming work. Requires you to think of things you wouldn't bother with otherwise—like why we say "rained cats and dogs." What in the world? Clichés are ghastly, and in terms of meaning, they are often nonsensical. There's hardly an easier way to weaken writing than by using unexamined clichés. Clichés can send the meaning of your work careening. If you are a professional, clichés make you seem like a hack.

My classes are still confronted by the list of clichés Elisa compiled for me. I could show anybody the list today, should they want to improve their skills at freshening language, or should they want the "punishment" students are challenged with once they prove they're lazy writers.

When Elisa graduated, I took a huge bouquet of Princeton orange roses to Commencement, for her mother. After the ceremony, I walked the crowd, scanning the few African Americans there. In twenty or thirty minutes of wandering and witnessing all manner of graduation joy, no sighting. I offered the celebratory bunch of roses to an Asian woman who looked like a proud grandmother. I congratulated her and walked home.

Turns out, the supporting CEOs had come for Elisa's graduation and had whisked her and her mother back to Omaha on the private jet they'd flown in on.

Both Ibby Caputo and Elisa Durrette are my small constellation of enduring relationships that Princeton gifted me. These two former students, and Toni Morrison.

Elisa and Ibby are almost as close to my daughter as they are to me, which is a sure sign of staying power. They both met my daughter as an infant, fresh from New Orleans. Ibby has survived a major illness, has resumed her career as a journalist, and has moved abroad with her outstanding Buddhist British husband, Damian FitzPatrick. Elisa moved to California and married a progressive lawyer, who works in a powerhouse position at a progressive nonprofit. With two Black women lawyers in the household, they are a fierce duo: collecting art, traveling widely, buying land. Lives set sailing on the power of Princeton. Living proud dreams.

In real time, Morrison modeled for me how to mentor Princetonites. Give them the half hour they came for and be real Black for them. The pressures of the posh white environment were extensive and obvious and unrelenting, but showing up as a Black woman, a creative person, a gifted teacher, an intellectual . . . I did what I saw Morrison do: feed their minds and engage their spirits and facilitate their feeling chosen. In the long term, though, I couldn't continue pouring all my energy and precision into the large population of students who had lives of ease, lily-white social networks, scant knowledge of the real America, and Princeton at their backs.

Fortunately, before I went to Princeton, I had worked with Ann Lauterbach, poet; Ann had a bright, whimsical smile. She often looked like she had a secret, even if she'd just shared the secret with you. It was up to you to take it in, to understand. Ann was my teacher when I was in graduate school, for my MFA at Bard College. Ann modeled lyric language beautifully and taught me important lessons about teaching and writing. One night out, Ann waxed poetic on students as friends. Some of us were expressing concern about befriending teachers, and

Ann objected adamantly. She indicated that many of her former students had become good friends. She encouraged us not to discount how much depth, openness, and vulnerability existed in the teacher-student relationship. They know you, she said. They've already decided they like you. Most of the road you have to travel—revealing yourself, presenting your preferences, making jokes (lame or funny), being on time or late—you've traveled with your students already. They won't judge you any more harshly than they already have.

Because Ann had taught me this lesson in my own teacher-student years, by the time I arrived at Princeton, I understood. Ann acknowledged how many mountains we cross trying to teach and learn with our best students. Without her early lyric meditation on the slow processes of learning about another human being, I might have rejected the overtures of my most devoted Princeton students, just on principle.

Immediately after the discussion with Ann, I mustered the gumption to befriend my favorite teacher, Archie Rand, who also taught me at Bard. Thank goodness for Ann and Archie. How much poorer my life would have been without Archie's exuberance and deep knowledge, his indomitable, uninterruptable, painterly focus. Archie Rand has been painting works in the Jewish tradition for years; his focus is near miraculous and really motivating to behold.

This kind of unrelenting focus was similarly a Morrison hallmark. When you witness this kind of focus in artists, you encounter steel, stamina, steadiness. Focus always shows, too, in the body and/or the volume of the work. For poets, sometimes this volume is vertical. How high does the poem tower? How low does the poem dig? But Archie Rand is a painter, and in his field, as for novelists, focus and control are manifest in volume and breadth.

Were it not for Ann Lauterbach, I might have missed out on my decades-long relationship with brilliant Archie Rand. He's taught me so much about color and about life.

My small coterie of Princeton students, who have marched along into the future with me, are a result of this late-night discussion, this modeled teacher-friend trajectory, which has enriched my life. There are many examples of this model (student to teacher to friend) in the history of artists in any given age.

When I signed the publication contract for *The Good Negress*, Archie and his lovely wife, Maria, celebrated by giving me a beautiful party at their Sunset Park house. Maria has gone, but she and Archie were supporters of mine since I first started to write. They sent my daughter gorgeous baby dresses when they received her one-hundred-days birth announcement. The book launch party was wonderful and memorable and full of sweet good cheer. Maria was a legendary hostess, and pianist George Cables came and played.

I was fighting with my editor at Algonquin pretty furiously at the time of that party, but I had kept the explosive arguments a secret. The rocky process was terrifically confusing and was taking a toll on me physically. I was ill at the signing party, but I had to keep secret how very sick I felt. Fortunately, I was at Archie's house, where we were all comfortable, we were a small-ish group, and people were warm and friendly with one another. That party put very little pressure on me. So, I pretended things remained tremendous. But I wasn't totally present, and I moved through the celebration in a kind of haze. Things worked out, ultimately (obviously). But at the time, I was woozy.

I have noticed as the years have passed that I feel called to waking whenever I hear Jaco Pastorius's "Three Views of a Secret." I check the listing, and it's George Cables playing. In response to that rise of energy, I turn up the volume. I imagine that the great George Cables played that tune on that launch party afternoon. May be. Otherwise, why the sense memory? Why the call to stop and listen; why do I notice this song, of all the tunes that play? The music is beautiful, and the lyric idea is luscious: three different perspectives on something unsaid.

THE ATELIER

One of the first times we talked after I arrived at Princeton, I asked Toni Morrison if I could come to her class. Crazy, nervy ask. She would not allow me. Of course I understood, but at the time, I would have loved to witness Morrison engendering writing in young people. Her approach to pedagogy fascinated me by its mystery. Was she calculated? Extemporaneous? Specific or theorized? But I never witnessed her working in a classroom, not once.

Yet I learned from her constantly, sometimes from her commentary or actions, sometimes from my own processing. Impossible to spend time with Toni Morrison, and not leave with my brain buzzing about something she'd said or suggested. She never disappointed. You just did not encounter people who spoke with the aim, the speed, the sailing precision. Archery-like in their chatter. And so, I listened; and I paid attention. Either we spent time just the two of us, or she invited me where there were crowds. When it was just the two of us, I experienced her mind up close: her brevity; her muscular, honed capacity for concentration. Her tendency to joke. Her searing insight, keen perception, compressed speech, swift decision making. Her wit, which even she enjoyed. I can't remember who we were talking about musically—someone whose music was initially unpopular, even derided, or condemned in the beginning, and then they changed the world. Maybe James Brown, or Aretha Franklin, or Nina Simone, or Sam Cooke. At one point, Miss Chloe remarked drolly and summarily, "The older generation always despises the music of the next generation."

An inarguable observation, delivered flatly and definitively, by Toni Morrison.

With characteristic (and often cutting) brevity, she could make a short statement, in the middle of a long conversation, in the midst of a conversation rising in heat, that could shut the whole matter down. That was my experience. This flat-footed acknowledgment of a plainly visible reality always caused me pause, to reflect on brilliance. Toni Morrison's ability to see was unusual, and innovative, and unique, and honed. Her mastery of language permitted her to deliver her insight, cutting through all kinds of muck—intellectual "quandaries," thickets, cheese. With erudite delivery, in her husky voice, she stated what could have been obvious to everyone.

Cross-generational musical disdain bears out in the reality everywhere. Eunice Waymon, aka Nina Simone, changed her name so that her mother would not know she was playing risqué music in nightclubs. Her mother could see the name "Nina Simone" on the brightest of marquees and would not suspect her daughter. Musicians are constantly breaking with the past, at peril well documented in biographies and histories. Families, schools, neighborhoods, churches live and fight to survive through rifts over music. Brawls inside households, over the tone, the volume, the profanity of the music. A Black boy was killed over music the shooter thought was too loud; the shooter—a different generation, a different race—thought he had a right to regulate. Once you hear Toni Morrison slice through a truth so briefly and accurately and *humanistically*, you wonder why you haven't seen or said as much yourself. Morrison was uniquely able to see and speak clean through muck or muddle, to create space for inventiveness, even as miasma dims the forward view.

Morrison brought a new teaching context into the Princeton Creative Writing Department, which she called the Atelier—a collaborative and immersive classroom modality. *Atelier*, a French word, references the kind of workshop where carpentry or woodwork is done. As many times as we say the word *workshop* as writing teachers, it's shocking that it took Morrison to drag the architecture of an actual workshop into our consciousness, via another language. A structurally focused word, *atelier* translates into "room to work." Morrison's vision of a workroom centered on a defined project. Both the process and the outcomes of creativity were emphasized.

Morrison chose to use the Atelier to bring creative artists to Princeton for short periods—a semester, a couple of months, a few weeks. Powerhouse creatives whose work she admired. Black (and other) geniuses whom she wanted more people to notice, from whom she wanted to hear more, with whom she wanted to work. She selected and invited artists to come to campus with an artistic project in mind, in which Princeton creative writers could be involved and challenged. Students could broaden their exposure to creative arts and personalities. Students could put art into practice. Artists from an array of artistic genres were engaged. When I asked Morrison how she developed the Atelier, she explained, "I have to make my courses interesting to me, too." I understood completely. You don't write at the Nobel level and affably continue the read-write-critique-repeat model of creative writing "workshops" set up for undergraduates. Change would have to come.

Morrison's innovation in an environment of plenty brought her assertive take on art and invention even more clearly to the fore. Her launch of the Atelier supported the ancient adage "Necessity is the mother of invention." In one of the most well-resourced teaching environments in the nation, Miss Chloe was a marquee member of a marquee faculty; in order to stay and remain engaged, she needed better courses. As usual, Toni Morrison was ahead in the game. Always thinking toward a future that evaluated, elevated, and extended the accomplishments of the past.

Recruitment for her "Atelier" at Princeton created a space for Morrison to acknowledge and engage with Black geniuses in other disciplines and allowed her to expose her students and the campus to other fine (often Black) minds. She went in search of artists and intellectuals she could champion; she brought them to Princeton to work actively on creative projects, with creative writing students participating. She chose professional artists like filmmaker Louis Massiah, musician Toshi Reagon. Well-known musicians like Yo-Yo Ma. Richard Danielpour. When Morrison had her celebrated and extended residency at the Louvre, in Paris, she invited and showcased Black Parisian musicians and poets, referred to in the press as poets and dancers "off the street."

Morrison chose writer Edwidge Danticat to participate in that amazingly curated atelier abroad. Morrison was thoroughly discerning, and she unearthed Black genius from wherever genius lives and thrives. In her observations and approach to broader arts, Morrison lived that idea she espoused: your freedom demands that you reach back and free someone else. She reached resolutely. The people she reached for—not just me—benefitted from her wit, her banter, her body of work, her direct gaze, and, most important of all, her choosing. Morrison actively sought out artists whom she might help our sluggish culture welcome.

Louis Massiah, whom I had known casually, I got to know more directly as a result of Morrison's recommendation, her almost-luscious recollections of his work, in the Princeton Atelier. Massiah made a movie about a Black nursery school in Princeton, allowing students in Morrison's writing class to put art into practice. Morrison spoke lovingly of this nursery school/kids project. Louis (pronounced LOU-ee) is another keen-eyed artist whose work Morrison championed. After Miss Chloe passed, Louis sent me a poignant note: "Yes, A.J., we have lost our champion."

The high point of my experience with the Atelier was the semester Morrison invited Gabriel García Márquez. The García Márquez seminar, called The Architecture of Narrative, was compressed into a super-short period—a few short weeks. The workshop met for a stack of hours, three or four days a week, for a few weeks straight. I had a pretty breathless conversation with Morrison about García Márquez's visit. I wanted to be in the seminar. No pressure. I wanted to just listen to what she and García Márquez would say about writing. I wanted to be there, if silent, back of the room.

When I asked to join the class, even as a wallflower, Morrison asked immediately, "Do you speak Spanish?" If I could have translated, I imagine I would have been of use, and therefore allowed.

"Not really. Street Spanish," I answered—half-joking, half-referencing my wonderful rememory of Nina Simone. Miss Chloe had no way of knowing my fond memory of Nina. Not then. And she did not perceive any joke in my "street Spanish" remark. She wanted me to define what I meant. I'd used a loaded word. The positive tone was audible, but still it needed explaining.

"No, you can't come to the class," she said. "It's just for the students."

"Do they all speak Spanish?"

"No."

I was not surprised. "Well, the class meets all day for days," I said, changing the subject slightly. "What do the students do about their other classes?"

"They'll figure that out," she answered curtly. "What do

you mean street Spanish?" she returned to the conversation at hand.

Nina Simone, I explained, used the phrase "street French" when I met her, and so I use the expression "street Spanish" after Nina. Asking Nina Simone about living in Paris was a question I prepared, and I had remarked that her French must be amazing. Though I was wrong about her French, I didn't regret my prepared questions. You don't want the conversation to stall during your one chance to talk to Nina Simone, or Toni Morrison, or James Brown, or whomever you admire. You have to be ready. You never know how anything will go with celebrities; you just prepare and hope for calm.

To have a chance to quote Nina Simone to Morrison was a special, generation-joining experience. To talk about having heard Nina in person, having had a chance to visit with her, to draw up that memory of the South Side, when I was quite young, and to recount that brilliant concert in Chicago. It was thrilling to have a great story to tell.

"I'LL INVITE YOU TO SOMETHING when he's here," Morrison promised, referencing García Márquez. So, the invitation to a Princeton dinner organized in his honor became my consolation prize for missing the whole García Márquez/Morrison Atelier. At the García Márquez dinner, there was a distinctive golden hue suffusing the room. I think they (or Morrison) had curated a warmer light than what we normally expect for events here in the United States. I can see them both crystal clear: lingering, talking, their exchanges cast in red and yellow, creating an evening tangerine. There was no fluorescence; this gave the room ambiance and soul. I stayed late. People had started to leave. I remember sitting at a table with the two of them. There were other people there, whom I remember only vaguely, as shadows. García Márquez said his nickname was "Paco." He doodled that on a card while we lingered. Later, I read that people called him Gabo. Did he have two nicknames, or am I misremembering what he told me? I envisioned him deep in the arbors of Mexico, like in *One Hundred Years*. I learned way less than I wanted to about García Márquez. My experience was like a movie: mostly visual, little translation. I had to settle for being present with the two of them, which was no small shakes.

Researching García Márquez's visit after the fact, there in the photo with Toni Morrison and García Márquez is an eager-looking, baby version of Jonathan Safran Foer. Just as I remember him: shining glasses, leaning forward, ever-present half smile, hair high over his head.

ONE SEMESTER AT PRINCETON, I was asked to teach a seminar on Morrison, on her work from a creative writing perspective. I agreed to do the course because, by then, I had come to view anything that involved Morrison as including her hand. We had a pretty pointed conversation about the seminar. She asked direct questions and seemed pleased by my answers. There were only four students, which she thought was a fine number. "Like a graduate course." The conversation we'd had about being so visible to Sterling Brown—when she and Florence Ladd and one other student were in class together: that is what came to mind. In the Morrison seminar, we reviewed and summarized and situated all her novels (then nine), but we closely studied a powerhouse three: *The Bluest Eye, Song of Solomon,* and *Paradise.* All the students had read *Beloved,* and in discussion, *Beloved* came up frequently. Our tiny seminar met in Firestone, the Princeton University Library. That we met in the library impressed her too. For the remainder of the semester, I was anxious that she might appear, but she did not.

Morrison asked me to meet her late one afternoon at the Woodrow Wilson School. As of this writing, Princeton has removed the racist Wilson's name and replaced it with "Princeton School of Public and International Affairs." Woodrow Wilson resegregated the federal labor force, unemploying and reimpoverishing so many freedmen. A betrayal. An official governmental abandonment of citizens like me and my foreparents, who were struggling and striving in Washington, DC. During my tenure at Princeton, the Woodrow Wilson School stood erect with its original name. A newer building, with its architecture of steps and glass on all four sides, surrounding an august interior.

Roy DeCarava, genius photographer, published an image of a young woman who stands up against some stairs, maybe bleachers. The risers span the horizontal plane of the photograph and accentuate the young woman's perfect posture. The woman wears a big smile. Black and white, of course, the photo probably dates to the early 1960s. DeCarava shot and printed regular Black people, and Black geniuses, for decades. A lot of people who could be characters in fiction, or their children, can be represented by DeCarava photographs. Also, like Morrison, DeCarava made you see what he saw. You realize he is showing you what you always see in your regular life and just don't notice. Morrison's work presented the pedestrian with the same power.

You learn from accomplished artists like Morrison and DeCarava that our everyday lives are worthy. Amazing that worthiness of self as humanity is something a person would have to "learn."

As Morrison came down the wide steps of the Wilson School, she reminded me of DeCarava's girl against bleachers. The whole background accentuated her posture. Descending those steps that afternoon, Morrison—her posture and position amplified—could have been trailed by a superhero cape, and she would have looked no different than I remember. We were meeting there as a starting point for an evening. I do recall that she asked me to come by at the end of an event she was doing, which I did. By way of hello, I said, "A superhero cape would fit this tableau perfectly."

"Who, me?" she answered/asked. She was coy, and laughing.

I answered that her sweater/drape could stand in for a cape, and she replied that superheroes wore bright colors. No subtlety, no grays.

"Imagine it orange" (referencing Princeton), "with a big purple 'TM' on the back." She could see what I was envisioning; she giggled. We walked along into the evening hour, into *flânerie*.

MISS CHLOE AND I WENT to Wild Oats, a boutique grocery store that was local to us, on Nassau Street. We'd gone to collect materials for charcuterie. Again, she asked me to make the choices. Was she trying to learn my palate? Was she disinterested in food somehow? Was she indifferent? Was she a person who liked all kinds of food? Knowing me, I collected olives, smoked gouda or mozzarella, an apple or two, stuffed grape leaves. Maybe smoked trout and sun-dried tomatoes. I remember thinking, *She's going to want crackers*, and then choosing some, probably with pepper.

Morrison ran into poet Alicia Ostriker while we were shopping, so Morrison and Alicia launched into an impromptu meeting in the front of the store. Morrison's progress through a place like that could be slow, impeded by well-wishers or admirers, or people who didn't often see her.

I was distracted. I was standing outside the checkout, in the narrow walkway between the registers and the exit. I had hurried down that walkway before, holding a screaming baby. This time I held the bag of what Miss Chloe and I had bought. Morrison and Alicia stood talking, making plans. I did not think I should interrupt Miss Chloe to say, "I'll wait for you outside." And so, I stayed visible, waiting, revisiting the most unpleasant memory of my whole Princeton experience. I was sure I had been in the store since my daughter's injury there, but only purposefully. No lingering at the scene. But on this antipasto afternoon, there I stood, waiting quietly and impatiently, caught up in my daughter's screams.

When she was fourteen months old, my daughter leaped out of a shopping cart near where I was standing, reaching for shiny magazines she could not read. Given her proclivities to leap and sail through the air, we thought she'd be a dancer. Launching out of the grocery cart, she had landed splat and then had bellowed and bawled and alarmed us to the point

233

where I had to hoist up the screaming, wailing child and hustle outdoors. She was not bleeding, but she screamed all the ride home, shaking the leafy green treetops. She screamed in the house, but then started to tire a little. I rocked her. Fed her *sopa*. She was knocked out, asleep. We watched her, checking to be sure she was breathing. She slept hard, for several hours, and when she woke, her one eye was the size of an avocado.

I rushed her to the big, local pediatric clinic, a place that was Princeton fabulous. Commensurate to those leafy green suburbs and the high value placed on the endless march of white babies and white children. A sprawling place with extended hours; you could go there until 8 p.m., without an appointment. There were multiple doctors working in the clinic, which made it an ideal place to take an injured child. I can still see the doctor from that day: Dark hair. Narrow face. Practiced smile. On the young side of middle age. Avocado eye or not, my daughter looks like me, and has since she was a small child. The doctor looked at the baby. Looked at me. Asked what had happened. I explained, and then I flipped. Was the nap a bad idea? How could I have let her sleep while a bruise rose up dark and mounded as an avocado? What if she had a concussion? I should have had her checked first. I should have rushed from Wild Oats to the physician, loud as she had howled.

He said matter-of-factly: "Don't blame yourself, Mom."

I did not immediately calm down, but eventually his words ricocheted and created a shift in my approach to pediatrics. This was not her first leap and would be far from her last. A broken collarbone was coming soon.

This young doctor set the bar high for my medical experience going forward. His response changed my entire approach to medical care for my daughter's whole childhood. Without knowing before that I would or could, I pressed future pediatrics for interactivity, engagement with and sensitivity to the parent, not just the child. Sensitivity is not ubiquitous. Not everyone is offered calming, helpful medical attention.

"The injury is not in her eye. It's the tissue around her eye," he said. "Her vision should be fine," he reassured me. Treatment: cold packs, cuddling. I added cocoa butter to the mix. Princeton created a medical expectation for me at the perfect stage in brand-new motherhood. Learned expectations, obtained at the sprawling pediatric clinic, designed for the Princeton and Lawrenceville gentry. Accidentally accessed by my baby and me.

As my daughter sped through her baby years, and then jetted through her childhood years, my standards for a pediatrician were not relaxed. I maintained my efforts to access compassionate doctoring—for my baby, for me, forever.

That Wild Oats store went away, ultimately. I've forgotten what it became. Maybe an actual Whole Foods? The poet Alicia Ostriker was another Princeton personality with a huge reputation, perhaps someone I should already have known. After they finished their conference, Morrison and I walked out to her Jaguar together. I had quietly survived the "stand here and wait for me," and the uninvited replay of my daughter's first serious fall. Nobody knew how rattled I was but me.

At the time, Miss Chloe had a little condo in Princeton. It was small and very brown due to paneling. Eventually, she traded up from that little condo to a big gray house on Nassau Street. Morrison didn't love the sprawling gray house, although the house better fit her role in the environment. Princeton was a world full of huge personalities, of stately, wide houses. And there I was watching, witnessing, trying to figure: Which connections should I make? What steps should I take? Would people remember me in her shadow? This is where the "standby" with Alicia Ostriker sent me. Was I really in Morrison's shadow, or did I frolic in her sunshine?

Fran Lebowitz—also a very longtime friend of Morrison's and a woman who is more than funny—is another person I met on the quiet Princeton pathways. When Morrison introduced me to Fran on a sunny day in an unremarkable season, Fran and Miss Chloe were having a visit in Princeton. Fran was driving a car so old it stopped foot traffic. Fran, who is a small woman, seemed large as the ages in her pristine antique car.

Miss Chloe, who believes in the power of the belly laugh, spent forty years enjoying Fran's humor and good company. These two ladies had a solid, impenetrable past. You felt their familiarity, their years of knowing, their rollicking humor. Fran is as funny as the moon is permanent, even with all its shifts of form. I have never seen Fran when she has not made me laugh within moments of our meeting. At Miss Chloe's memorial at St. John the Divine in New York City, I greeted Fran. We talked about who had been more integrated into her life, Morrison or Fran's mother. The question itself informs; we all revere our chosen familiars, separate from those we are given.

I thought to ask Fran whether she still had her antique car.

"I still have her," Fran answered. "She has her own apartment."

Hilarious, and I laughed, even though the person who can afford to house an antique car in New York City is a person who can afford their preferences. I didn't dwell on the car or on the car's NYC digs. You could see that Fran was grieving, mourning Morrison. Celebrating Toni Morrison—that was our focus that important afternoon.

WHEN MISS CHLOE TURNED SEVENTY-FIVE in 2006, an elaborate birthday party was held for her at Princeton. A merry evening with ample catering. Glittering people happily gathered. The clink of glasses and the aroma of well-cooked food cast an air of limitlessness. "Happy 75th Birthday Toni Morrison" was written in chocolate cursive around the rims of the dessert plates. There were *scores* of chocolate-rimmed plates, placed in front of us by uniformed waitstaff.

Oprah sat at the head table, and spoke at this celebratory dinner. She wore drop diamond earrings, seemingly big as plums. They shone like beacons, so bright they seemed to wink.

Oprah loved herself some Toni Morrison. Four times I heard Oprah speak in person about Morrison's work and contributions. Each time, Oprah was animated and vigorous, her eyes alight.

At the chocolate plate party, Angela Davis was seated at my table—next to me. Whose idea was that? Maybe Miss Chloe's. Who knows? Angela Davis and Toni Morrison were friends for decades. Their origin story is seeded in Angela Davis's activism and in Morrison's belief that Davis could write an important book. The two of them, Morrison and Davis, shaped Angela's book together, and the book sales continue today. Their relationship emerged in the 1970s, and at the end of Miss Chloe's life, their relationship endured.

I was not prepared for the conversation pressure; I had not been forewarned. I believe Angela and her partner came in late, before Oprah but after the speeches had started. I have seen Angela in Morrison's orbit many times. I have always been cordial and complimentary and polite. I often received news of Angela from Byllye Avery, MacArthur fellow and founder of the National Black Women's Health Project, now the Black Women's Health Imperative. Byllye, and her partner, Ngina, have participated ably as my daughter's lesbian grandmothers. Byllye and Angela Davis go way back, as friends and American activists. Had I been forewarned, Byllye is the person I would have consulted to plan my "conversation with Angela Davis." But the dinner was a long affair, and the information I had in reserve about Angela was not dinner table conversation. I just wasn't prepared for an evening with Angela Davis, and I felt real pressure.

My table talk strategy became to engage pretty generally with everyone (which I did), while Angela felt like a flame by my side. I could not ignore the heat. Not my style to falter in conversation, but I worked to involve more of the whole table in discussion, instead of doing what made sense and chatting according to the seating chart. I don't know if Morrison had spoken to Angela about me. I don't know whose idea it was to seat us this way. (I don't know if Morrison knows my name is "Angela." "A.J." is the only name she ever called me, even when she sang.) Several times during the evening, I found Angela Davis staring at me, and I could only wonder why.

In the future between then and now, Angela Davis and I have had a few low-pressure exchanges. But for the hours we were trapped at that table, in assigned seating, I would have needed to plan in advance. I had reviewed nothing. I was blindsided. Flat as a butter knife.

Morrison seemed to have a wonderful time. She received a whole trove of presents, which made the individual present seem pointless. I had begun to question whether gifts made sense for Morrison.

MORRISON'S FONDNESS FOR GIFTS, and her propensity to receive mountains of them, eventually stopped me from trying to buy for her, especially when there were crowds. When she left events like these, someone carried her loot for her, hauling a sack like Santa Claus. There were mishaps with gifts for her, and then there were times when you had the sinking feeling that what you had brought now resided in a mountain of indistinguishable good wishes. Who knew whether what you carefully sourced and labored over would even be noticed, kept together with its card? I transitioned to bringing gifts only on low days or slow days. I also responded to her direct requests.

THERE WERE TWO REPEAT REQUESTS Morrison made of me, when I asked, dutifully, "Should I send you anything?" Or, on rarer occasions, "Should I bring you anything?"

On a regular day, she might ask for flowers, which I'd source and order as carefully as I could. These could not be standard flowers. I'd had to find a couple of boutique florists, near enough to deliver but serious enough not to be FTD. Her asking for flowers ensured there'd be another conversation, because I'd have to call again later to find out what the flowers I'd sent looked like, whether she liked them, whether the florist had included the colors and blooms we'd discussed. I often asked for calla lilies, as they always make me think of Katharine Hepburn and her lilting, aged announcement about these rare-to-me flowers, in bloom. I'd be checking to ensure the flowers I discussed with the florist were close to the flowers she received, and then I'd decide if they were worth my money. I often requested arrangements low to the table, instead of high vases that you have to crane to see around.

Morrison loved flowers, she knew flowers, she grew flowers. Her first novel began with a season when the marigolds did not blossom. In *The Bluest Eye*, that there were no marigolds laid the groundwork for a story too battered for blooms, and barren of nurture.

In life, I provided the best flowers I could source to Miss Chloe, a lady who so appreciated them, and who had characteristically keen discernment about gardens and greens. Lots of luscious beauty for Ms. Morrison, for Miss Chloe. No carnations or chrysanthemums. No daisies. No baby's breath. No cheap, near-disposable glass vases.

When I lived in New York, I had my favorite florist. Fonda Sara, proprietor of ZuZu's Petals, could be relied on to deliver remarkable and unusual beauty. Artistic arrangements for discerning artists. Fonda's "bouquets" were guaranteed to raise the level or the ante. Morrison reacted with love and joy when Fonda's flowers were delivered to her home in Tribeca. Novelist Cathleen Schine and I can date our loose but long-term friendship to flowers arranged by Fonda Sara. I didn't know Cathleen then, but once, in *Mirabella* magazine, she compared *The Good Negress* to Austen's writing of women and interiors. I tracked down an address to send her flowers, as I thought that was the most amazing comparison to make. Life brings surprises, and genteel gestures are still applauded, are especially remembered; they even launch relationships. Though, in a world of artistes, you have to find florists and booksellers and sartorial splendor in order to make such gestures memorable. Especially in New York City and LA. You have to refine every edge. Cathleen, experienced with both east and west, said they were the most beautiful flowers she'd ever seen. That the flowers nearly floored Cathleen did not surprise me. Fonda Sara's artistry had already been proven on Toni Morrison.

MORRISON'S MORNINGS WERE FAMOUSLY RESERVED—as were mine, perhaps in imitation. Our dates happened always after three, after five, after dark. In all the years I knew her, I don't believe I ever saw or spoke to Morrison in the morning. Except once.

I was visiting her at a hotel in Oberlin, Ohio, eleven miles from where she was born, in Lorain. The Toni Morrison Society was installing its records at Oberlin College. Morrison invited me to come visit, and my ten-year-old daughter and I planned to drive up from Washington, DC—so *far* for one driver and a ten-year-old. But I told myself, *This is your pilgrimage to Lorain*. After I mapped out the trip, I shifted gears and, in spite of the cost, bit the bullet and bought plane tickets. I rented a car and drove to Oberlin from the airport, feeling real elation when I passed the road sign showing the Lorain town limits. I had two kinds of precious cargo on that trip: my kid and a bag of freshly baked yeast rolls.

Rolls are folk history. Hot bread rises under my own hands. No sourcing. Just planning and kitchen alchemy. Morrison and I were both down for that. Comparing what we knew about this women's work, in our history. Because rolls take forever to make, and take forever to master, they are prized. Rolls made from scratch are increasingly rare. I am referencing rolls you start with yeast.

I learned to make rolls from my great-grandmother Ma Goldie. Born in Sweet Home, Arkansas, Ma Goldie cooked for one white family every weekday and Saturday morning, for twenty-nine years. Ma Goldie was paid, meagerly, which is a smidgen of improvement over the historical exploitation of enslavement, of stealing people's lives and labor and progeny, not a wage paid.

After three decades in the white family's kitchen, my grandmother could no longer travel across the city by bus, early in the morning, only to stand on her feet all day and produce hot meals like clockwork for a family of six (not hers). At the end, the white family said goodbye. My grandmother left the site of her employment with no pension, no severance, no retirement. No financial send-off into old age.

For Ma Goldie, the segue from a child of enslaved parents to an independent person did not free her from demands for nurture and feeding by people who claimed she was not worthy. And yet, Ma Goldie's mastery of the kitchen, and her efficiency therein, was legendary, alchemical.

From Ma Goldie, I learned to bake dozens of yeast rolls for the holidays, a seasonal specialty for which I and my family have become well known. Rolls are, at minimum, a fourteen-hour project, yeast to table. (This time frame excludes the shopping.) I committed to carrying on this tradition, mostly to testify to Ma Goldie's decades of neat kitchen wizardry. Morrison celebrated the craft and the time and the art. My great-grandmother made rolls with stunning effortlessness. I've strived to get to that level of mastery, but the truth is, making rolls, for me, is work. I can make the bread taste effortless, but flour makes me sneeze. The clock is always ticking. Sweat runs down my brow. You don't want dinner waiting on the bread.

Morrison had family experience with rolls made from scratch, referred to them as "yeast rolls." Yeast rolls are often mistaken for biscuits by the uninitiated or people inexperienced with either yeast rolls or language. Morrison knew the difference between a biscuit and a roll. Biscuits have craters and rely on shortening and baking powder. Biscuits take fifty minutes, from decision to removal from the oven. Rolls are smooth and depend on yeast and rising. Managing just the dough can take the better part of a day. Yeast rolls depend on their maker's attention and on knowledge of how to knead, how not to overdo.

Some cooks consider yeast a finicky ingredient. Unless you are primarily a baker (which I am not), you have to understand yeast, and its process, as it contributes to building bread. At the grocery, planning to make rolls, I always buy double the yeast I need, carefully choosing from two packaging batches. Invariably, the yeast gets to work during the wee hours—of either the night or morning. If the yeast were to fail, there would be another opportunity, relative both to replacement yeast and to time. Rolls require mounds of sifted flour. If you are making rolls for a large family Christmas, you will sift fifteen pounds. Our sifters do not have a squeeze bar, they have a hand crank.

Flour will not be contained. White clouds leap and swirl and hang in the kitchen air, settling in the corners, settling in the drawers, uncomfortably coating your tongue and getting caught, snowing your hair. You will shower the flour away later; now you are focused on the temperature and elasticity of the dough. You have to observe what the dough is telling you, by its temperature, by its looseness, by its height. It's important to knead sufficiently, but you must be extra careful not to overdo. When the dough gets tight, it gets tough. Toughened dough won't rise, no matter your plans. Rolls require two different rising periods, in a warm, not-drafty area. Overzealous kneading ruins the second rise. Timing matters. Keep the dough warm.

Reaching the first rise can take up to three hours. After the dough has doubled, cresting its container, you smack down (gently) the ballooning part, and release the yeast-fueled air. Then the dough needs to be flattened with a rolling pin, in smallish sections; you work with plate-size portions. When I apprenticed under my great-grandmother, we used jelly jars to cut the rolled-out dough into proportioned circles. Cutting with the jelly jars was my job exclusively. After my grandmother was gone, I became chief roll-maker. I visited Williams Sonoma and bought stainless steel cookie cutter rings, with sharp rims. The jelly jars and the rings cut with the same uniformity, but the rings require less pressure. With the rings, you can work with the wrist, forearm, even triceps. With the jelly jar, you have to work from the shoulder. Twisting the jar makes the cut, not pressing the jar down.

Before they're buttered on top, cut and folded across the middle, and laid out on cookie sheets for the second rise, there's always an issue about where to cook the bread. Everybody wants to eat rolls hot. My father looks forward to holidays almost *because* of the rolls. He and both my sisters will stand by the oven waiting for hot rolls. My father can eat a half-dozen rolls before you can say "Are they ready?" While the bread is cooking, you always know where my father is. Standing by the oven. Full stop.

Morrison was having a family dinner in Lorain. Family dinners tended to make Morrison giddy. Private time, though not alone time. We arranged that I would meet her at the Oberlin hotel at 10:30 a.m. I stayed up the whole night before our flight, working on rolls. I baked the rolls, let them cool, and packed them carefully in parchment, in dozens. I filled a small shopping bag with four dozen fresh rolls, and at the crack of dawn, I headed to the airport with my daughter. My daughter's dreads were baby locks then, three or four inches long. The kiddo was charged with making sure the rolls made the trip. Her earnest sense of responsibility has never left my mind. She was careful with the cargo that could not be crushed and could not be forgotten. She respected her mother's hard work.

Morrison recognized roll making as Black woman's labor, as a throwback to the kitchen work that fed white southerners, and as a skill that kept Black people either half or all the way alive. I think five or six times in the course of our relationship, I hustled up a rasher of hot bread at Morrison's request. For this, I spent a whole day in the kitchen tending to the rising. And then, at the end, I'd wipe up flour for days.

That one morning in Ohio, the only morning I ever spent

with Morrison, my daughter and I took the first flight, we collected the rental car, we drove past Lorain and then to Oberlin. Morrison's son Ford came downstairs in the hotel to collect us. I introduced him to my daughter and remarked that I had not heard him coming at all. Ford and I know and recognize each other; he and his mother often traveled as a pair. I learned on that morning: You don't hear Ford coming. You don't hear his breathing. You do not hear flip-flops clapping against his feet. My daughter and I were waiting in hotel lobby chairs, and he walked up on us, in a silent way. I was stunned he was wearing flip-flops, because how.

Making small talk, I said, "Hello Ford, I didn't hear you at all."

Without hesitation, he remarked, "He who walks silently will live a long life."

I imagined that I looked either surprised or impressed.

"You never heard that?" he said. "Native American."

I nodded, and we started on our way. We followed him and his silent shoes upstairs to his mother.

There were three or four very lively young women there. They were her nieces, she said, introducing us. The nieces had come to give her a pedicure. The pedicure was already in process.

We spent a couple of hours visiting. Six women, one room. Morrison central, arranged, queenlike, in a chair. Much chatter—about family; and about Lorain; and about Washington, DC, where my daughter and I lived. The nieces were curious about who we two were. Or, Miss Chloe thought we should explain. She bluntly interrupted my meandering story to say I was her friend from Princeton. They were po-

246

lite and welcoming, all far more adult than my daughter, but younger than me. We talked about the Toni Morrison Society, the events planned for the evening. Miss Chloe inquired of my daughter—the various and sundry interrogations made of children (age, school, interests, intentions, hobbies, sports, books you've read), mostly to see whether (or how well) the child will speak. The child had spoken well at all her ages; then, in front of Toni Morrison, was no exception.

For the family lunch they were having that day, the four dozen rolls were ready. My daughter got credit for doing her carrying job effectively; they had journeyed amazingly well. I was tired, having lost sleep, wanting the bread to be as fresh as possible and not day old. Rolls are a labor-intensive gift. You have to feel some affection to take the project on.

That chatty morning in Oberlin, fresh off her pedicure, Morrison nearly skipped away with her Whole Foods shopping bag filled with rolls baked in my kitchen, hundreds of miles away. Her nieces followed her out, like chicks. I never had a chance to meet Miss Chloe's dear sister, whom I would probably have addressed as Miss Lois. But because of that Oberlin visit, I believe she had a chance to taste my rolls.

Handmade yeast rolls are a throwback. Morrison loved the kind of folk remembrance making rolls represented. I can still see the vision of her reaching to take a bag of fresh rolls from my hand and go liltingly off to her engagement (or home), with one of her contributions mine. That's what happened that Oberlin morning. At the end of our visit in her Oberlin hotel room, I tried to suggest the best way to reheat them. I was going to tell her to wet a towel, to wrap the rolls and let them steam-heat. Morrison put up her hand, shutting me up quickly: "Child, we know how to handle hot bread," she said.

When Morrison first learned I made rolls, years before Oberlin, we were discussing an upcoming holiday. She interrogated *me* to see if I knew the difference, to see if I was making the reference to yeast rolls correctly. It's a huge faux pas in the Black culinary tradition to refer to rolls as biscuits; only people who don't cook, or who don't know the folk tradition of cooking, would make this mistake. Morrison understood the cooking, the rising, the difficulty, the tradition, the centuries of demands for unpaid family feeding. Time had brought us less fraught experiences of nurturing: The anthropology of the Black holiday table. The improvisational reality of the Black family dinner. An extant, chosen menu. An opportunity for plenty. Giddy anticipation. The gathering of the children, the grands. She and I both considered making rolls almost a lost art. Who isn't proud of preserving a dying art?

By now, I have taught my daughter and my nieces to make rolls. They are five or six years into their apprenticeship. They are a team, and they have a system. They can make fifteen or sixteen dozen rolls and still enjoy the holiday. Though they do not use jelly jars, they are still reaching back at least a hundred years. During the fifties and the forties and the thirties, Morrison's era of maturation, most of what you had you made. All work was done by hand.

Dr. Eleanor Traylor, Professor Emerita in English from Howard, is one of Morrison's oldest colleagues and friends. Dr. Eleanor and Toni Morrison were junior faculty at Howard together. Dr. Eleanor reported that once, Toni asked her what she thought was the greatest invention in the world. Toni Morrison insisted the greatest invention of all was the sewing machine. The suggestion has much merit. The sewing machine swept into the household and liberated how your clothes got made. The sewing machine mechanized factories. The sewing machine reduced the seemingly endless work heaped on girls. The sewing machine has been in constant use since it was invented.

Understanding and preserving dying arts, seeing ourselves in truth: as makers, as experts in feeding, in family survival, in kitchen alchemy. Engaging young people into Black culinary history, offering up roots as expertise. This would be the lined-up labor of kitchens that Morrison watched or experienced as a child, that caused her to react to rolls with glee. Rolls often make me think of Morrison now. Grief travels unfettered pathways. Memory calls the kitchen home. Near to Lorain, I see Miss Chloe that one Oberlin morning, in unsunny Ohio light, sauntering toward her afternoon family reunion, with my offering in hand.

WE WERE ALL IN OBERLIN that weekend because of the Toni Morrison Society. The organization, celebrating Morrison as a literary giant, had been searching for an academic home suitable for present needs and future plans. Morrison suggested Oberlin, and so the Society made a meeting there, to explore possibilities and possibly review facilities. I wasn't as closely involved with the Society then as I am now. While I traveled to the meeting, at the time, it was less because of the Society than because Morrison asked me to come.

Morrison received so much fêting in her lifetime. All well

deserved. By the time we got to know each other, she was well known and celebrated and a respected, sought-after artist and intellectual. I came to understand her interest in spending time without numbers of other people. No crush, no noise, no crowds, no stage she had to occupy.

One afternoon in her office at Princeton, Morrison narrated an upcoming moment having to do with the Toni Morrison Society. I was new to her world then, and I wasn't exactly aware of what the Society was or did. Morrison explained the group to me and referred to its members as "lovely, studious, competent ladies." She seemed proud of them, and said that she loved what they were doing. Over time, she discussed the Society when there was a matter of moment, and then one day she point-blank suggested I go join in. This was a direct suggestion, or a direct request. And so, I made contact.

THE TONI MORRISON SOCIETY IS just as she said: a scholarly group of women serious about the author they'd organized to honor. There are societies associated with pretty much all the great authors in history. The author societies are organized under the auspices of the Modern Language Association, the scholarly group for teachers and researchers in the humanities, including literature. There's a Faulkner Society, a Welty Society, a Twain Society. And as the Toni Morrison Society members know and have acknowledged, Toni Morrison is one of the greats.

There are author societies operating nationally and internationally to encourage study of the works of established and esteemed authors. American author societies are numerous, though these groups promote and preserve the literature only of American authors. The coalition of author societies comprises the American Literature Association, begun in Baltimore, Maryland. Begun at the annual ALA meeting in 1993, the Toni Morrison Society invited the participation of scholars and lay readers, and through the reach of their programs, and due to the international renown of Toni Morrison, the Society also enjoys international attention and encourages cross-cultural participation.

The Toni Morrison Society is a thoughtful, inventive group. This was Morrison's feeling, though she seemed coy in her commentary. Now I better understand the way Morrison's remarks about the Society seemed filled with positivity in the beginning and increasing wonder as time went on. The Society was growing and becoming active as I was learning Morrison's landscape. As time passed, the work of the Society grew more targeted and more powerful. Morrison's esteem for the Society grew along with the organization.

Dr. Carolyn Denard, an American studies scholar from Georgia State University, founded the Society and has served as its board's chair. Dr. Dana Williams, dean of graduate studies at Howard, is the current chair. Both these lovely women were welcoming when I showed up at their business meeting. I said, "Toni Morrison sent me." That may have had an effect. The Society has been impressive in the work it plans and does. For many years, it has developed programs, involved Ms. Morrison, engaged with her ideas, and celebrated her name and her works. Toni Morrison, I can attest, loved the whole evolution.

I have been to so many Society events. Since Miss Chloe "sent me," I have tried to stay involved as best I can. Sometimes,

I wish I were a better archivist—so I could keep events and dates straight. Sometimes I wish I didn't have whole families living in my mind, cowboys suspecting store men, running children getting burned by flame. An emptier mind might also help. As it is, I go where I can, I remember whom I've met, but the events themselves run together.

THE SOCIETY HAD A THIRTY-FIFTH anniversary celebration for *The Black Book*. That was in New York. Farah Jasmine Griffin was there, with her students working the event. Edwidge Danticat was there, too, as was Tayari Jones.

During one of the sessions, in the late afternoon, a woman stood up from one of the tables and said she was going back home (to California) and divorcing her husband. Because all of us were sitting at tables and could be seen, I remember concentrating on not dropping my head. I did not want the woman to imagine or deduce what I was thinking, which was: *Oh Lord, here come the crazies.* So, I sat upright and didn't make eye contact with anyone. Other folk, mostly women, were turning around in their chairs. The woman speaking had stood up, so you could get a good look.

She went on: "While I've been here, I've been reading *Song of Solomon* again, and I just realized I'm my husband's third beer."

By then, the call-and-response had begun. People were saying all kinds of girlfriend things—to the woman and to one another. *What? What did she say? Third beer? You're divorcing over beer? She's divorcing over beer? Why is she talking about divorce in here? Say more.*

Now, this is the kind of situation that makes me laugh. To see a bunch of ladies lean into a brand-new crazy-man story. I was breathing deep by then, pressing my lips together so no sound would emerge.

The woman who spoke had reached into her large handbag. She took out a tattered copy of *Song of Solomon*. She opened to a page and read aloud. (Since this event, I've kept this passage marked.)

She was the third beer. Not the first one, which the throat received with almost tearful gratitude; nor the second, that confirms and extends the pleasure of the first. But the third, the one you drink because it's there, because it can't hurt, and because what difference does it make?

The room rose into a minor uproar. The reader was offered all the finger snaps and moral support that immediacy could provide. She was soothed by strangers. She was encouraged and applauded. There was much conversation and much noise.

I don't like beer, and I'm not often around people who drink beer. I'm a loner is mostly why; I don't mind that people drink. But I did find the divorce announcement shocking. I found the reading of the passage humorous, and I found the reaction of the assembled audience amazing and hilarious. The whole situation has not been forgotten. I can still see the woman, I can still see the harsh room light.

This lady is a fine example of what I mean when I say, "If you read Toni Morrison, it will change you." Maybe not so thoroughly. Maybe not so abruptly. I hope not so disruptively. But her books are ignition; you must get ready to roll.

THE SOCIETY CELEBRATED MORRISON ANOTHER year with a big book called a Festschrift, which contains letters and commendations and carefully scripted wishes. A collection of direct messages. All to go on record. These books are archival, commemorative, and prized. The event where the Festschrift was unveiled was crowded with Morrison admirers. I am told the book was one thousand pages long; I don't think this is an exaggeration. (Not one of those hundreds of pages is mine.) The Festschrift celebration was held in a huge auditorium somewhere in Washington, DC. In the huge auditorium there were built-in benches along one side of the cavernous space. There was a woman sitting on a bench by herself; I noticed her because I was removed, too, observing from the edges of the crowd. The seated woman was startingly recognizable. I thought to myself, bluntly, *She looks like James Baldwin in a skirt.* You had to do a double take, which I did. When I looked back a second time, she was looking at me—and so, courtesy demanded that I mosey over and introduce myself.

"Hi, there," I said, sitting close enough to be heard. "I'm A. J. Verdelle."

"Hi," she answered. "I'm Gloria Baldwin."

"Gloria Baldwin?" I said, as she smiled, looking radiant and unquestionably Baldwin.

I was right about who she was. And she knew me. Imagine my surprise. She'd read my book. She had my book on her shelf, she said. We proceeded to get to know each other, there on the bench, disinterested in crowds. I sat close enough to be heard, but not so close as to encroach. I tried not to focus too much on Jimmy, although I was basically looking at a less consternated version of his face. We spent a huge chunk of time talking and laughing, and staying out of the fray. I think I must have told her how pleased I was to meet her, how glad I was to see her, four or five times. Repetitive. Gushing. I was completely thrilled and stunned to be chatting with James Baldwin's surviving sister. It seemed the greatest serendipity, and it eased the pain of my not understanding what the Festschrift was, and for missing my opportunity to be included. Meeting Gloria was a huge gift. We have maintained contact with each other since our evening spent together at the edges of a great crowd.

At the Schomburg, where Baldwin's papers are archived, there is a letter Morrison wrote to Jimmy after meeting his sister, Gloria. Morrison refers to Gloria as a woman of a "certain timbre." We don't meet women like her much anymore, Morrison wrote, alluding to Gloria seeming to be a pillar and observer, from a different, more resolute time. I had the same feeling about Gloria, and for me, she is a grace that came along with Miss Chloe.

At the same time that the Festschrift celebration was in process, Carmen Gillespie, a Morrison scholar at Bucknell University, was editing a book to celebrate Morrison's four decades as a writer. *Toni Morrison: Forty Years in the Clearing* was what Dr. Gillespie's book was called. I had been working hard to contribute to it, and I was also coordinating contributions by Florence Ladd and Mary Nelson Wilburn. I interviewed them about their college years at Howard, and about their poetics with Sterling Brown, and about their kerfuffle trying to wrestle with the approach to Shakespeare in a Black university English department. Mary and Florence and I could have, and should have, submitted to the Festschrift, but I had been informally appointed "leader," and I was so focused on the submissions for *The Clearing* that the Festschrift dropped off my radar. A miss.

The Festschrift night was celebratory and loud. I'm glad I had sense enough to get to the Festschrift evening, because that event gave me Gloria Baldwin, who has become one of the wise women I reach for—when the season demands or when Black women's wisdom is what I need. Or when I just want to check in on a special woman, in her wisdom years, who looks so much like her brother, she takes you almost out of body, watching her, and listening.

At Morrison events where there were hundreds, I retreated to the sidelines. It was daunting to watch the alacrity of Morrison's legion of fans. Stunning to watch. Everybody leaning toward, reaching toward the great Toni Morrison. Gloria and I hung back together that night. I can still see her in the dim sideline light—retro and formal and smiling like Jimmy, prim in her navy jacket and skirt.

I valued the gift of meeting Gloria, and we have kept in touch. One afternoon in late summer, my daughter and my partner and I visited Gloria at her house. We were so glad to be there; I was thrilled for Gloria to meet my daughter, and for my daughter to meet Jimmy's sister. My daughter has said to me about Gloria, and about other folks she met during her childhood: *I wish I'd understood who she was, or he was . . .* This is how time works: you cannot learn until you grow.

When we arrived, Gloria said right away, Jimmy's money bought this house. Such a fine legacy to imagine—Jimmy's books, still seeding real estate. Once the front door was closed, I drew in my breath. There, in Gloria's front room, over a reception table, hung a portrait of Baldwin, painted by Beauford Delaney. At the time, I thought the one I was seeing was the only one. Turns out, Delaney painted Baldwin multiple times. The table and the painting placement gave the whole setup an altar flavor. I almost felt like I should genuflect.

It was a full-frame canvas, with bold oranges and yellows in the background; blue and ochre and sienna combining to create Jimmy's face. Painted by a master artist, a character from the Harlem Renaissance, preserving the youthful countenance of one of my stone-cold idols. Jimmy Baldwin, master writer man.

No one could have told me I would see that painting in person in my life. The painting was like double exposure in so many ways: two men, two careers, two expatriates. Two siblings, two eras, two sides—earth, and paradise—both represented.

Just as it's hard to cover Morrison's artistry and community without talking about James Baldwin, it's impossible to talk about Baldwin without referencing the great modernist painter Beauford Delaney. In Morrison's eulogy for Baldwin, she celebrated and thanked him, suggesting that she positioned him as a predecessor, a forebear, a person who broke ground where she traveled.

It's hard to know or imagine whether Morrison considered Baldwin a contemporary, or an antecedent/mentor. I know that Baldwin and Morrison had conversations about literature, which I imagine were rich and propulsive, based on my experience having conversations with Morrison about language. Morrison always treated me like I knew what I was doing, and from the incidental remarks she made, I imagine Baldwin treated her the same way.

Beauford Delaney was a mentor and supporter of Baldwin's, and in Delaney's old age, Baldwin behaved like his son. Beauford Delaney, born Black, and dark-complexioned, and artistically inclined, in 1901, in Knoxville, Tennessee, had always been artistically engaged and productive; his younger brother, Joseph, was also an esteemed painter of their time. Delaney spent most of his adult life in New York and was a "card-carrying" member of the Harlem Renaissance. When Jimmy Baldwin moved to France from New York in 1948, Beauford Delaney had been a painter and a bohemian and an intellectual and a gay man, working the New York art scene and traveling with the Greenwich Village bohemian crowd. Delaney was productive, and private, and exceedingly well-known in artistic circles. He counted Stieglitz, painter Stuart Davis, painter Georgia O'Keeffe, poet Countee Cullen, and writer Henry Miller among his friends. Delaney moved to France in 1953, at the age of fifty-two. As queer Black male artists and expatriates, Delaney and James Baldwin became very close in France, and held each other in great esteem. Baldwin wrote that Delaney was his first evidence that a Black man could be an artist. This I totally understand; before I met Morrison, she was evidence for me.

American writer Henry Miller, whose work I've not much enjoyed, published a chapbook in 1945 called *The Amazing and Invariable Beauford Delaney*. This is the only work of Miller's that I've read start to finish. As a chapbook, it's admittedly quite short. (I've started other works of Miller's, but beyond Beauford Delaney, our interests do not match, Miller's and mine.) Miller attesting to Delaney's talent, and devotion, and near mysticism, documented an open and cross-racial respect that was barely visible during the 1930s and 1940s, when Black artists were post-Renaissance, and white artists were going along their merry ways. A perpetual bohemian, Miller's motivation to write and sell this pamphlet about Delaney is hard to define. Perhaps the little chapbook was written to support Delaney, who was known to run out of money. Once, when he ran out of money for materials, he famously painted on his raincoat. There is a Delaney composition—*Untitled, 1954*—which has materials listed as "Oil on raincoat fragment."

Or, alternatively, perhaps the chapbook was written just out of curiosity, since both Miller and Delaney were part of the (mostly white) Greenwich Village crew. Miller was known for his "curiosities."

The copy I have of Miller's chapbook on Delaney was republished by the Studio Museum in Harlem, to accompany their retrospective of his work in 1978, a year before his death. In spite of this exhibit, and even with Baldwin's adulation, Delaney's work was heralded and widely respected by artists, and not all that well known by others. Delaney was considered an artist's artist, during his era, and beyond. Delaney was known for his focus, his devotion to painting, and his figurative and abstract artistic phases—including his "yellow period"—European years during which he became enamored with the color yellow.

When attempting to verify that the painting I remembered was actually as I remembered, I learned that Delaney painted Baldwin multiple times. I had not known. Gloria reported that the Delaney that I had seen, that she had so prominently displayed, is now donated to McDowell, to grace the James Baldwin library there. I'm thrilled I first saw the painting in Gloria's home; I could not have imagined that I would see an original Delaney outside a museum, with one of my writing heroes staring expectantly and confidently out of the canvas.

Like I said, I wanted to genuflect.

After Delaney's passing, Baldwin brusquely referenced the very hard life Delaney led. Baldwin also conjectured that "in a less blasphemous time," he and Delaney could have quietly been considered Master and Pupil. Delaney as the Master, and Baldwin, the Pupil.

I totally understand the pressure to name how you relate, and also how your chosen names can be derided by your era, your time, how other people (will) read you. All the years I was friends with Morrison, I felt her restraint. She did not want to "help me" with my writing. She did not want us viewed as "master and pupil." She wanted me to deploy my own agency and recognize my own range and power. A big charge that takes big time to internalize.

ALL I LEARNED FROM MORRISON cannot be neatly packaged. She taught me straight-up lessons, but she also seeded my curiosity, and she created conditions for my orbit to expand. The people I met because of her, the things I know because of her, include Gloria, and Beauford, and some real truths about reach. Morrison taught me, by modeling, that the artistic intellect is like a web: it finds and situates in high corners, is spun out of the way of approach, and it captures and holds whatever comes high and passes through. Whether you have a name for what you see or what you do matters little. Effort and devotion, focus and control—those are the matters that count.

UNCOVERY

Decision making accounts for a huge part of writing. Writing requires that decisions be made about words, characters, sentences, settings, paragraphs, point of view, events, scenes, drama, outcomes, beginning, middle, end. And that's not the end of the near-infinite list. Some of these many decisions are made multiple times as we revise. Learning to make decisions, and to do so without languishing or lingering, is a critical skill for writers. James Baldwin famously said that writers have eighty million decisions to make. (So get busy.) The number is not an exaggeration. So, those of us who intend to write need to build our decision-making skills. And we need to make all those decisions against our human backdrop—the ticking clock we know as mortality.

One of Toni Morrison's steadfast writing lessons: You have to make whatever you write believable. That's your job. If you can imagine it, then making it believable is a function of your focus, of language, of your ability to make images and language speak clearly to each other so that a saturated story passes through to your reader. You need to see as much as is possible, given your insight and sight line and care with words. Your reader needs to see what you see.

I had yet to learn what I know fully now: that all writers and all artists must be intensely autodidactic, self-directed. Morrison expected that writers would take on the task of independently teaching themselves. Regulating their own lives, their own writing practice, their own schedules. The writer—like any creative—must create a product or project in a form that effectively serves as an outlet for their ideas. Your work must interest you, must intrigue you. You must shape your work so that it engages you. No better precision than that. "Uncovery," practice, self-teaching, discovery—all these are ateliers on the road to mastery. As we travel the road to mastery, ateliers are places to tarry—to read, to study, to discuss, to collaborate, to fence, to encourage, to remind.

MORRISON LOVED TO TALK ABOUT her own work, though not necessarily in casual conversation. Interviews represented a platform for her, attention she rightly felt her work demanded and that international attention and scholarship proved true. She would answer your questions. She would also judge the depth of your reading, the breadth of your understanding, whether your questions were stupid. You had to know Morrison's work to do a good interview with her. You had to know Morrison's work as a whole to be her friend. She would squint at you, and dismiss you, if you came lame. She was exacting. She had high standards. She did not suffer fools.

That Morrison had a fire at her Hudson house created big buzz and real news all across the literary community. Writers, like people, have fires. Maxine Hong Kingston had a fire at her house, and Morrison publicly and empathetically encouraged writers to send books to Ms. Kingston, to rebuild the writer's very necessary library.

When Morrison's house burned, there was worry about the artifacts of her monumental achievements. The archivists at Princeton sprung into action, and there was commentary about what had been saved. Eventually, there was an exhibit. Archives in the making. We were encouraged to visit the Rare Books vestibule in Firestone Library, to take a close look at the salvage of the typewritten manuscript of *Beloved*. Charred pages were flattened, their remains pinned under glass.

Morrison's postfire manuscript of *Beloved* showed damage, carefully catalogued. Under glass, near the entrance of Rare Books, you could view her Courier-typed pages. Burn marks, edges singed, words sucked into flame. Standard pages embered into irregularity. A fire-licked, storied manuscript. We visitors gawked at the fragments. How close the future came to total loss of the original. We stood there, before the salvage, observing pages that had been on their way to ash, brown burn stubbornly referencing destruction. You can imagine hot tongues of fire searing her chilling words, lapping at her stone-cold position in the canon.

Surely, the curators had chosen and arranged the flame-damaged pages for maximal effect. Not lost on me. I had a few moments when all I could do was stand stock-still. I put my hand to my heart as if pledging allegiance. To what? To the miracle of its being only half-burned? To the Morrison manuscript, however partial, however partially saved? To the curatorial choice to show burned text, and to alarm us all with the shock of almost-loss? To the waving flag of reimagined history? To *Beloved*? To see the burned pages was to look at a consummation of experiences: preparation of a world-shaking manuscript; preservation of the record of the work; near loss; our fixation with preservation of those works we've deemed important; a record of a house fire. These were hallowed pages, and this was an absolutely knee-weakening save. I can still see the glass case; I can see the pages pinned. Some sentences complete, and others with clauses burned away.

On Wednesday, December 5, 1997, I had my inaugural reading at Princeton. Morrison had been asked, and had agreed to introduce me. A crew from *60 Minutes* came to campus to film Toni Morrison in action and chose to film my reading—to show Morrison at a lectern, before a crowd. Morrison looked to be lecturing from the podium, as if she were teaching, but she was really introducing me. She may have looked as though she were lecturing, but that is not how creative writing classes at Princeton were taught. Our classes were small, held in classrooms with soft furniture. Fifteen students, max. This event was held in our auditorium, and my goal had been to fill more than a hundred seats. Goal achieved. I still use the announcement cards I made for the event, as bookmarks.

The Princeton Creative Writing Department hosted readings for the college and the wider community on Wednesday afternoons—readings by visiting writers, faculty, and, in late spring, graduating seniors. I was nervous and gobsmacked over Miss Chloe's introduction. We were just getting to know each other; there were signs we could grow close.

I had been anxious and often in a zone as I prepared for this important reading. I practiced and put voice marks on my pages. I had been working on my cowboy novel; I had written "Six Prayers." I thought I should read a sampling, but I called Morrison to ask her opinion.

"Should I read from the book I'm writing—the cowboy book," I asked, "or from *The Good Negress*?"

Her answer: "Read what you have to sell."

Bam! I began to be impressed with how succinctly she delivered advice. I read from *The Good Negress*.

My reading was a rare appearance for Morrison in the auditorium at 185 Nassau. I soon learned that she hardly ever attended the Wednesday readings. Whatever Morrison said about me that day was heard only by the audience and that *60 Minutes* tape, not by me. I was delirious, drowning in nerves. *To follow Morrison to the lectern and to read in her presence!* She had not heard me read before, but I had been on tour with the novel. I had practiced. I aimed to read like a professional. My family was there; Ed Bradley was there; a healthy audience was there—but to me, I was reading to Morrison. I wore a red pantsuit.

The *60 Minutes* feature on Morrison was already in production when my reading took place. Ed Bradley had come as the *60 Minutes* correspondent. This was a grand surprise, though Ed Bradley knew that this was my night. With a production team making the arrangements, Bradley had been given the heads-up. The segment on Morrison aired the next month. Morrison's brief remarks that day about my work were silenced by a voice-over. The narrator of the segment summarized Morrison's importance and her illustrious career. On the day of my reading, she and Ed Bradley both let me know that they felt they were making a strategic decision, to record what Morrison had to say about the brand-new novelist A. J. Verdelle. Miss Chloe considered that she'd done something useful and unusual, helpful and permanent, and in my best interest.

I view the voice as part of the work we writers do, and so, I practice sending words out into the air in soothing, carrying tones. People have said to me for years, *I could listen to you read all day*. That's my goal, to be received that way.

My family drove up from Washington, DC, in two cars. We were milling around shortly after the event. I signed books, introduced Morrison to my family. That was a heady afternoon, and the work leading up to it had not been insignificant. The audience was fuller than usual, I would come to observe and understand. And after that date, I never once saw Morrison in that auditorium again. Eleven semesters of Wednesday readings and only one sighting of Morrison—at an event to introduce me. Hard to fathom, but real nonetheless.

After the reading, she seemed happy and impressed, which was a relief. In the hall outside the auditorium, I said to her, "I love Ed Bradley. He's the very definition of suave and debonair." Morrison widened her eyes and looked at me winsomely— inquisition and recognition together. Miss Chloe and I could set each other giggling by ruminating, by dragging language forward, by a targeted choice of phrase.

Morrison gave me a side-eye—maybe my first of those as well—and then she cracked up. She laughed heartily and aloud. She leaned forward a little, the way we are compelled to when we feel laughter deep in our bellies. It's almost like a little bow to the joke that has slayed you.

"Suave and debonair" comes from the 1960s or '70s. An ancient age in television advertising. A pitch for razors. Selling and romanticizing a clean shave. To get men, through their women, to dream of being Dean Martin, or Frank Sinatra, or Sammy Davis Jr., or Harry Belafonte, or Sidney Poitier. (As if a shave, or its razor, could make you glamorous, or Hollywood.) If you were me, or Morrison, apparently, you might just think of Ed Bradley, who milled around with us as his crew packed up.

I'd been carrying around the phrase "suave and debonair" for years, but I'm not sure I'd ever used it in a spoken sentence before then. I wanted to praise Ed Bradley; I wanted to reach for language that reflected his era, his dates. Born in 1941, Bradley was a decade younger than Miss Chloe; I'm sure she watched his career balloon. I knew him only after he was already confirmed as a genius in journalism. Ed Bradley and Miss Chloe both shook up the status quo in their disciplines, bringing their Black brilliance to bear.

I met Ed Bradley during my New Orleans years, and our recognition of each other spilled over into New York. What I found out in New Orleans was that Ed Bradley knew and loved jazz, that he was a friend to, and investor with, George Wein and Quint Davis, both impresarios and founding executives of the New Orleans Jazz and Heritage Festival. George Wein also founded the long-running, high-impact Newport Jazz and Folk Festivals. George and Joyce Wein were phenoms and pioneers.

More germane to my literature experience, Ed Bradley and literary agent Marie Brown grew up together in Philadelphia. Ed and Marie were tight, very close friends. Out at clubs or concerts together in New York City, the two of them would tell anyone who would listen about their young years together in Philadelphia.

Marie Brown is legendary in her own right. When I was starting out, I sent her my manuscript—before I realized that sending in a fifth or sixth draft, for me, amounted to a premature submission. Marie offered some advice that was enormously helpful. *Make sure everything you see is on the page.* This is a variant on Morrison's articulation *Make sure what you see can be believed.* I referred to Marie's advice, which came before I knew Toni Morrison, as a technical assist. When we see a character in socks and a yellow dress, we will often present the yellow dress and not present the socks. Both are telling, both need to be there. We have to figure ways to enmesh our visuals in our action. We have to bring all the visual to the page. When we begin, the page is blank, after all. Anything the reader sees or knows is because the author lays those images down. We offer up our vision, which must rise up off the page. A child in socks is different from a child with bare legs is different from a child wearing white tights from a package.

Marie Brown was a Black agent when there were none. She changed agenting for Black writers everywhere. Marie worked almost singularly, like a pioneer, representing and pitching Black books and authors to the New York publishing establishment. Ed Bradley, her old friend, was tall and lean and stood out in a crowd. He aimed (successfully) toward sartorial splendor. His voice was lovely, basso, compelling; usually his eyes were shining. He pierced his ear and wore a diamond stud on air. Ed Bradley was a superstar, and both Morrison and I were giddy to have him at the reading in Princeton. His being there had nothing to do with me and everything to do with Morrison. I was invisible, mostly silent to the *60 Minutes* folks, but Ed Bradley already knew me. Toni Morrison was getting to know me. When he left, Ed Bradley said, "Don't forget about this footage, kid. You, at the beginning. It's in the can."

I read from *The Good Negress* then, and I still read smatterings of *The Good Negress* now. Who could have predicted then that my cowboy novel would languish, or that Miss Chloe's advice would not dim? Perhaps I could have predicted the latter. *The Good Negress* has done well, and has served me well. It's been in print in paperback for twenty-five years, basically without interruption. It has changed publishers twice, gotten a beautiful new cover, and is taught in college classes.

MISS CHLOE LOVED LAUGHING. She seemed to view laughter as a higher-end human experience. In her novel *Jazz*, Morrison writes, ". . . laughter is serious. More complicated, more serious than tears." I get that; it's so much more ordinary to sink into sadness, or distraction, or woe. To insist on humor, to laugh at will—this is what's hard and rare.

In my youth, I got into so much trouble for laughing. Grown folks took such offense; they always felt put upon, that I was mocking them, laughing at them. I was laughing at what was happening, consistently inviting trouble. I remember this as the toughest lesson of my childhood: containing my amusement. I found lots of actions and statements and figures of speech riotously funny. I found spelling mistakes hilarious, too. As I matured, I became more successful at suppression: I could laugh uproariously in my mind but present a straight face to others who shared the scene.

More than once, Miss Chloe caught amusement in my eyes. I'd be startled to find her apperception of my gaze. But we both thought some things were funny in contexts where others might not. We had big laughs together, in person. Laughter can be serious relief.

I never once cried around Morrison, and I cried only once in my life for Morrison or about Morrison. Morrison never cried in my presence. When she announced, "Slade is gone," her eyes welled up and went shiny. Later in that same conversation, when I mentioned the confoundingness of the children's books she and Slade had published together, she chuckled; we laughed. *That's the whole point*, she let me know, done with her hint of tears.

She talked about Slade before and after he passed. When I asked about his health, about what had so fatally happened to her second son, a man his young age, I got a word salad, surprise. Her words were crisp and separate, tossed together,

drenched in grief and loss. His ailments, his beliefs, his refus-
als. Rare, this scramble of words, structureless and trailing
off, dressed in a semblance of togetherness. I expressed my
sympathy. I tried to be unafraid of the pause, so that Miss
Chloe would feel encouraged to talk. Miss Chloe talked about
him painting, his paintings, his work, his short life.

In her way, or in a way, Morrison reminded me of the value,
as an adult, of sitting quietly. All the *Be still, Sit still* you get as
a child pays off when, as a grown-up, you can present quiet
to, or for, somebody else. You can let their mind caress a loved
and active past. You can listen. You can wait. The wise one
eventually delivers. In my meetings with Morrison overall, I
said much less than normal for me. I hear myself chat, banter,
quip all the time. Making small talk. Making jokes. Teaching.
From writing, we learn the power of the pause; from Morrison, I learned about power and pause in person. I am neither
afraid nor made uncomfortable by pause, by silence, by moments where thoughts make their connections, rendezvous in
air. Some pauses are pregnant and worth the wait.

I LOVED HOW MORRISON USED that word, *gone*. I never took for
granted her intentionality. The great breadth of her choices
helped raise the significance of using that word. A folkloric
word. The phrasing lingered, and echoed. *He is gone. She is
gone. Slade is gone. Ed Bradley is gone. Lois is gone. Miss Chloe
is gone. Morrison is gone.* That phrase, "is gone," was language
Morrison used religiously: to offer news of passing, to open a
moment of reflection, usually referring to a person she loved
and missed, who had recently made their transition. She said

"gone" pointedly and with deliberate pause. Coupled with a name she loved and treasured, rolling off her tongue. She said, for example, "You know my sister died. My sister, Lois, is gone." As for Slade, the words were presented like an invitation to a moment of blaring silence. Like, *Now let's have a visitation*. An announcement that they're gone is like an invitation to send them up. To talk about them, to acknowledge what they've done, what they brought to the table, what you should know, in case you don't know already. Send them up, raise them up, testify to their having been here, and having been real, and having made their way from where they started to where they ended up, to where everybody who knew anything knew who they were, and where those who knew who they were were fascinated. People who are gone, to use Morrison's lexicon, had a whole lot to do with us when they were here. They are gone from our lives and from the world, and they had power when they left. People who are gone are gone against our will. People who are gone travel on a wind you can feel. You—and maybe only you—feel the waft of air that comes with their rememory. Your mind rides a witnessing current: she was here; she spoke to me; she had expectations; she was glad and sometimes mad. You cannot avoid, and do not want to hide from, rememory of what they did, of when you knew them, or when you last saw them, or when you experienced the power in their name.

MISS CHLOE STARTED COMPLAINING ABOUT how her back hurt while we were still in our early years. At the time, I did not know what exactly to make of her complaint. I didn't think much about her age, which was silly. I hail from a slow-to-medicine family. Our dear Ma Howell passed from a bad reaction to a new drug. We do not auto-trust doctors; nor do we auto-follow the directives of allopathic medicine. Historically speaking, there are concerns. Also, medicine is so chemical- and scalpel-driven; these procedures seem a last resort. For diagnoses, we depend on doctors just like everyone else. We tend to try plants and food as medicine first. We try to keep our bodies whole, standing back from the immediate incisions and removals and anesthetics. We do not necessarily believe that doctors know the best answer to every single thing. Sometimes, just like with the dictionary, you have to read down to the fourth definition, or the most traditionally linked remedy, to find an option that doesn't require strangers medicating you unconscious and then taking scalpels to the parts of you that you can only hope are correctly indicated on the medical charts and written communiqués. You hope they won't operate on the wrong hip, or do somebody else's procedure on you while you are forced to sleep—naked, exposed, and cut open—inside a cold room.

Over the course of a few years, Morrison and I exchanged and discussed all kinds of hot water–based treatments, arnicas and creams, homeopathies and relaxing mugs of hot bone broth. I fancied I was researching and delivering poultices, handmade in small batches.

I WAS IN MY THIRD YEAR teaching at Princeton when I found myself excitedly, delightedly pregnant. The Creative Writing Department did not want to grant me time off; I had planned to have my baby in New Orleans. I had come to Princeton from New Orleans, where I owned a house in the French Quarter.

I had planned to bring my baby home to St. Philip Street, between Rampart and Burgundy. My daughter would have outings to Congo Square, which is the only place in the nation where it was legal for Africans/slaves to drum. She would travel in the stroller to Armstrong Park, and to the Mahalia Jackson Theater. She would see the Mississippi River in baby vision and watch her first New Orleans Jazz Festival riding the crook of my arm. She would understand the feel of hot sun and humid air on her skin. She would be able to identify with the music. Because my plans had changed, because the invitation to Princeton intervened, I happened to be in New Jersey when the baby blossomed. Princeton and New Orleans do not compare, in my mind. I was not interested in accidental geography for my daughter. From my house in NOLA, we could walk to all the jazz spots and to dim old houses where whole nights were spent socializing, earnestly discussing art and music and film and New Orleans; long origin and art stories were told. Everybody wanted to share their relationship with the old city. Points of discovery. Points of departure. Dates of return.

New Orleans is a city with a long, palpable past. The community feeling—exemplified by second lines, and social aid clubs, and music, and camaraderie, and living history—makes New Orleans more compelling than most geographies I've visited in America. My experience in New Orleans was a highlight of my life and a boon to my sense of self as an African American. My plan to have my daughter there was not easy to abandon and seemed too important to subordinate. But Princeton, I was told, grants no extended time for maternity.

I called to ask Miss Chloe's advice (after frustrating exchanges with the department). Morrison's completely support-ive response to my plan for birthing could easily represent the most profound of her interventions in my life. Morrison en-couraged me to do as I chose, to pursue my own plan. What she said was—cue husky voice—"They can't tell you where to have your baby."

Brief and direct, as usual. Bolstered by her response, I told my department director I was leaving for the spring semester. He could decide whether I should come back. But, I said, I am going "home to New Orleans," so that I could have the birth for my daughter we'd planned. Amazing to consider, retrospec-tively, how accustomed people have become to controlling other people's lives. Crazy that a supervisor at work should *decide* such a personal decision in someone else's life. Thank goodness for Morrison; she shielded me. I imagine the director pegged me as Morrison's interest, and that influenced the ultimate out-come. I was encouraged to return in the fall, which I did. My daughter's place of birth signifies and relates to our culture. Drumbeats and real heat. Not a manicured campus, all insular and subdued. Being a toddler in the Princeton sandbox was a good way for the baby to graduate from babyhood. Being born in New Orleans is permanently defining and cannot be erased.

The Princeton story is all about graduating, no matter who you are. My daughter went to baby school at the YWCA in Princeton. Her "school days" (four a week) started at 9:30 a.m. and ended at 11 a.m. Hilarious. She saw all the other kids going to school; she stood at the screen door saying, "Wan go, wan go."

I signed her up and dropped her off, and our babysitter,

Mayra, picked her up and took her home, so I could teach. At the end of the school year, they had a graduation for the babies. The teachers made mortarboards from construction paper, yarn for tassels, and take-out paper bowls for the caps. I was stunned that the paper bowls fit their little heads. Their heads looked larger to me. But the teachers at that little school were veterans with babies. They knew the bowls would fit and would make cute/hilarious stand-ins for mortarboards. The babies slid into their next year by coming down a sliding board on the outdoor playground. They could not have been more adorable, at their first "graduation."

Princeton was where I learned that one of the principles of the YWCA was to combat racism and inequality. When I went to sign my daughter up, the facts were spelled out in the paperwork. Eliminating racism and empowering women are their basic principles. *Hooray!* I thought. *Here's my money. Here's my child.*

I WENT TO NEW ORLEANS in January, and in April, on the day after my birthday, I had a baby daughter. My doula suggested that I book twelve consecutive weeks of "help with the newborn." And so, for twelve weeks, we had a schedule of infant tenders, starting with my mother and ending with my aunt Betty. Farah Jasmine Griffin came. My older sister, Brenda, came. All of them rocked the newborn so I could sleep or write or venture outside, hands free. My younger sister, Adrienne, had two young boys already, and so she didn't come.

Laurence Fishburne was in the Quarter near to our house one night that summer, when we still had help with the baby.

My partner called from a nearby watering hole, wanting me to come down and join her, shooting the breeze with "Fish." I walked to meet them, because in the Quarter, you could walk everywhere. You felt joyful in the balmy New Orleans nights. You really do hear horns and wisps of music as you meander in the dark. That night, I walked five minutes away from the baby, who was being watched by our helper of the week. In the French Quarter, you could amble around in the night lit by streetlamps; there were usually others, out perambulating too. Fishburne was wearing a wine-red velvet maxi-skirt. Of course, we talked to Fishburne about our new baby; that's most of what I talked about in spring of 2000. Fish said that in countries in Asia, the baby is not announced or presented until the child has lived one hundred days. I loved that. So, based on that long night's conversation, our daughter's birth announcement read: "100 Days, Planet Earth."

We dressed her and propped her up on a pillow that was near as big as the baby. I sent an announcement to Morrison, on the Hudson; she had been such a source of support. Without her husky pronouncement, who knows whether I would have made the trip back to my house in New Orleans, that I'd bought with my kiddo in mind. I like to think I might have gone back on my own, that I would have continued to challenge the department director until I won. But Miss Chloe's classic brevity shut the whole worry down.

Fish and my partner and I hung out until dawn. Like pre-baby days. New Orleans, particularly the French Quarter, is a place where you can walk out at night into a live music scene. You can be steps away from where you live and ride the music into reverie. To see Laurence Fishburne walking dramatically down Royal Street as the night peeled into morning was stunning; his sartorial choices unforgettable. Walking dramatically into the dawn fits with thespian practice; Fishburne took to the center of Royal Street, departing. I had given him a copy of *The Good Negress*. The next week, he called me on the phone and left a message, in character. "Hello A.J., this is Lonts," he said. Lonts is one of my minor characters, who is really named "Lawrence," as rather a nod to Morrison's Cholly. The culture—we know its inflection points; we recognize each other. My brother, consummate actor, could recognize and speak into a whole revelation in one sweep. Fishburne saw Lonts like I saw Cholly. His message amounted basically to *I hear you; this could be me.*

When the birth announcement finally went out, we were flooded with good wishes and gifts. Susan Taylor, of *Essence*, sent such fine equipment. Boxes and boxes of baby stuff. Babies have about eight times their size and body weight in stuff. Babies must be accommodated and protected from the elements, shielded from sharp edges and from tumbling down. Susan was like charge card grandma, sending accoutrements I might not have thought of. We had a blow-up circular raftlike thing that cradled the baby from loose head to curled-up little legs. When I think of my daughter as an infant, I see her happy and watchful, in that blow-up raft, which she loved. She could see everything and not be strapped in. Susan sent a high chair, too. I thanked her then, and I thank her now, twenty years after the fact. Susan sent me things I didn't know I needed, but I learn from all comers. Wise women are always welcome. In the journey of my own life, there's a special lane reserved for women who know the score.

Princeton was a fine place to be a new mother. The sandbox was right outside my door, in faculty housing. My daughter could get herself out the door and to the sandbox on her own by the time she was two. She loved sand, and I wanted her to learn independence. I encouraged her, from an early age, to be about places she'd like to go. I could see her in the sandbox from the back door or from the kitchen window.

Morrison and I had some upfront conversations as I watched myself develop as a mother. She mostly spoke about her grandgirls. Morrison had three granddaughters; the youngest two are near my daughter's age. One afternoon at her Hudson house, we were discussing the girls' generation. I had met Miss Chloe's young darlings, and I had my own little darling to watch and nurture and be amazed by.

"Guess what I'm going to have them call me," Miss Chloe announced, almost abruptly.

I might have replied, "What?" or I might have just widened my eyes. I remember realizing that I was experiencing Morrison invent a name in real time. If there is one aspect to Morrison's work that for most of us writers is minor but that for Morrison is major and bombastic, really, it's her approach to naming.

"I'm going to have them call me 'Grand.'" And then she started giggling. She thought that was hilarious, and of course, her laugh was infectious, and I laughed, too—mostly to see her so pleased with her choice. To see her planning. To see her name herself for a new generation. To see her naming proclivity in real life.

Now, for babies, "Gran" would be pretty easy and somewhat normative. Surely, this word would slip off their little tongues and would seem like "Gran," short for "Grandma." If Ma Howell had decided to give herself such a name, she would have coached us: *Gran-duh. Gran-duh.* I don't know whether or how Miss Chloe coached her grandgirls, but I know that in the planning, she took great delight.

Call me Grand.

THE GOOD NEGRESS, MY FIRST NOVEL, covers mostly how we parent and caretake differently for boys v. girls. Some people argue that my novel is not about gender differences, but about education. To other readers, the novel is about "a way out." Some people say it's a story about language. I accept all these interpretations. We contain multitudes. To my mind, you protect the boys from idleness and from the police. You protect the girls from lack of ambition, from what Dr. Mary Bunting referred to as "a climate of unexpectation." Girls face daunting expectations of enclosure; they're overbusy, premature caretakers, and often duty-bound. Boys have more freedom all around, which for Black boys is wholly different from the freedom associated with (white) boys who are preferred and permitted. Black-boy freedom is created from disregard, disengagement, and, frankly, lack of care—which, for regular Black boys, often leads to struggle, poverty, and imprisonment. Black boys are not permitted to be free. As mothers and caretakers of Black boys, we try to sculpt or manufacture a frame of freedom for them, moving forward with their promise in mind. While this motivation is understandable, particularly as an antidote to societal vitriol, the freedom we teach them gets proved to be false. And then there is fallout, widespread despair.

One afternoon when we were together, late in our relationship, Miss Chloe asked whether I'd had a boy or a girl. I was startled she didn't remember, but she had her own preoccupations. This was after her mobility had started waning. I can still see her sitting, straining slightly to turn. I answered, "I had a girl. You met my daughter in Oberlin, when the Society was moving there."

She didn't stop to recall the time; she wanted to make a point. "I was going to tell you if you had a boy to give money to the Fraternal Order of Police. You don't have to give a lot, but when you give them money, they send you a sticker to put on your car. Usually, if they see the little sticker on your car, if they still decide to make the stop, the sticker slows them down. Slows them down a little bit," she repeated, speaking and gesturing distractedly.

Toni Morrison. Sitting, not moving much, giving me advice about how to slow down the police, in case they stopped my Black child while she was driving. Morrison had started to behave as if she were giving last advice as life advice. I remember having a thought about her putting an "I Support the FPO" sticker on the back of her green Jaguar. She looked as earnest as I'd ever seen.

My daughter was years from driving, the age of her

grandgirls, but Miss Chloe wanted to give me this information while it was on her mind.

We try to protect them, but their treatment creates despair.

THE HOUSE I OWNED ON St. Philip Street, between Rampart and Burgundy, was yellow. Writer Sarah Broom has made her mother's yellow house in New Orleans famous—a house destroyed by Hurricane Katrina. I understand and sympathize. I had to give up my own little yellow house after Katrina, too. I had returned to Princeton; I had tenants. But Katrina perforated my roof. The house became unlivable. I did not have the means to go there, or stay long enough to get my roof repaired. I could not find, for more than a year, any contractor to repair it. I was able to sell the house, as it was, because it was in the French Quarter, which was built at an elevation that has helped it survive floods since the 1700s. I was glad to find a buyer. The yellow house is not an uncommon sight in New Orleans. The houses in New Orleans sport their own palette—bright, pastel, changing colors all down the street. New Orleans is visually and aurally and historically a very special American place. I am unwaveringly grateful that Morrison's clear voice kept me from acquiescing to the insistence of my supervisor that I could not leave for the semester. Without Miss Chloe's advice, I may not have realized I could just say no.

LUMINARIES

Morrison attracted many luminaries to Princeton. I might have been briefly considered a luminary myself. Really, though, I was just a workhorse, and an acolyte, and a writer developing a theory of revision that has served me and my students and clients in spades. Being around Morrison all those years made me think about writing much more carefully. We talked about writing, so I had to lean into my own insights. I had to make sense of my thoughts and strategies in order to be able to engage with the unyieldingly great writer and great communicator before me. Revision as an art form has been described as my approach. I am grateful for the student work that provided canvas, or context, for me to theorize and strategize about revision. I always believed I could revise my work into shimmering beauty and, with my students, worked on aiming for the same. Always wanting to experience and elevate art, I benefited from Morrison's star power, and I went to see as many of the luminaries as my time there made possible.

Oprah came to campus to tape the *Paradise* book club event. I attended the event, held at some kind of university mansion—big windows, small panes, trim all painted across; huge sunlight, which seemed fitting. The event was held on a sunporch, where a whole cadre of Black women gathered, partook of fruit and tea and crumpets, and situated themselves like paragons of respectability.

I was not invited, initially. I called Morrison to ask if I could go. "What do you want to do there?" she wanted to know. "Watch," I answered. I was envisioning Peter Sellers sitting hungrily before his beloved television while he ostensibly ran a country: *I like to watch*, I thought of joking, but I didn't. Miss Chloe could be very businesslike, and references to minor, dated movies would be dicey in a hot, preparatory moment.

Morrison gave me a time to meet; I went into the event early, as her guest. Her son Ford came, with a young woman he introduced to me as CeCe. That's how young we were. Known in mature circles as Cecelia Rouse, in 1998, CeCe was Ford's future wife. Their two daughters are young women now. As of this writing, CeCe, now a mature and accomplished economist, has joined a presidential administration for the second time. She has also been dean of the Princeton School of Public and International Affairs, formerly known as the Woodrow Wilson School. CeCe and I were wallflowers together that day. There is so much power in wallflowerness, especially if you are paid to dream.

OPRAH IS AS MUCH A presence as she seems. A force field surrounds her. Intelligence (and busybodyness) crackles and simmers as she moves. Morrison was eager and delighted to talk to Oprah's readers; she loved the assembly—many of them Black women, she mused, when we got a chance to debrief. There was unusual excitement and notable orderliness to the book club women. Neat and done up, ready and steady, Black women in the group conjured the spirit of Black club women of the past. Then, in the (segregated) club women era, books were rare and expensive and erased us. Groups of Black club women quietly represented us in their local enclaves and strove to bring promise to our future, through all the segregated centuries. All the while making notes. In the rooms Black club women occupied, our "books" were in handwriting, our fleetingly recorded stories in the hands of a studious few. Black club women were attentive and organized and devoted to the work of groups—which often was acknowledging how our lives were evolving (or not). Their dedication delivered—so that women like Morrison and Oprah (and I) could be who we would become. Black club women arranged themselves into upstanding, near-secret societies that upheld the truth of our humanity, and they did not mind doing so in gathering spaces we orchestrated and held dear. I do not know how the book club women were recruited to Princeton, but like Black club women of old, they were decked out, armed with history, and definitely on the scene.

At the low-key and dignified *Paradise* taping, the food was opulent, piled high. Fruit enough to feed an elementary school. The couple of dozen women there seemed honored, even awed, in the presence of two queens.

I was delighted to witness this discussion of *Paradise*, my absolute favorite of all Morrison's books. *Paradise* is about triumph, and certainty, and determination, and generations. The story covers an all-Black town built by formerly enslaved people. Black town developers, visionaries, are sometimes equated with "Exodusters," as written about by historian Nell Painter. Exodusters was a quasi-biblical name given to Black freemen who went west (to Kansas) in the interest of free or cheap land, just as whites went west in the interest of free or cheap land. They journeyed away from the brutal South, formed communities, chose stopping places, built homes and infrastructure, such as it was in that time. Black people accumulated their own tools, constructed their own towns, governed themselves, lived the way they deemed moral and corrective. Eventually, their moral code was trampled by time marching over them. And so, ultimately, they find themselves old men on the wrong side of the present tense. The book is so complex, and the time for the filming was short. CeCe and I watched the goings-on together, quietly, from the edges.

The multiple sets of twins in *Paradise* amazed me. Deacon and Steward are older male twins in the forward storyline; in the backstory, there are antebellum twins Zechariah and Ezekiel, who are forced, by gunshot, to dance. Biblically named, Zechariah and Ezekiel are casually known as "Coffee" and "Tea." After one is hobbled during the dance by gunshot, the twins become separated and estranged.

We talked about *Paradise* separately and often. I raised the rarity of twins as a comment on the book. Morrison answered, "Twins run in families. A lady I was in maternity with," she reported, "was having her third set of twins."

We have only one set of twins in our family, and to watch how they're simultaneous and subsequently divergent has been a wonder. Our twins are still teenagers, albeit in a racially tumultuous age. Morrison's twins live long lives in what we have viewed as a brutal and intolerant past. Both pairs of Morrison's twins—Coffee and Tea, Deacon and Steward—grow together into age, and then they suffer shame, and separate. An inventive stroke of narrative, beyond the births.

MORRISON TAUGHT HER STUDENTS THAT research needed to be used only in ways that added to the humanity of the characters. Rachel Kadish, novelist and essayist, was a student of Morrison's at Princeton. The two of us met, Rachel and I, as colleagues at the Lesley University MFA program, where we both teach aspiring writers. According to Rachel, Morrison taught her how to align her work more closely with her own interests and passions, and how to conduct research that focused on hu-manness. Morrison challenged Rachel to extract the aspects of the voluminous and dramatic arcs of Jewish history that could inform character *behavior*. What can you use about the past or its artifacts that will define your character's drama and shield? What do you find in the research that helps you know how and why your character might hide her letters, or toss her hat, or hurry to recapture carefully cut velvet rose petals caught up in the wind in the town square?

MORRISON ALSO ATTRACTED LUMINARIES to herself, to her person-ality, to her reign over literature and letters. She could have crossed the country dozens of times, and traveled to foreign climes frequently as well, responding to the many regular folk and great minds who wanted to hear her speak, or read, or an-alyze, or prognosticate. To protect herself and her energy and her work, she said a lot of no.

When you invited Toni Morrison, and you hosted Toni Morrison, you had to have infrastructure. You had to have your systems, your people, in place. While Morrison was still mobile, she often traveled without Ford. Without him as a buffer, organizations had to put their own buffers in place. Occasionally, people who knew me would get an appearance agreement from Morrison (most often to honor her). Then I'd get a call, asking me to come and be buffer.

Byllye Avery, founder of the National Black Women's Health Project (now the Black Women's Health Imperative), helped her organization plan an event to honor Morrison after *Paradise*. Because Byllye and her wife, Ngina, are two of my few inner-circle folks, and because I am all about *Paradise*, and because I knew and could stand near and could talk to Miss Chloe, Byllye called me to be buffer, and to be on the program. My job, Byllye said, was to be near Morrison so she wouldn't be deluged by strangers, to make sure Morrison had everything she needed, and to let them know if she didn't. I was also to help make sure Morrison got to the stage at the right time. The organization was relieved to be able to hand off the Morrison handling. I was fine, or so I thought.

This event took place in 1998, in Washington, DC. So, our relationship was not yet years deep. My years bopping around backstage in the jazz world had taught me to "move artists," to "do edges," and to be prepared with conversation of interest to the "star." I brought those preparations to the evening. It was a festive evening. We all gave remarks, leading up to Morrison's turn at the podium. I believe Angela Davis was on that program. I know actress S. Epatha Merkerson also presented. She left her copy of *Paradise* with me afterward, to get signed and send to her. It was my first time meeting her. I remember thinking, *How does she know I will?* (I did.)

I wore a white Kevin Simon tea-length linen dress, which had long sleeves, a wave hem, and beautiful statement buttons that fastened the dress front, from neck to hem. The buttons were graded shades of sable; framed against the white linen, they looked like sliced gemstones—agate or tigereye. It was fancy.

I bought my performance clothes in New Orleans during those years, from a woman, Jann, who had asked if she could "dress me." She had a lovely, eclectic shop on Royal Street, in the Quarter. To go with the Kevin Simon white tea dress, Jann had given me socks with crocheted lace edges. I loved them; they were unusual; they reminded me of childhood; they went great with my dress.

Miss Chloe did not like the socks. At all. I was surprised she chose to comment. My clothes, my choice. But she thought they messed up the dress. She thought they made me look childish. She thought they were "strange."

Over time, I came to realize that this was early in my career, to her. (I started my second career when I tried my hand at writing. I'm not sure she knew or cared that I had been a statistician before.) I had already had all the dress code arguments I planned to have in my life. I had worked in corporations where the unwritten rules could get you killed. I was in my mid-thirties, way more than grown. I liked my socks. I think she saw herself as advising me, a newbie to the public. I think she saw herself correcting my understanding of the professionalism of the greats.

"I love my socks," I said pretty jovially.

"Are you listening?" she answered. Snappish.

This was the end of the conversation. I managed to do the work I had been asked to do. I managed to maintain my composure and also to maintain my high regard for the outfit I had chosen. I don't think Miss Chloe ever again critiqued the clothes I wore. I'm accustomed. My taste is particular. My clothes are always loose and comfortable and gorgeous—according to me.

I think my expectations for how Morrison and I would interact in the future were diminished that night. She was cranky. She was biting. I was working, and so, mostly mute. I remember going home and thinking, *Jeez, we had a fuss.* I put S. Epatha's signed book carefully in a Ziploc bag, until mailing.

When I next saw Miss Chloe, in Princeton, it was as if it had never happened. I can guarantee that every time she saw me, I was wearing socks. None as pretty as the pair I wore to grace my Kevin Simon. (I count this as half a spat.)

GENUINE COWBOY

When Morrison asked me what I planned to call my cowboy book, I answered, "Meanwhile Back at the Ranch." Miss Chloe paused and, not smiling, said, "Make sure you keep that title." Keeping the title turned out to be the least of my problems.

The editor who acquired the cowboy novel during an exciting, if unexpected, auction was offered a promotion very shortly thereafter—a new job, at a different publishing house. She moved on to her future soon after the sale. Because I had been interested in the editor and not the publishing house, my agent cancelled the first contract, and we moved on to my second-favorite editor; their house bought the book and paid back the first publisher. The exchange happened but was not seamless.

With this new publishing arrangement, all manner of fresh hell broke loose. Notes I received were small books themselves. Maybe I didn't do enough race-splaining, but I was asked to reconfigure my Black cowboys. Repeatedly.

My cowboy book went through three major revisions—each took about three years. We make countless revisions at our private desks, but the editorial reviews and responses—those are the major hauls. After each, and after a long wait, I would receive detailed notes back from one (white, woman) editor or another offering me direction or advice in seventy-five or so pages that they had "worked very hard on." Their perception and mine got no closer together, and so, I left the whole morass alone.

My cowboy heroes continue, even now, to be important to me. We authors are our characters' one chance at life. If their story will be told, I must do that work. The record of Black cowboys—written by the victors, men committed to erasures—has been whitewashed. Uncovery—researchers and archivists, descendants and carriers of the tradition, have estimated that there were upward of twenty-five thousand Black cowboys. Historians suggest that one in four cowboys were Black. Their stories were denied and sidelined. Western Black businessmen, who also did exist, were also erased in the whitewashing of the West. My Black cowboys walked shoeless and bootless on the westward trail, transitioning from bondage to freedom on bleeding feet.

I dreamed of cameos: Barney Ford, a Black businessman credited with building the finest hotel west of St. Louis, the first hotel in America to have electricity; and William Biggerstaff, who was a self-made man and hothead who died in a duel in Helena, Montana. Maybe he could have lived a long(er) life and could have been known as a hero of the West. Instead, he got mad, agreed to an outdoor gunfight, and ended up shot dead. Information about Barney Ford is findable, though his race is not often foregrounded. William Biggerstaff also becomes known without too much digging; the most famous photograph of him is in his casket. His death image proves that he was present during the "opening" of the West.

I wanted to write the Black/brown side of the whitewashed West. This myth of the white West has been only occasionally examined. Issues seeded long ago are still alive. See history books for texts on omission. See John Wayne as a swarthy white dream. See Louis L'Amour, whose whole oeuvre turns on this axis. See Quentin Tarantino for a Hollywood version of Black "freedom"—with guns, *Django* in specific.

THE LONG MISSIVES FROM THE (white women) editors plagued me overmuch. How I imagined a Black male hero might not match the visions the editors had of Black men. Could they imagine a Black mythic hero at all?

When I submitted the first draft of the cowboy book, my agent, Wendy Weil, called to discuss the manuscript. She'd read all 602 pages.

"It's magnificent, original, inventive, and huge," she said.

The heft of those four words left me almost wordless with surprise. Her comment exhibited planfulness—predetermination about how to describe her experience of the book. I wrote those four words, in capital letters, on a large index card that day. Taped the printed card up in my tiny office, where it stayed for years, through more revisions; through the sliding piles and torrents of colored paper. My fitful creativity. I used Wendy's pronouncement to motivate me through subsequent drafts. Wendy read and gave me draft-by-draft advice. Wendy thought that the "dear friend" storyline was intriguing and too thin; she asked me to expand. (Dear friend's name was "Rita Jones.") And so, I expanded this character—a Black woman on the Plains who learns that, two days' ride away, another Black woman had arrived on the sparse landscape. You can imagine what happened.

After the next redraft, my agent, Wendy, opined, "Oh no. Now dear friend almost has her own story. Maybe you should remove dear friend altogether? Maybe dear friend is her own book . . ."

Wendy died after revision number three.

One of Wendy's assistants, an agent-in-training, called to tell me on a Tuesday morning that she had sad news, that Wendy had passed over the weekend. I was in the gym in Lexington, Kentucky; that year, I was a visiting writer at the University of Kentucky. The caller ID on the phone read, "Wendy Weil."

"Hi, Wendy," I'm sure I said, a towel around my neck, sweat detoxing me and hydrating my skin, making me feel lighter and euphoric.

The news sure shifted my condition. I stood stock-still in the center of the gym floor, arrested on my way from fly-weights to the locker room. The gym spun around me; I wondered if I could move my feet. White Kentuckians walked by me, incurious.

"What happened?" I finally asked, dragging myself back to the present from a faraway place.

The agent-in-training told me that Wendy had been calm, that she had been sitting in a chair, that she'd had a heart attack and did not seem to have suffered any pain. This news was reassuring. My first worry was grimmer: Wendy alone at her house in Connecticut, where she spent many weekends. Wendy realizing her predicament, trying to get help, being found, expired, in a reaching, grasping state.

Shortly after the announcement call, my former editor (at the new house) called to talk about Wendy, to express her condolences, I presumed. In the course of our short conversation, she reported, "You know, Wendy was reading your manuscript when she died."

This remark again immobilized me, briefly, then enraged me. I was not sure what I should do with that information. What did the editor want or imagine? How did the editor think I would interpret her remark or revelation? I've only told this story a few times, in part because of "symbolism" so blunt it seemed engineered.

Now, here's a lesson I myself can share: Do not read your life as if it's fiction. This will drive you crazy. Life is not neat the way fiction must be. Life will not adhere to plot outlines. Life is not symbolic. Our minds create symbols to keep our intellects active. Life has nerves, many more than fiction has pages.

Why did the editor call to tell me that Wendy had died while reading my cowboy book? Had she decided on a symbol in her mind? If so, which symbol? What did it mean? Or was she gossiping? Was she telling me just because she knew? She had received information and decided she needed an outlet? Or did she decide this was something (she thought) I needed to know? (Who knows her reasoning? I did not ask, choosing to go no further down the path in her company.)

During the six or so years of editorial exchanges, I thought, *I don't understand these people.* All these years later, it's still true. However, I appreciate the statement's having been made: It's archaeological, in a way. It's an artifact that goes with the artifact of my cowboy drafts. Dusted with a fine white alluvium of wrangling and confusion.

OVER THE YEARS, THE EDITORIAL back-and-forth over the Black cowboys had come to seem strange, near surreal. Why am I negotiating what a Black man, or a Black community, should be like? In fiction set in an imagined past? Who can best incubate this Black dream?

I reserve the right to my imagination. I demand to imagine the hero of my dreams. I can write a fictive story that models, manipulates, or mocks the myth of the white Westerner "winning his way" to land and nationhood. Genocide notwithstanding. In my vision, Native Americans do not go invisible. The white cowboy soothes no one as he sings. The white cowboy pathologically avoids the drum. The white cowboy shoots because he is anxious and afraid, too lazy and too cocksure to learn language enough to negotiate his interests. The white cowboy also loots.

Every three years for nine years, I submitted a new revision of the cowboy novel. Each time, I received a new novella-size memo in response. Feeling frustrated, and struggling not to sound that way, I had a conversation with Miss Chloe about needing another agent. Wendy had died; the book was adrift and seeming to get no closer to bookshelves. "I don't know," I babbled. "I might have to try to move this book again. I need an agent to help me untangle this thing!"

She listened. She still had patience, though the patient days were coming to an end. She sent me to Rene to get Lynn Nesbit's number and expressed her approval for me to call and use her name. I did; I sent the manuscript. I talked to Ms. Nesbit a few months later on the phone. She seemed to be in a car when we had our conversation. That's a big talent you've got there, she said. I didn't know what to do with that, and so I thanked her, and time marched on.

Morrison and I discussed the Lynn Nesbit conversation, and I had to explain the "conflamma" around the novel again. Morrison said resoundingly, "You don't need an agent. You need a lawyer." My turn to say, *What?*

By way of explanation, Miss Chloe practically blurted out, "Bill Clinton did his whole book deal—from start to book sales—with only a lawyer and no agent."

At that time, my mind just about shut down. I didn't say, "I am not Bill Clinton." I did not ask whether we could talk about steps I could take at my level, about steps that made sense for me. I did not ask, "Are you suggesting I call Bill Clinton's lawyer?" I just let the whole thing go, like a kettle blowing steam. Eventually, the mist and heat dissolves in air, and you cannot verify that the steam was once there.

Later, I came to view this as an intellectual *Bluest Eye* moment. Morrison was making a valid suggestion, and I could not even hear. She didn't say or mean "Get Bill Clinton's lawyer." She said, "You need *a* lawyer," and that I could have done. But at the time, I was so done with the situation that I just put what she said out of my mind.

After Morrison passed, memories of her came cascading. The two of us here, Morrison there, Miss Chloe telling me . . . I did not remember the lawyer conversation at first. It came back to me one afternoon in October, weeks after she had gone. I was in the kitchen. I was near where we had spoken on the phone. I think passing through that very place of conversation at that time of afternoon brought her back. I was about to prepare dinner when I heard her say again, "You don't need an agent. You need a lawyer."

I had to stop in my tracks that afternoon. Sit down. Collect myself. It had been at least seven years since she'd said that to me. I had not taken her seriously; I had dismissed this blunt advice. Yet, now that she was gone, here it was again. She had mentioned Clinton, which made me feel small, compared. And so, I had chosen to feel small, instead of taking her point.

This October afternoon, I finally wept. I had been visited by so many memories, so many silent reels of her in motion, so many moments of laughter and silliness as we launched our little language jokes. I had stayed focused on the gift I had been given, the grace of years of experiences with Toni Morrison. No matter that she welcomed and accepted me, I saw myself as different, and nowhere near to the future she imagined for me. I separated myself from her grand success, and I could not see myself except as a satellite to the grand life she led. So much of what she advised, I had valued but had not done.

I STARTED TEACHING AT MORGAN STATE and kept writing quietly. At Morgan, I face brown students in rows like eggs, near to my daughter's age. I work to tickle and open their minds. I work to unearth curiosity. I try to get them to see language as the conduit. I try to bring some world to them, to interest them, so that they can go out in search of something they hunger to know or to do. I am acutely aware of the short time I have to convince them that they need to awaken to the breadth of life. I remember my young hunt for where book language was spoken.

AND FINALLY, THE SPEAKERPHONE

I leaned across the kitchen counter, dinner prepped, things looking and feeling ordered. I was in a rare moment, to be angling so early toward the end of the day. But when I'm planning to call Morrison, I have to get everything out of the way. She often gets my head spinning, depending on what we talk about. So, I don't call without making sure I've done all I have to do.

The light of evening was imminent, I could see from the graying outdoors. I felt fluttery and unusual—somewhere on the continuum between elated and distressed, between terrific and uncertain. It was 2012. I had submitted a third major revision of my cowboy novel. My revisions had been completed in small segments, around the child and around my students. I had not felt as hopeful as I wanted to, but I forced myself toward optimism, after the huge effort, a big submission, a new book in the balance.

I had made no decision to tell Morrison about this third revision. But on the wind of this accomplishment, I was ready to attend to other important tasks on my list. Making a call to Miss Chloe was like gray scale, a preprinted item on my running list of important things to do. Once a season—I tried to keep to that schedule. I was sure the revision and my resulting sense of positivity, or productivity, prompted my timing, but I was completely unprepared for how the call went.

I had no real agenda; I was just making my regular reach. Just a few minutes in, that evening, and days afterward, went careening.

"Why aren't you publishing? Are you not writing?" she asked abruptly.

My thoughts scattered immediately. My mind shot into defense mode, in spite of the calm and satisfaction I had been feeling. *She's raising her voice*, I thought nervously. *Miss Chloe is yelling at me*. I wondered then: Is she on speakerphone? I checked the clock, wondering if she was still in her office working, rather than having turned to what was usually her early evening *flânerie*. Always, we'd had an easy intimacy, sotto voce conversations. A reprieve, repartee in the afternoon. Not this.

First, I stammered. Then I reported on the new revision. I sounded lame to myself, and Morrison nearly sucked her teeth. I was frustrated, and I admitted as much. I knew that the persistent pressure to do this or that must be coming from some work I had not yet done, but also, my editor's directives were often contradictory, and seemed so micromanagerial, especially for people not writing the book, or writing books at all.

She did not want to hear my long explanations. She wanted me to publish. She knew I had a book, and so, my absence was on me.

Mentally, I was still wrestling with how distant and amplified she sounded. "Am I on speakerphone, Miss Chloe?" I asked.

Yes, she answered, and went on talking. First speakerphone conversation.

In my mind, she floated up to the corner of a room, held

aloft by hot air. Demanding a defense from the upper reaches of a perfectly appointed salon.

I did my best to explain: "I've done three major revisions. I don't know what else to do. No, I don't want to keep rewriting to their suggestions. I'm just teaching right now. My kid is a teenager. I'm just teaching, and raising the kid."

Pause. Morrison was unhappy, but we did not problem-solve. Although, at the time, I did not go petulant; I did go mostly silent. I felt flummoxed and stung. *This conversation was bound to happen*, I told myself.

In short order, we changed the subject, but neither of us was willing to limp through the aftermath. Very unusual for our calls to end quickly, but that was the day. In general, we kind of luxuriated, chatting. After that afternoon, I did not call her for years.

I made no blunt or definite decision that I would not call again. But the speakerphone conversation really rattled me, and I retained the perception, for weeks and then months, that she screamed at me. Of course, I could not really say for sure. The microphone in the speakerphone could have been the culprit. Whether or not she was purposely loud, she was distant and she was sharp.

And I was full of dread at starting a fourth round with editors who confused me and who seemed themselves confused about my Black cowboys, about the heroes I envisioned. I had no question about the viability and importance of my Black cowboy heroes. I see cowboys, runaways, refugees, hauling their way west—fleeing the torrid, brutal, chattel-driven South. I heard my late agent reciting, *magnificent, original, inventive, and huge*. And yet, there was no book.

Maybe I wasn't writing well enough. Always a nagging thought. Maybe the (white) editors could not perceive or believe the myth the story rode in on. Possible, too. Maybe my writing style was hard for them to perceive clearly enough to edit. Who knows?

That conversation with Miss Chloe was a bolt-blue afternoon. Like a mirror in good light. I heard resignation in my voice. Going through the motions of revising given the editorial dissonance was like spending a new day standing at a closed door.

AFTER MORRISON PASSED, AND OUR conversations started to interrupt my days and my routine, her suggestion about getting a lawyer, about Bill Clinton, came back to me. I realized that she had just wanted me to unhinge myself. She did not say, "Get Clinton's lawyer." She did not even say, "Be like Bill." What she said was, "You don't need an agent to solve your book problem. Get yourself a lawyer, and keep moving."

When Morrison said this to me, I didn't really hear her. I couldn't see myself in a Clinton sentence, and so I dismissed myself from the context. When her voice came to me, when this suggestion was a memory, that was when I wept. All my grief for Miss Chloe had been encased in gratitude, and so, I had not cried. I was hardly even sad. I was glad that I'd gotten to know her and to experience her amazing mind. But the recollection of yet another piece of advice not taken . . . I then had to face the weepy consideration that, perhaps, she had believed in me more fully than I had in myself. Sobering.

This was when I had a kind of *Bluest Eye* moment intellectually. Her recommendation, her example, involved Bill Clinton, a famous and erudite former president, a white male. Almost instinctively, I separated from the topic at hand. I viewed Morrison as making a mistake—to suggest that I could do what Clinton had done. It's crazy. The view from here suggests that I had a problem. That I had dealt with my manuscript as if I needed to take orders. I didn't.

I'm not cooking. I'm not charging by the plate. I'm trying to tell a story, best I can.

I knew now what to do: exactly what she'd said. *Instead of hanging round where the language I spoke isn't spoken, move to a different crowd, where the lingua franca is shared.*

IN THE WEE HOURS, I acknowledged that I might, maybe, have another chance with my cowboys. For the record, I have never in my life stopped writing. I started writing once I understood the sentence, and I have not stopped since. Writing and publishing differ in agenda and in scope. Both are capable of celebration and of battery and of all in between. At its core, writing is an individual contract, requiring intellect, commitment, and heart (or confidence). According to Morrison, writing mostly requires focus and control. Publishing is big, public-facing, an institution, a place of intrigue, often a series of machine steps, a lumbering mystery to the uninitiated. Publishing got the better of me.

MORRISON SEEMED TO THINK I should be able to sort through the publishing thicket. That I should be bold enough to come barreling in with my book. To my mind, that would have been miraculously, or magically, or with some measure of *her* ease. Over time, I've come to think she wanted me to be determined, to refuse to give up or be held up. She wanted me to move confidently, to match my confidence to my competence. She wanted me to be more aggressive, more demanding. She wanted me to shake whatever the hell was the tree.

If I did not believe in my writing, in my intelligence, in my work, then what did I think she was doing with me?

WHEN MISS CHLOE SCREAMED AT me through the speakerphone, I wanted to dissolve. But the truth was, I could not negotiate the publishing business. She wouldn't help, and I couldn't figure what else to do but do the book over, per these (sequential) editors' advice. The many do-overs had gotten old and pointless. I explained to her that I wasn't sure what would happen with the book.

Her frustration and her raised voice led to our long recess. I scarcely admitted to myself or anyone else that my failures had provoked me to put our friendship on pause. I had no new monographs to bring to the table. My scattered pages and unfinished books were as present and as weightless as air. Only finished work ages well. I could not keep presenting myself without new work. That was my takeaway.

Toni Morrison and I had two and a half spats in seventeen years. This was one of them.

ANOTHER OF OUR SPATS WAS almost all theater. We are sitting in the river-bathed light at her Hudson house. I remember its being early-ish, like lunchtime—an unusual time for us to be together, but when I traveled from far, there was some time flexibility.

We had moved from her downstairs kitchen to her sitting room, with softer furnishings. She made a few comments about her house—about its having burned, about what was lost. She went on to discuss the rebuilding and the peeve she had about having closets and cabinets redone and done wrong. Basically, she was complaining about contract work, or contractors. A pretty standard issue, apparently, when you have "work done" on a house. Complaints you'd be sure you could make to a friend.

My response was not what she expected: "I'm glad you own property," I said. "I'm glad you had the means, the money to rebuild. I'm glad you have this beautiful house and that it has such value. I'm so glad you had the financial skill to have a place that's yours, so you could do what you wanted."

She glared at me. She didn't speak immediately, I remember, but the tone of our visit had changed. Some people have fires, I almost whispered, and they have little teeny houses; rebuilding is out of the question. Or they don't have insurance, or it's a rental or an apartment. Those people can be just *out*. Out on the street. Out of luck. I did not say "outdoors," but I could have, quoting Sula. Quoting the inventor of Sula.

By then, Morrison was so far from outdoors, the quote would not have been relevant. She had the postfire house on the Hudson; she had the loft in Lower Manhattan; she had the condo first, and then big gray, in Princeton. All these places I'd known. Her Hudson house was whole when I visited those few times. There were quirks of her rebuilding that she did not like and that were not correct. I did not know how to sympathize with a person like Miss Chloe, who had a view of Manhattan across the Hudson River, which was basically her front yard. Her kitchen drawers and closet sliders did not function as she had intended or planned. Fault the closet assemblers or the contractor. Call them back, demand redress? Not everything goes smoothly. My wrong reaction to her story of the fire was one example of our chafing. She was unhappy, but I was not. I was glad, finally, that she had talked to me about what had happened in her house. I loved when she talked about herself, her life, her houses, her boys—both of whom were men the whole time I knew her. Her sons are near my age.

Not everyone does what they're expected to. Each person chooses differently. No circumstances are the same. The time we spent together was the time we had. Her voice on the phone, her few sentences at mobbed public gatherings, her giddy delight at some spoken phrase, some folkloric idea crammed into literary English or blanketed by literary language, some reference to rolls.

Not having enough sympathy for her contractor failure, her ill-fitting drawers turned out to be our half spat. Later, when she seemed to be unwilling to help me break through the logjam with the cowboy novel, I became both frustrated and embarrassed. This was a real spat, a whole spat, separate totally (and starting on my side) from the half. Our separate expectations had us both glowering in our own way, and drove us to subsequent silence on the subjects that riled us.

I did not understand the advice she was giving me, which seemed oblique. I also could not face the distance that was growing between her expressed faith in my ability or potential as an author and my own inability to produce another book. Mine was tragic frustration, and hers was cryptic insistence. What she wanted me to do was refuse to be halted. No matter the outer obstacles, she wanted me to tack on an interior certainty; to not be swayed. She wanted me to barrel through on the strength of my faith in myself and in my work. She did not want to help me; she thought she might be a crutch. She wanted me to prove myself to myself—and thereby, to everyone else. To her, I had already proven myself; any people in my way should be bulldozed or left behind. She did not want me to face a future where my career looked like (or was) something she had made. She wanted me to use my sight line to envision a future, to go right ahead and upset the social or intellectual order. She wanted me to do as she had done: write confidently, consistently, and kick doubt to the curb.

Whatever the source of doubt, she felt it should be dispensed with. Toni Morrison did not traffic in doubt.

I KNOW YOU TRIED, MISS CHLOE, in your silent way. You tried listening to my nattering: Maybe it wasn't the editors, the dissonance between my Black cowboys and their white fantasies. Maybe it was the writing. My writing. Maybe my writing was too circuitous. Maybe, maybe, may be.

I can still see you looking at me, your pizza midair, your mouth agape. *Am I not here with you?* That's what your look seems to be saying, screaming, shouting.

The answer: *Yes. Yes, yes, yes.*

Standing at the Gate of Goodbye

Eternity comes for all of us eventually. When infinity came for Toni Morrison, I had no reason not to be ready. When the text announcing her passing came across my phone, the future turned irreversible and, in an instant, became forever.

Sometimes, we just don't see people anymore. Sometimes, the last time you saw them is the last time you see them ever. Even people we love. Even people we want to see. We have to live with that. We mull over the dearness of the departed. We linger with our visions, we close our eyes. Whether briefly blinded or totally blindsided, closing our eyes and reaching for stillness contributes to our equilibrium and to our healing. On the dark screens of our interior, we can see our memories from forever. Sometimes, we laugh at a sighting of our visions of then, of you *then*, of us back then; our happy times freewheeling round our mind's eye. Sometimes we weep for same. Some moments pulsate with our gratefulness, our memories alive and periwinkle and sparkling. Or fuchsia and glowing. Or matte blue. Or champagne.

As long as we are clothed and in our right minds, our memories refuse to die.

CODA

In the last full year of Morrison's life, the new Center for Fiction, in Brooklyn, held its inaugural fund-raising dinner, at Cipriani's. This cavernous establishment in Lower Manhattan serves as a site of "coronation." Glittering literary events are held at Cipriani's annually. Big prizes, like the National Book Awards, take place in this hall. A place so vast, with ceilings so high, that the ambience contributes to the awesomeness of the occasions. I have attended a number of publishing events there, including two National Book Awards dinners and this Center for Fiction dinner. The room holds hundreds of people. In connection with the high-stakes events that are scheduled, the room can seem daunting or fabulous, either one. On its venerable corner in Lower Manhattan, with its columns and stone steps at the entrance, you can experience breakthrough moments or glassy, surreal moments. Especially if you face that slick, reflective corner in the rain. Especially if your nerves are roiling or firing because you have to eat dinner and engage in table talk while you wait to see who has won—you can feel even more doe-eyed. You feel caught in the light.

The Center for Fiction had elected to honor both Morrison and Sonny Mehta with Lifetime Achievement Awards during this first of their fabulous fund-raising dinners. Though most sojourners in the audience (like me) had come to see Morrison, and though many New Yorkers in publishing had come to see Oprah, who was to speak about Morrison, Morrison did not come. We were informed of this early in the event. A woman came to the podium and announced that she had "sad news." A number of us looked up with alarm. The woman's voice was so wan and her word choice so cliché, we thought she was signaling that Morrison had died. The audience of hundreds started immediately to hum and rumble, as the speaker reported that Toni Morrison was not feeling well enough to attend. Scores of people rose and made their away after that announcement. I myself could only stay in my chair for a few more moments. The woman had given me a fright, which turned rapidly to worry.

How ill was she? Was she home? *I need to call her.* That's all I could think. *I need to call her.*

And so, to contain myself, I stood and meandered the narrow aisles. Many were making their way from their seats toward the capacious entryway and the gargantuan doors. I joined the milling to meet and greet.

I started by looking for Robin Desser, editor at Knopf, whom I had wanted to be my editor way back when the cowboy book was fresh and sizzling.

BECAUSE I HAVE SURVIVED THOSE aggravating years, I can say now that "losing" Robin as a potential editor was part of the string of mishaps that sank the trajectory of my cowboy novel early. When I asked Wendy, my agent, why Robin Desser was not in contention to work on the book, Wendy explained to me that all the publishing houses fit under one or two or three overarching companies and that under these umbrellas, imprints, or houses, did not bid against one another. By the time we discussed this, the deals were already on their way to paper.

The "deals" part of publishing aggravates me, as an author,

because the conversations happen absent my input and over my head. Not negotiating for the editor I'd asked for raised my temperature and, frankly, pissed me off. As a writer who doesn't know the insides of the industry, all I see are outcomes. The innards of publishing are as mysterious to me as intestines. So, over the years, I've taken my outcomes like a brave soldier, and unhappy though I might have been, I've carried on. Morrison would not approve of this approach. If I dared speak to her about such poppycock, she would not lecture me; she would barely listen, and then, at the end, she would likely suck her teeth—*sth*, as in the beginning of *Jazz*. Or, if we were together, she might side-eye me. Morrison knew way more about editing than I will ever learn; she thought I should be more assertive. She thought I should plow through. I could barely interpret her directives. I had no solutions then.

MISS CHLOE AND I NEVER formally negotiated our relationship; we participated and watched ourselves evolve. Neither our progress nor our process was planned, and the foundational years of our relationship, which happened at Princeton, were whimsical and spontaneous, especially in retrospect. Mostly, I'd ask questions, and she'd answer yes or no, and then we'd move forward based on that outcome. Less frequently, Miss Chloe would make a request, and I would answer yes if I could; and if no, I'd answer by inaction. I do not ever remember saying no to Miss Chloe aloud. Overall, I think I did a decent job of setting limits; I didn't set myself up for failure by trying to do more than I could.

Early on, we could see that she would not formally mentor me, she would not directly teach me, and she would not review/comment on my incomplete work. I so wish I could have been edited by Toni Morrison. Who wouldn't wish that acuity, that mind, that pencil across their page? But that era was over for her. I was too late. We would not have that kind of relationship, either.

And so, I committed to watching closely, listening carefully, and remembering well. Miss Chloe taught me so much—when she spoke: through her questions and commentary, her brevity and levity, her sometimes cryptic, snapping remarks. When she wrote, the lessons were infinite. And most important, I learned from being around her: that her carriage and acute perception had both reached the level of profound. Not always, but often, she was performative. In public and at her offices, presenting the great author. At teatime, she could be Miss Chloe. Much of what I learned from Toni Morrison, she modeled at teatime. The gift was being near.

THE LAST TIME MORRISON AND I talked about my cowboy novel, I was trying to explain that even if I got the book to an editor and publisher who would get the book out into the world, I'd need to redo the book. Morrison was not hearing it. We were on the phone.

"What?!" she said brusquely and abruptly. The temperature was high between us that day.

I should have interpreted her question as rhetorical, or as a side-eye. Instead, I tried to answer. She said nothing as I stumbled on. I remember thinking as I was talking, *She doesn't want to hear you talking. She wants you to publish. Full stop.* And yet, I prattled on. Eventually, I started talking about Michael Cunningham's book *The Hours*. About how quoting authors of the period in the architecture of the narrative now seemed the benchmark for setting stories in the past.

She entered the conversation again after I raised the architecture of *The Hours*, which was a relief. I was starting to wonder if she was going to say anything more at all. After a short narrative architecture moment, she said, "I don't know what this has to do with you." This time, I decided not to answer; I was so relieved not to be talking. She went on about my babbling about new conventions, about maybe having to start again. "Did you finish the book or not?" she asked me. A totally valid question: once you finish, you don't start again.

After a pause showed she expected a response, I said that I'd changed the book so much, based on opinions I now think were off target. I basically admitted to having to go back to the earliest version of the book and work from there. *Magnificent. Original. Inventive. Huge.* You don't get those words often. Neither those words nor that draft should be forgotten or let go. I remind myself.

Morrison was unhappy with this conversation, and I myself was flummoxed. A rare moment in my time with Morrison, when I was glad to disconnect.

I DID NOT FIND ROBIN DESSER that night at the Center for Fiction in Brooklyn. I had not seen her in twenty years, but I asked around. I was told she was there, but perhaps she was part of the early exodus.

Finally, later, I saw Robin at Miss Chloe's memorial, at

St. John the Divine, in November 2019, so many months after my search at Cipriani's. That afternoon, I was distracted and had forgotten what I intended to say to her nearly a year before. She was in a row nearby where I was standing. I asked her name. "You look so familiar," I said. She answered, "Robin Desser," and I giggled. I had not recognized her at all. I was sad that afternoon, and I gave myself a pass for all the things I didn't say, or couldn't say, or could not remember. I decided, though, that perhaps the editorial shenanigans were—for me—part of what Jimmy Baldwin references when he says, "You don't get the book you wanted."

I SAW SO MANY OLD friends and compatriots that evening in Brooklyn that my anxiety over Morrison's health was abated for a second. (That dinner happened in December 2018. We could still hug each other then.) Michael Cunningham and I have been friends from the Provincetown writing community, and though we see each other infrequently, our times together always flash with intensity. We are admirers of each other's good works. One summer, when we were departing Provincetown, Michael said, "Bye-bye, Queen." Of course, I left smiling as a result. Another time, he called me Queen in public. So much love and admiration in that one word. He spoke with brevity and punch—a Morrison stroke. He lifted my spirits at the start of a long winter. It's natural to be fond of people who bring you good cheer.

So, at the Center for Fiction dinner, being able to embrace and exchange life updates with Michael was a huge highlight of that evening. Michael, as usual, had more dramatic news than I. But I had been raising my daughter, and he had been working and writing and out among the glitterati. Michael was not informed that *The Hours* had been a butterfly among the sticky autumn flowers. Now he knows.

Cipriani brings with it an echoing level of noise. You practically have to raise your voice and lean in to hear anyone you might speak to. Among the literati, eye contact goes on overdrive, every exchange begins with a nod. We embraced, Michael and I; he was brief with his dramatic news. I could not possibly have told him this story then.

Edwidge Danticat and I also found each other and walked around together for a few. Edwidge took me to see Glenville Lovell at a table, another writer I had not seen for eons. Glenville, Edwidge, and I had been brought to NYU by Paule Marshall, when the three of us were first published. We'd had a reading together, and the great Paule Marshall blessed all three of us with her attention and clear-eyed grace.

I spoke also to Colson Whitehead, who was at a front table. I spent a few minutes at the HarperCollins table, with my editor, Tracy Sherrod. As always, I was happy to see and talk to Jackie Woodson, who introduced me to Leah Haber; Jackie and I also see each other infrequently, but as with Michael, our brief encounters are warm and enthusiastic, laudatory, loving.

At the Toni Morrison Society table, Bahiyyah Maroon sat next to me; she had traveled from California and told the story of having wanted for her entire adult life to meet Toni Morrison in person. She said she'd decided to come to New York so she could see Morrison and Oprah together. She was dressed in such clean, sharp white, her clothes seemed almost ceremonial. She and her friend were the only people at the table who weren't members of the Toni Morrison Society. She had been looking so forward. When the woman announced at the microphone that Morrison wasn't coming, Bahiyyah said, right away, "*Sth*, I waited too late." A comment on mortality. Ruing a moment her life almost caught. I think we all interpreted the experience of missing Morrison as a reference to mortality. The whole timbre of that big room shifted.

All of us had journeyed from our corners of the country. We'd each paid a thousand dollars to support the brand-new Center for Fiction. Morrison was absent (though alive). Sonny Mehta was present, and I was glad to hear him. He gave a detailed address about his long relationship with literature. He stood as a publishing giant, discussing being a boy reader and then a young editor in Britain, being commended for a lifetime of accomplishment at Knopf. This was the first time I'd met Sonny Mehta; he was short in stature, wispy in weight, yet his accomplishments and reputation were huge, and fit the room, the celebration, and the erudite audience assembled. Morrison had spoken to me about him, always mentioning his name with quiet affection and discernible admiration. You could hear dense loving history in the way she said his name. She'd spoken to me of only two people with that kind of reverential, first-name-only, near-whispered affection: Sonny, meaning Sonny Mehta, and Ruth, referencing Ruth Simmons. Sonny and Ruth were answers to questions, were tags on her long-term experience. *With Ruth. Sonny said. Sonny called. Ruth came. Ruth was honored.*

I was thrilled finally to meet Sonny Mehta, even if at the end of the night. He was chatting with the fiction winner from the year before. He was seated at the front, center table. He said he knew my work, which surprised me. He reached to shake my hand. Though I am not generally a handshaker, I would not refuse Mr. Mehta. His hand was startling, cold, *freezing*, really. That was the moment I thought of, when I heard of his passing in December 2019, just months after Morrison: the augury of his freezing-cold hands.

MARY EMMA GRAHAM, A MEMBER of the Toni Morrison Society board, came from Kansas. I had spoken to her by email, on Society business, but to see Mary Emma's face was helpful and reassuring. Frazier O'Leary, also a member of the Toni Morrison Society board, had recently been elected to the DC School Board. I thanked him for his service, as a little language joke. Frazier had driven up from DC; he left immediately once the announcement was made that Morrison would not be there.

Oprah came in the back entrance, striding past our Society table to the microphone. She wore flats and customarily bedazzling earrings. This woman—a child of the Deep, mean South who had become one of the richest Black Americans and one of the richest women in the world—loves Toni Morrison and always steps up for Toni Morrison. And so, there she strode, bejeweled, showing up yet again to testify for Toni Morrison.

After the announcement, I couldn't sit still; nor could I eat. I just wandered around the auditorium, having conversations. Some of the reunions almost made me cry. Mitchell S. Jackson is my old pal; I hardly remember when we first met, but we always end up giggling together. He'd brought his partner, a poet, and she had made a custom fragrance blend called Beloved. The bottles were attached to a glossy plum cardboard backing, and "Beloved" was written in gold script. So impressive. Inventive. (I told Miss Chloe about the fragrance vials when I called. I told her I was sure they'd send her swag bags, and she should look carefully so as not to miss the Beloved fragrance.) I met Tommy Orange, who won the First Fiction prize.

I spent the afterparty in Chelsea with Rachel Eliza Griffiths, poet and photographer, who was in my writing class in Province-town; Salman Rushdie, whom all the world knows; Mitch Jack-son and his inventive partner; and Tommy Orange and his lovely wife. If I had not gotten so discombobulated by worry over Miss Chloe, I would simply have had a sweet and smiling time. As it was, the evening ended, the night wore on, and I could not sleep.

The train ride home was ghastly. I thought about all the trains I'd taken to meet up with Toni Morrison, and those times were clearly coming to an end. I had not been able to eat at the dinner; I'd spent my time chatting, and besides, my stomach was doing flips and turns. On the train, where there was nothing to compare to the thousand-dollar plate, I drank hot tea and tried not to feel morose. I got home and started pacing. Clean-ing. Putting things away. I began to plan what I would say if, when teatime came, I got Morrison on the phone. I wondered if I should say, "I know it's been forever." I wondered if I should say, "We all came to the dinner, and were so concerned when you weren't there." I wondered if I should say, "I had to call to see how you were feeling." I wondered if I should just begin with a mea culpa: "I know I haven't called you in so long . . .

At 4:15, I dialed the number, and it rang only a few times. She picked up, and I said, "Hi, Miss Chloe, it's A.J."

She answered so quickly, she almost interrupted me: "A.J.?! I haven't heard from you in years!"

It seemed to me she should know how distressed I might be. She hadn't come to the dinner! There'd been hundreds of people waiting to see her, not just me. I had been out of the loop. I had forgotten the legion of requests, the dozens of awards, the many people and organizations who called and wanted to honor her. I had to explain to her which dinner I meant. I had to explain to her that it had been the night before. I had to explain to her how awkward and awful that "sad news" preamble had made us feel.

She didn't dwell on the dinner, or my worries, or the wan announcement. "Well, I'm glad to hear from you," she said. "You know my sister died?"

Just like forever, I found a place to listen, and I listened to as much as she would say.

That publishing dinner, and Morrison's absence, prompted my last few conversations with Miss Chloe, our last short season of sharing—wisps of winter and spring on the phone. Miss Chloe and I had a coda to our long relationship. Our long hiatus ended only because of the Center for Fiction dinner. Thank the fates.

Was I Kind?

One of our great graces was that we got beyond the religion fissure. We could really have fallen apart therefrom. When I saw Miss Chloe's final film, *The Pieces I Am*, I recognized some of the same tenets of Catholicism that had thrust me into a childhood of questioning. The Catholic practice of confession and declaration of faith are part of the presentation in the film. You have to know Catholicism to recognize the stages, preparation for transitioning from one life to the next. But there they were, in all their glory. Profession of faith. Confession of sins. Penance, of course, is private. The catechism came rushing back, because the lessons ingrained in us as young people can be neither retracted nor unlearned.

Jessica Harris, an African American food historian and cultural critic, reviewed *The Bluest Eye* for *Essence* and interviewed Morrison when the book was first released, back in the 1970s. Jessica reported that she had had a chance to speak to Toni Morrison decades after their original exchange. Harris reminded Morrison of the *Essence* interview and could see that Morrison did not remember.

"Of course, she wouldn't remember," Jessica says, "after all those years. But you know what she did say," she went on. "She asked me, 'Was I kind?'"

Of course, Jessica was startled and impressed by the question. I understand why. Sounds like readying for the Rapture or, less histrionically, for the other side. I've had so many experiences with Morrison. I know how she can jettison just a few words and rock you back on your heels. Morrison looked right at you and then reacted precisely and intimately to the moment she was in. Morrison didn't remember Jessica at all, but she had a soft and telling question about her own behavior, decades after the fact. A quintessentially Morrison moment. Cutting to the chase.

So many people have Morrison stories. They should be collected and curated. Published. But this question to Jessica aligns with catechistic Catholicism. You scope out what you might have half-done or overlooked or done wrong. At the end, you want to right yourself. In preparation. This is how Catholic religion is taught. Morrison had a long history of being snappish. She could very well have been cutting, as she had been perceived sometimes, and not always incorrectly. She was right to ask "Was I kind?" If Harris had answered no, which she did not, I imagine some penance or atonement would have followed.

In Morrison's last years, you really had to go see her. There was no alternative. She wasn't really traveling for me to meet her anywhere. I did not feel I could afford to just up and go. I heard about trips Angela Davis made; I was envious. I had a daughter I was putting through college, and like all my life, I watched my coins. I planned to stop in New York and see Morrison on the way to taking my daughter back to school in Massachusetts. My trip was scheduled for late August, and Morrison transitioned before the month came to an end. I had thought I might see her one last time before she left this world.

Every time I talked to her, she asked me to come see her. I promised I would, and I intended to. She asked for flowers, which I sent, and which cost me a pretty penny, though less than a road trip. In her last conversations, Morrison talked about her aches and pains, her feeling that her body had betrayed her. She had renovated (twice, in the time I knew her) her house on the Hudson and had installed an elevator, to give her access to her upstairs. I'm not sure I'll ever unhear her say—so petulantly, so full of disappointment—"I'm just in this elevator." This blunt and desultory statement let me know that her walking days were past. These words are pretty much emblazoned as the last words she said to me. I'm sure they were not the very last, but that's how they resound.

Mourning Is Mind Altering.

Carmen Gillespie, the scholar of Morrison and Walker who taught for years at Bucknell, died suddenly and almost inexplicably shortly after Morrison. We hope that loss of a hero did not radiate out fatalities. This could happen in fiction, but we hope not in life.

Communal mourning experiences were organized in many corners for Ms. Morrison. I heard that the day she died, there was a night parade in her hometown, small-town Lorain. What an old home–seeming practice, taking to the night streets. In New Orleans, the funeral parade is an institution, which means even when it's disorganized, it's organized, because it grows out of a system that has requirements. A New Orleans funeral, jazz parade, includes a designated parade route, which necessarily travels past the house where the person lived. In New Orleans, there are horns. In Miss Chloe's case, I can only imagine that they walked past where she might have been a little girl, or past where her sons spent summers. I would have loved to be in that number, paying homage by streetlight; walking in Morrison's memory, companionably, in the dark. I imagine that there was quiet, which can be its own song.

I was in Baltimore, and I had been fine, forever, with just us two. And so, when there was one, there was also none other. Because I did not "put my feet under the table," as we say in our community, the main ceremonies of Morrison's mourning excluded me. I cast no blame. I know I stay too far removed. I was also soon to be bruised, slipping on the back steps in a moment that felt important if only because of the bells that were ringing. Groups of women and readers, and others whose affinities I cannot name, gathered in outposts and bookstores and houses and galleries—took to the night by streetlamp—to celebrate Morrison's release from gravity.

Missed Connections

Especially when my mind is full up of fiction, I can get pretty loopy, and I miss connections I should be making. When I talked to Morrison near Christmas 2018, she sounded a little loopy, too. I wondered if she was taking loop-inducing medication. She was giddy, though; she said, "Everybody is coming here," meaning to her house for the holidays. I asked her if she wanted me to send anything. We decided on rolls. I planned my shopping and baking schedule, planned when I'd need to cool and wrap and overnight-mail. I went on December 22 to see what time the last pickup would be on December 23, so that the rolls would arrive on December 24. I made my rolls, cooled them, wrapped them, boxed them, got them to the post office, and worried that you could still smell bread rising through my packaging. The postal clerk said they would be delivered on the twenty-sixth.

"No, no," I corrected him, "I want to send this Express Mail." I knew it would cost a fortune, but I was prepared, and in the back of my mind, I felt that this was my last dispatch.

He restated: "It will arrive the twenty-sixth."

And so, for my forty-seven dollars, the box would arrive *after* her family gathering.

"What time did I need to be here," I asked, agitated, "to get this there by tomorrow?"

"Yesterday," he answered coolly.

I was upset, near abject, but I sent the package anyway. What was I going to do with all that bread? Perhaps it would still bring her some good cheer, perhaps with leftovers, or maybe she would laugh about my missing the target.

I didn't call until days after Christmas, but before the New Year. I expected to hear whether the rolls had been of any use. I spoke to Miss Chloe and asked about the box, and she said it had not arrived. Miss Chloe seemed a little loopy again that day, and I wondered for the first time whether I should check in with someone else. I described the orange sheet of paper that I'd written the address on, and I explained that if she got a lot of packages for the holidays, it might be sitting around (spoiling). Food decays with scientific fanfare and could attract a whole kingdom of crawlers. The number of days bread takes to mold should have been emblazoned knowledge from my youth. But I was much more preoccupied with having been unsuccessful with this minor point (of bread delivery) in what may have been for her a major time.

The few times I called back, the package was not referenced—and then, eventually, Miss Chloe wasn't answering anymore. I imagined she was in the hospital, and so, I called intermittently. The mailed box of bread became eternally MIA.

Miss Chloe was back and forth to the hospital and, later, rehab. When I talked to her anymore after that, it was by accident.

I'd call every few weeks, usually a couple of days straight. And once or twice more (only), I got a chance to talk to her. I still had that cell phone number she asked me not to use. I did not use it, although I remember staring at the number in my contact record. I don't know what happened to the rolls I baked for her for her last family Christmas. Reduced to green dust, 100 percent allergen—even if boxed and wrapped in plastic bread bags and, inside, wrapped in parchment.

The bread lost in transit, the effort lost to its intention—these signals let you know that the energy has shifted. The curtain's coming down.

ALTHOUGH MORRISON LIVED A LONG TIME and achieved the richest of outcomes in the one life she was given, so many of us were brokenhearted when she passed. All we should have done was celebrate her life, but many of us were shot through realizing what an influence she had been, admitting what star power she had, expressing our regrets—having hoped to meet her, having wished to see her in person, having wished to see her one more time (my story). After August 5, 2019, memories of Morrison rose up in my daily life like silent films playing projector-less in air. I'd be sitting or walking and, unbidden, I'd see somewhere we'd been, or recall something she'd said, or see her in some posture, joking, ribbing, snapping somebody quiet. One by one, memories of her showed up and reminded me of the length and breadth of the time we'd had. I would have to demand to recall her voice. Mysteriously and amazingly, most of my memories showed up silent. I was happy to watch. I think the point of the silence was to make the point that she had passed.

IN A DREAM, I WENT into Shakespeare and Company, in Paris, the legendary bookstore with the blue door. In reality, I'd taken my daughter to that bookstore when her locks were fresh and new and she was having her first visit to Paris. I took a photo of my daughter in that doorway; she was wearing one of her favorite childhood traveling coats—a lavender number with patch pockets. This photo of "the baby" with her brand-new locks is an iconic image from her childhood. Second only to the "100 Days" photo from her infancy. My daughter stands framed by the doorway, looking full of wonder. The photograph could only have been taken by someone intimate with the child; the look of trust and invitation is unmistakable.

Spencer Reece, poet, priest, and almost like a brother, has had this photograph of my daughter on his nightstand in all the places he has lived, including his parish, center city, in Madrid. Father Reece says he looks at this photograph every day; it reminds him of the "profound promise of youth." I remember positioning my daughter in the doorframe. I set the image up for later, for posterity, and that spirit comes through. I imagined that when she and I talked about this trip, we'd talk about the Pont des Arts, the Pont Neuf, *pain et chocolat*, her locks, our birthdays, and Shakespeare and Company. Eventually, she'd have this image to help with understanding the literary and philosophical metaphor of doorways. We have a series of doorway photos, and the blue-door image anchors that collection.

In my dream, I carried the experience of the new locks and the iconic photograph as history. The dream was therefore anchored in the real. When I entered the store in the dream, Morrison was there. She was wearing a black skirt and white blouse, which meant this was Morrison from an earlier era, younger than when I knew her; she never wore a black skirt that I saw in person. There was no event going on at the bookstore; I was lured in by the books in English, by the legend, by the welcoming lights. I had been out strolling the Paris streets, serenely and independently. I had crossed the Pont des Arts. I was on no timetable. I was loving the Paris streets as dusk descended and the streetlights came to life like small moon after small moon. Since this was not real, we could have traveled there together, but the dream held to the logic of our lives, not to the magic of a dream. I noticed her, but determined not to interrupt her. If I caught her eye, I'd speak. I went to the section where her books were lined up; there were English editions and French. I pulled down a copy of one of her titles; the dream did not foreground which title it was. The book cost $190. I was wistful, and I put the book back. I decided I didn't have extra money to buy the book at that price. Morrison grew hot under the collar, not because I couldn't buy the book, but because she found it aggravating that I didn't have the money. Her look of consternation stone cold woke me up.

MORRISON AND I TRAVELED TOGETHER only locally. We never went any farther together than a few miles around Princeton. Otherwise, I traveled to meet her—where she lived or where she would be or where she asked me to arrive.

Spending time with Toni Morrison by myself was her choice and my education. I used to joke that she wanted just duets. We experienced each other inside her reputation and separate from her public significance and stature. Just us two became our routine; an automatic intimacy was created by the unscripted air. Although I remained in awe of her all the time I knew (of) her, I also remained somewhat mystified by my times with Toni Morrison, by my experience with Miss Chloe, by the realities of our proximal years and our silent pause.

George and Joyce Wein, a white Jewish promoter and an African American woman, were married when interracial marriage was neither a good look nor a safe strategy. They became spouses and business partners who created and managed the Newport Jazz and Folk Festivals and La Grande Parade du Jazz, in Nice, France. Joyce Wein was one of my biggest supporters; she absolutely loved *The Good Negress*; Joyce spoke to me about moments in *The Good Negress* almost the way I spoke to Morrison about *Paradise*. It was flattering. Joyce was closer to Morrison's generation, and yet she befriended me. I was interested in George and fond of him because of Joyce. I will never forget that Joyce came to my baby shower. It was held at Cassandra Wilson's apartment at 555 Edgecombe, in Harlem. Jazz aficionados know that a number of music greats passed through that fine building, including Cassandra, in her era; including Duke Ellington, in his. Joyce made herself the recorder of the gifts and made a neat, careful list so that I could properly write thank-you cards.

George and Joyce were legendary and smart—individually and together. They were a legendary duo in the jazz world, the music world, the folk world, the festival world. They hired Duke Ellington, Thelonious Monk, Miles Davis, lots of jazz cats—that's how old school they were; that's how long they lived. There are photos of George with Louis Armstrong. When Black American musicians traveled to Nice, George had handled their books and contracts; he set times and payments. Joyce handled feeding the bands.

Joyce had an amazing sense of humor, and as an educated Black woman, her sense of history was rich and real. Joyce didn't mind discussing the "early years," and she could tell great stories of struggles survived. Joyce was fond of saying that she and George liked and loved each other, but "it took me fifteen years to get him to marry me," she'd say. She was honest about the hesitation being about family and society. External pressures created "the longest courtship."

Joyce often told stories about sourcing and preparing food for the likes of Ellington, Monk, Mingus, and their bands. Hungry men eat volumes. According to George, some of the cats he'd booked said that the best part of the gig was the food. That the food was why they came back to Nice year on year. They were thrilled to eat (Joyce's) soul food in France.

In addition to their home in New York, the Weins had a home in Nice, a stone compound on a hill on the French Riviera. An astonishing place for me to find myself. The Weins' house in Nice was not too far from where Jimmy Baldwin lived, in a little French town called Saint Paul de Vence.

In part because of Joyce's praise of my writing, George inquired whether I could help getting a book done that he wanted to write. I later found that I was another in a long string of writers whom George had approached about the project. I agreed to try, and he and Joyce promptly arranged a trip to France for my partner and me; we stayed at their house. They purchased our flight. Before that trip, I had no concept of the French Riviera. Before that trip, I had never seen an olive tree.

The trip was mostly social (for everyone but me). The house was full. Balls were being hit on the tennis court, and I was trying to wrestle with George's thousand-page draft. The imbalance was tough, but I tried to invest in my end of the bargain.

While we were there, George arranged for us to visit James Baldwin's house, a property now owned by the government of France. The house wasn't open; it was not a museum, as it should have been. The house itself is walled—very French, and just what Jimmy Baldwin might have wanted or needed. In the years since his passing, the house has sprouted near fences of wild, tall weeds, grown to above human height. Behind a wall of stone covered by a wall of weeds, James Baldwin spent nearly twenty years padding around that farmhouse—thinking, drinking, worrying, entertaining, and writing all night.

The visit to Jimmy Baldwin's house seemed surreal, and I remain grateful for the journey and the sighting. George knew exactly where to have the driver go. That's as close as I've been to Baldwin's presence on the planet, beyond the blessing of his work, his lookalike sister notwithstanding, though she is her own radiant, special person.

That George Wein and James Baldwin knew each other also endeared George to me. Joyce was first; Jimmy was second. I was unable to cohere George's massive draft into a manageable book, but for George to ensure we saw Jimmy's stomping ground made the work worth trying and made the trip unforgettable.

George and Joyce took us to other small French villages and to Monaco. We traveled on hillside roads with hairpin turns that made the U.S. landscape look safe as spoons and skillet flat. We went to a dinner party at the house of one of their painter friends, a Frenchman named Tobiasse. French dinner parties are legendary, often intimate, with a much holier emphasis on food than my American experience prepared me for.

The luscious leisure of the French dinner party actually informed my time with Miss Chloe. I tried to model my time with her based on the different style of engagement that comes with dinner with friends in France. Both Morrison and I were fond of France. Though the two of us never remotely approached replicating French food, I was perfectly able to invoke the feeling of French company around a French-made meal when Morrison and I spent our afternoons or evenings doing our friendly, literary duets. I tried to slow down time for the times we spent together. I consciously emptied my racing mind and chilled out my bustling worries. I tried to turn down the volume when I was with Miss Chloe, as if at a leisurely dinner at someone's home in Nice or Saint Paul de Vence. To consider the fresh food, the aged cheese, the warm light, the warm apples. To accept and observe the well-appointed plate. To admire, appreciate; to eat mindfully and quietly. Deploy your best manners. Observe the ceramics, the designs, the mealtime conventions; enjoy this other country. Experience the night, the ambient light; the rich, old wine; the drive in the dark; the shadows of the olive trees. When your mouth is not full, contribute to the conversation.

Dinner on the French Riviera is the kind of invitation I imagined I should offer to Miss Chloe. This was not an invitation I was able to proffer. I do not think I ever invited Morrison anywhere. Everything we did was at her invitation. I simply did not consider that my life had the infrastructure to support her huge personality and theatricality. I remember a time I wondered, *Can Morrison even fit through the doorway of my house?* A ridiculous question, of course. She could. But her aura would have had to fold and squeeze and bend between outside and indoors. In my estimation, Morrison needed grander and better appointments than I could provide.

RECOLLECTIONS OF MORRISON CAME AS I ironed, or fell asleep, or eased awake. I had to remind myself that I now lived in a world where these memories were the most alive experiences of Morrison I would have. I wrote this as my way through my remembered slants of light.

"You iron?" she said to me once. I can see myself standing there, pouring water for steam, a heavy turquoise tablecloth folded across the ironing board. Late afternoon, around five in an autumn season. Telling time by the hue of evening.

"Yes," I answered. "Ironing makes me feel calm and reminds me of my grandmothers. Besides, I buy cotton clothes."

"Do you iron sheets and pillowcases?"

"Sometimes, but not usually," I answered. I have had a few spates of ironing bed linens. I usually iron cloth napkins and tablecloths for when the whole crew gets together, during giddy holidays.

IMAGINARY PICNIC

Sometimes, like two writers on a playdate, we would imagine together. We dreamed up outings that I suspect we both knew were unlikely to happen. We planned menus. We were quite elaborate, deciding on food, discussing how the food would be prepared, dividing contributions between us, deciding on the best time of day for such a party. Planning for the patio, or the dock.

Once, when discussing a picnic, we spent quite a bit of time discussing deviled eggs. How many? The ingredients. What secret ingredient? Avoiding boiling them green. I may have admitted that people loved my deviled eggs.

I'm not sure I answered her question about what I put in my deviled eggs. I always hesitated spouting recipes. This reticence has nothing to do with Morrison. We moved quickly to potato salad and how long it takes to make. *Can't rush the potato salad.* The potatoes have to be boiled through and then cooled through. The cooling finalizes the cooking and helps create an even texture in the potato. These two steps make potato salad a two-day project. Not everybody can accept that, and so the potatoes are often underdone and glassy.

Morrison wanted to know whether I made yellow or white potato salad. I answered yellow, but was careful not to add "of course." I admitted to not being fond of white potato salad— not enough flavor. We then moved on to the next important choice: cubed or smashed potatoes? I admitted to creating careful cubes. I did not admit to how neurotic my mound of even potato cubes could look. Cubes crumble in the stirring, but most remain, and when I'm done, the bowl looks catered.

I said I'd make one or the other for our "picnic"—potato salad or deviled eggs. I agreed to bring my famous party wings. Then we turned to chocolate strawberries. Should we order them premade? Did either of us have the chocolate dipping sauce already? Where would we find large enough strawberries, if we started out with just the berry, chocolateless? Should we have another dessert?

I did not raise the question of tableware or a picnic basket. First, in her enormous house, with its dock over the water and its patios on multiple floors, she had to have a basket we could use. Second, this was pretty surely an imaginary picnic, anyway. Food you can imagine, and sustain a conversation. Tableware—not as sexy or compelling. Tableware does not make you hungry.

A fine picnic. A cooking conversation. A skate through folklore, stopping in the kitchen, looking in the pots. A dream. So easy when you can just imagine the plan and not have to grocery shop or turn on the stove. Or start potato salad two days in advance. Factor in the drive; factor in keeping the potato salad cool. I could have made it there, but we were spinning a story. Our menu was as close to real as this date would get. I didn't mind imagining; there was only one drawback: Miss Chloe does not sit across from you. You're only talking on the phone.

In the end, so many of her familiars tried to inspire her, encourage her, urge her outdoors by raising the allure of her dock. She had a swing. She could sit and sway over the Hudson River. She could eat there if she wanted. *Don't you want to (get up and walk and) go outside, Miss Chloe? Aren't you still enamored by your daily view?* We were more excited than she.

THE PLANET WITHOUT TONI MORRISON is a changed place, and as Barack Obama so pointedly acknowledged, we are glad that, for a time, we all shared the same air. We got a chance to see her in action. We got a chance to hear her husky voice, live. We got to watch or hear her answer questions in ways we would not or could not. Who else could compare or align oppression with forcing someone to their knees, in order to make the oppressor seem tall? *Are you really tall? How do you feel about yourself when we stand up?*

Our whole culture owes Morrison honor. Toni Morrison subjected so many of our situations to the bright disinfectant of sunlight, splashed across the open page. She laid down powerful words and standout characters. She showed a genius Black mind at work. She reimagined, reinvigorated, and revisited our past so that we all could have a chance to see what we, unencumbered, could imagine. Morrison demonstrated what those of us who might have been tactically or accidentally free could become. If only we could imagine ourselves fully literate, fully liberated, allowed, or even lionized.

MEMORIES BARRELED DOWNHILL IN THE beginning: The last time I saw her. The last time we spoke. The last things she said. Our hilarious times at Princeton. Her big parties. Dinners. Her love of celebrating. Congregating. Seeing what people would do. Her undisruptable focus. Her pencils. Her gaze. Her sardonic gaze. Her "don't you dare" gaze. Her "you must be joking" gaze. Her "are you joking?" gaze. Her "you did not just say that" gaze. The signals that time was up—on the phone, for the visit, and now for her very life.

NO QUESTION TONI MORRISON USED her grand imagination to change what and how we read. For some readers and writers and scholars, even for entrepreneurs, Toni Morrison changed how we think. For people like me, Toni Morrison changed how we live. The material of our history passed through her imagination and emerged like second sight. Morrison challenged herself to make the best that she could envision or imagine come alive and seem real on the page. To make others see and believe was the task of her hand. Insight makes imagination practical and observable. You recognize what your imagination helps you perceive that is too rarely acknowledged, if noticed at all. What can you see in the actions and gestures before you that suggest ideas or emotions beyond the actual sight before you? Insight drives imagination through to the physical. All struggles or pleasures that are physical resonate with the human soul. Insight as a practice is imagination on the march.

ON THE FRIDAY AFTERNOON OF Miss Chloe's funeral Mass, I slipped and fell on those rain-slicked steps, in back of the Baltimore row house I was still getting to know. Because I fell, I hold a crisp memory of that wet and humid afternoon: landing on the landing outdoors, going down, my thoughts slowing down to watch me. I recall, even now, thinking, *Geez I'm glad these steps are wood*—more porous, less punitive.

Scanning where I hurt, trying to register the totality of my situation, checking mentally for broken bones, I tried to bring myself upright. While I was worrying and wondering over potential serious injury, the bells of the church in my village rang three times. St. Casimir Church in Canton, in Baltimore, rings out the time on the hour, starting at eight and ending at nine. Bells all day. Upstate in New York, Miss Chloe's service was graced by a clear and sunny sky, I was later told. Miss Chloe's

Mass and subsequent gathering was disbanding at the time I found myself falling. Residual creakiness and struggle from that fall did not immediately go away.

One of the questions I asked, once I heard from Gloria Baldwin and from Louis Massiah, was whether church bells rang at Miss Chloe's Mass. At Dr. Eleanor Traylor's "mourning afternoon" in September, there were programs. There, I read, her service closed with organist and bells.

On Writing

Writers do not miss the beat or loop of bell ringing. We scaffold events, or situations, or change, with the kind of signals and sound effects that bells bring to bear. After an incident or an accident, a sound, a sight, or a rare passerby might expand the experience for the character and, thereby, reinforce the moment for the reader and for the story. Writers loop the story back on itself, giving the character another go at redemption, at thriving—or surviving—through the crisis situation, moving the character hopefully forward. In life, we ring bells on joyous occasions, at momentous times: to fill the senses, to fill the air, to preserve and reinforce the memory, the experience. As it happens, truth gets serenaded.

We writers involve everything useful in the scene. We use the moon and plants and the whole wall of windows. We use the bunny running across the grass in the dimming evening. We use the fall down wet wooden steps. We arrange and nurture symbols and sounds, messages and murmurs, butterflies and bells. We use the whole universe of the story so that the universe can speak through the storyline and the story can teach some truths about life. We sweep our vision around the occasions and environments of the narrative, and then we must deploy both *focus and control*, Morrison said. We carefully, judiciously, add pearls to the pile as our readers reach for wisdom. We cajole, we admonish, we affirm; we offer our best authorship to the ever-pressing question of what life means. We push ourselves to lean on the author inside authority. We. Ring. Bells. We let robins loose on the town.

In his crisp and inimitable fashion, James Baldwin said, "You never get the book you wanted, you settle for the book you get." A truer thing has not been said. We start out believing we are writing one story, and then the characters we invent begin asserting themselves. If you are writing from memory, once you start to write, recollections stop reclining in the shadows and step into the sunshine of your mind. Our characters and/or our memories will make demands of us, once they learn from us there is a page, or a canvas, or an outlet of any kind.

Our characters must take on the tone and the shadows of where they live and what they do, which is not the same as how and where we, their inventors, conduct the business of our lives. And our memories cannot be separated from their time or slant of light or reason for being. Our memories cannot be separated from where they happened: the rooms, the cars, the concert; the couch, the bed, the chairs. We writers have to separate our industry or our era or our angles of perception. What we write has a life outside the confines and air-conditioning of our lives. Characters blister their feet on the roads in *their* environment, their era. We writers have to recognize, and sometimes set aside, the lens of now.

DURING THE YEARS THAT I danced with cowboy revision "memos," documents so long they seemed accomplishments to their authors, I did have a chance to discuss my Western and its morass with Morrison. And she shared a lesson she said she had learned early in her career: *Never sell an unfinished book.*

Amazing advice. In publishing, an author whose work is in demand is the person who can sell an unfinished work. I communicated as much, and Miss Chloe answered, "Yes. True. But I did that once, and I'll never do that again." Truth is, when you sell an unfinished manuscript, the publisher buys what they *think* they will get from your ten or twenty or fifty or even one hundred proposal pages; they buy what they *imagine* they will get from who they believe you are. Morrison argued that a finished book is what it is. When editors get what you finish, the book might not match what they imagined. And then, where are you? What happens to the book that exists versus the book the acquisitions editor dreamed of?

Further, when you write, timelines take on a nattering quality. Creativity doesn't privilege July or August, or any month or date. Creativity behaves like it knows its own significance; creativity will send the music only when the writer is listening.

As African American artists, our music is foundational to our history, our ancestry, our artistic development, our progress forward, our American birthright. We could not be contained musically, even as our alliances with words were forcibly disrupted, and our access to materials regularly denied. This is why New Orleans became so important to me—the engagement with music spans our whole American history, and raises tendrils of Africa, from the dances, to the drums, to the social interdependence, to Congo Square. In New Orleans, as an African American, you can learn so much about you—about who you have been, about what you can sing, about what your knees can do. Our history lives in the humid air, in New Orleans—the bad history, and the good.

I met James Brown once in New Orleans. James Brown gave a night concert at the New Orleans Jazz and Heritage Festival, and I watched from backstage, courtesy of a pass provided by my producer partner. Meeting James Brown in person was an unforgettable moment. During the concert, there was a cake brought to the stage for Mr. Brown's seventy-fifth birthday. Most people would consider seventy-five old-man-ish, but there he was, sliding and screaming and sweating onstage, falling to a knee, being draped in a cape, faking a walk off, and then turning round, revving up again. Shoes polished to a mirror shine. Horns blaring with trademark unity and precision. Everybody sweating; the whole audience screaming and singing. No one screams as rhythmically, as iconically, as recognizably, as James Brown.

Morrison was more a whisperer than a screamer, but to those of us who read, Morrison was equally an icon and a leader. Morrison is to literature as James Brown is to popular culture. Both of them were—in their respective, artistic fashions—the personification of "I'm Black and I'm proud." Both of them spoke with great, breezy, and unquestioned authority to their devoted audiences. When either of them spoke, we all listened.

I had five, at the most ten, minutes with James Brown. I listened to him talk, and when there was a pause, I asked him how he felt about his influence, about his enormous effect on all the many people. Many of the people James Brown influenced are now living years in which their futures will be far shorter than their pasts. Even though people—and especially artists—who are in the know, all have a take on James Brown. The late, great, multivalent Greg Tate was working on a book on James Brown when he transitioned. I heard the book is finished; it's bound to blow our minds.

James Brown was not a humble person, but he wasn't smug either. He was actually slight—not tall and not thick, at least when I saw him. I was thrilled to observe his stature, his glistening hair, and his pointy shoes up close. When I asked him about his enormous effect on generations, and on so many geographies, he said, "I know I raised all y'all. I'm godfather to everybody, I know it, and I'm proud."

Morrison raised the consciousness of huge swathes of girls, at least those of us girls who read. Morrison also had a huge effect on men who read too. Former president and icon Barack Obama famously said that reading *Song of Solomon* taught him how to be a man. No more enormous or significant, or more laudatory, compliment could be made. In the film *Barry*, about Obama as a young man, as a student contemplating law school, there is a meditative scene where the title character settles in for the night, with a cigarette and a well-worn copy of *Song of Solomon*. You know you've ascended to the summit and planted your flag when, as an artist, your work has influenced not just the people, but their president. James Brown and Toni Morrison both had their art and personalities carried from the adulation of the ordinary citizen, into the hallowed halls of power. They were both fully aware of how their works radiated outward. This was their intention, and they both met wild success.

MORRISON'S WORK AND CAREER PROVE that the work of writing is thick. Viscous. Saturated. Thorough. Nothing that exists is out of bounds in writing. Both the page and the human mind hunger for invention and surprise and tales of unlikely accident or survival. You can write about whatever you can conceive. At the same time, you should keep some rules in mind. That's what Morrison was saying way back before, back at the first reading of hers I attended in that Boston church. *You have to know what you're doing.*

Morrison taught me so much about writing, from her work, from her answers to my questions, from our casual conversations. Her decades of steady work, her awareness of her talents, her devotion to her projects, her risks of thought and expression and reimagining, her unyielding pursuit of mastery, her plain, inarguable genius—all these demonstrate what we who come post-Morrison can put into practice. We are writing after Morrison. This is an immutable reality. We can learn what to do, from Morrison, from other writers, from pursuit of our own curiosities.

Ask questions. Be curious. Follow your own mind deep into the dark forest.

Remember: Darkness is protective. Rely on what you know, not what they say.

WE HAD THE MOST FUN one night in Princeton; we played an invented almost-game. If we had to name it, we'd have to call it "Imagination or Technique?"

Again, I had planned my questions in case our conversation lagged. Morrison had invited me to visit, but she had also ordered pizza, which I did not expect. I was overdressed for dinner. But since we had time face-to-face, and we weren't out in public, we ate and had a freewheeling conversation. I started by asking about Dovey, who had a man visiting her garden. You get the sense that the man is a ghost, but the narrative doesn't say. He just appears. Dovey is glad to see him and goes out on her porch to wait for him. He reappears a second time. And then again, a third, I think. I chose this as a starting place. I'd mention situation after situation in *Paradise*, and ask, "Is that imagination or technique?"

She was tickled at first, by my formulation. I can still see her amusement, her surprise. Her stopping the progression of the pizza to her mouth to register that I intended to go on. Her eyes lit up, and she laughed when she realized the components of the questioning. When I got the answer "technique" more than once, I exclaimed. I fell back (dramatically). I said

"What?!" several times. We stepped through a number of dramatic flourishes in *Paradise*, with me posing this dichotomy as the answer frame. She was entertained by the moment, and I certainly learned. There were many more answers of "technique" than I expected. Excellent news.

We went some rounds. Not a whole dozen, but more than six. We laughed the whole way through. She laughed, I think, to discover that I had question after question. And then she laughed at the moments or the objects/episodes I chose to ask about. She definitely laughed about my response when her answer surprised me. Of the evenings we spent, and of all the spontaneous conversations we had over the years, this little game we played was my favorite of our times together. We were not that experienced with each other then. This happened in Princeton, in the paneled condominium. We may have gone out that night, afterward. The answers to my questions helped me think about writing. A lesson tailored to my particular queries. I know she must have thought, *Who goes around asking this kind of question: What about this? What about that? Is it imagination or technique?*

Imagination can only be nurtured; technique can be taught, identified, explained.

Imagination is personal; technique is public information. As Morrison suggested in the very beginning, there are things to be learned. What do we call the aspects of writing that can be learned? *Technique.*

Toni Morrison's voice does not quiet; nor does it become less salient or significant. Now, when I'm in a situation for which she once gave me advice, I make a more conscious effort to follow the advice she gave. The time has come in the universe when I can't ask any new questions; old advice will have to suffice. For all the advice that this writing has shown I did not follow, I've still got marching orders. I know what to do.

MORRISONIAN APPROACHES TO NARRATIVE swirl around me now, carried on the current of her post-departure weather. Morrison plumbed the limits of every narrative technique. From sentences to scenes to perspective to point of view, Morrison always aimed to do more than the basic, better than the obvious. For Morrison, for example, a sentence was like a vise—far beyond routine, boring subjects and predicates. Noun and verb are but the beginning of what a sentence is and does. This Morrison demonstrates. The sentence locks you into a framework, which becomes increasingly particular with each new sentence. Each sentence we writers construct, in any given story, eliminates more possibilities than it allows. In this way, sentence by sentence, each story becomes particular, becomes the specific, one story it is.

THE GOAL OF FICTION IS to suggest truth. In other words, fiction should seem true as it's read. Morrison's fiction—in which she invented fantastic and impossible characters and events—seems true. Even though you routinely encounter flat-out-impossible goings-on, she has worked hard to make her visions seem tactile, tangible, real. Morrison causes us to believe in people who are as unreal as fairy dust. Every one of us knows Beloved is a ghost, even as we empathize with her terror, her speechlessness, her mother hunger. We all give Beloved the space to be an angry teenager. We permit her vengeance. We empathize with her desires to disrupt the ongoing household. We buy in; we watch the shed go red; we accept the ghost deflowered.

MORRISON WROTE THROUGH SOME OF the real dilemmas of our history, saturating and enlivening our past. Morrison wrote towering stories, complete with the closest details. Issues so minuscule we hardly notice—though, on the page, they resonate. Pea-size bubbles in a boiling pot. People who grow reliable hot peppers. Women running for their lives, early in the morning, being chased by men with guns. If you look, you will find specific reflections on complex and straightforward human endeavors, including handling atonement and forgiveness (complex) or cooking soft-boiled eggs (straightforward). You can find full treatises on slavery, naming, Reconstruction, and the Jazz Age. You can find secondary treatises on the Korean War, Black posterity, Black women's friendships, mothering. You can also find ribbons, and red velvet rose petals, and a clearing in the woods where a woman can preach.

Four hundred years of territory covered in Ms. Morrison's works. The scholar Paula Giddings made this observation first—that the novels written by Toni Morrison cover four hundred years of American history. The whole of our time in America. Paula Giddings worked as an editorial assistant at Random House, in Toni Morrison's editorial era. Giddings remembers typing parts of Morrison's first manuscript, *The Bluest Eye*.

MORRISON FAMOUSLY CHOSE AS HER project to write without "the white gaze." To focus on our single side of the doubleness Du Bois uncovered. Just as you cannot consider Morrison without Baldwin, or Baldwin without Delaney, Du Bois needs acknowledgment as a Morrison forebear. His was the dual consciousness she decided to forcibly separate. His genius theory is what Morrison interrogated. Jimmy Baldwin and Toni Morrison apparently began the gaze conversation, literally. Theirs was a discussion not of sociology but of reaching for an unsullied point of view. Baldwin imagined a small, white man sitting on his shoulder, critiquing, as Jimmy wrote. Of course, "the gaze" is far larger, more suffused, and more omnipresent than a critical voice, whine loudly though it may. The gaze is a camera more elevated than your shoulder. The gaze is atmospheric: the gaze can situate itself at any height. The gaze is the fundamental permission.

Morrison has been accused of "not writing about white people." In the early years of her career, Morrison was asked, or urged, to write "a real book," meaning, a book that included white people. The stunning myopia. Or sheer brazenness. It's hard to tell which. For the record: When oppression is included, oppression = white people. When the slave catcher comes, that man is white. When the lash splits the skin, the hand that aims the splitting lash is white. Ditto when there is a flesh-for-work transaction at the graveside: the body at the end of the member is white. Just a man collecting the quarters he claims due.

Toni Morrison spoke of her project more gracefully, more poetically, more accurately as writing "without the white gaze." Truth is, the contemporary connotation of "without" is inactive—as if you just leave something behind or by the way-side. For Black people, "the white gaze" is hegemony suffused with racialized malintent. There's no escaping what's atmospheric; there's no way to leave a context that contains you. The white gaze is no small matter, and no joke. In fact, our experience is largely under the umbrella of investments in our demise.

The effort Morrison undertook to forgo the white gaze took work. Future students, or critics, or scholars will study her body of fiction and say that she abandoned or retired or dismissed or avoided or refused the white gaze. It's also fair to say she sent the white gaze to the background, or made the white panorama a backdrop. Morrison's approach did not render white folks omitted or invisible. Though, oddly, that the question was asked at all suggests that unless in the foreground, white folks in the narrative are invisible to white readers.

The scope of Morrison's vision observed and encapsulated the whole scene, the whole context, the whole era in which the story played out. All the people appear: Black people, white folk, Native Americans walking miles. In some stories, there are islanders. In others, there are children from Brazil.

WRITING OFTEN IN BODACIOUS OMNISCIENCE, Morrison crafted points of view huge as skylight. Celestial-level vision over-top human behavior—she positioned the gaze up there. Even when her points of view dip into the mind—say, of Malvonne—omniscience reappears. Morrison created seeable casts of characters—people we can remember, whose names we can call and whose behavior we can call out. We have infinite options to offer our empathy, or sympathy, or sisterhood, or wishes for protection. As in life, there are also targets for fury. Morrison invented waves of three-dimensional, real-seeming, socially connected, living, thriving, bleeding, striving, reaching Black people. Hundreds of them have her chosen names. In her novels, whole cities, whole neighborhoods, multiple generations of Black characters perform and reference reality. Scores of people. Not every soul in her works is battered (by oppression) to dramatic despair or nothingness. Some are. The men who went day after day to apply for jobs in *Sula*—these men are an example of the battered. But there are also plenty of examples of the free. For the majority of their lives, Deacon and Steward, Morrison's old-men twins, are free. Reverend Misner would declare himself free: as would likely Sula, Nel, Soane, and Dovey. This list could go on. Pilate might say, I'm free *now*. Sethe could have thought Beloved was free.

Morrison thought deeply and wrote capaciously about both the physicality and the interiority of our lives. Our physicalities are contained, but our interiorities sing and reach and tumble and dance—just like all God-given spirits, especially those that answer to our names. Issues raised in the works of Toni Morrison are often complex and sometimes intractable and occasionally free-floating—not unlike the matters of our lives.

MORRISON IS GONE NOW. AND SO, my sight line has shifted. Before, I knew our high points and low points, our vistas and valleys. Now, also, our open and finale, all clear. A door closes when a person leaves the planet. A curtain drops. You must take your next steps from the audience. You must march yourself out into an altered world.

Louis Armstrong and Ella Fitzgerald sing a famous duet of the jazz classic "Summertime." The song covers cotton, and heat, and an era few of us consider fondly. And yet, Ella's lustrous voice sails over gorgeous lyrics, echoing the horn solo Louis Armstrong has just played. After Ella's measures, Louis Armstrong starts to sing, his voice and throat raspy from dogged years behind his horn. As a young boy, Louis Armstrong hustled for pennies on the streets of New Orleans until he was picked up as a waif and deposited in a colored orphan's home. Not unlike the boys in Whitehead's *The Nickel Boys*, Louis Armstrong, genius, found himself trapped in a nightmare, living out the tragic childhood of an American legend and an international celebrity. Ella Fitzgerald also survived a harsh (Black) childhood, and was homeless when she won Amateur Night at the Apollo in 1934, at the age of seventeen. The prize was a weeklong show, but because Ella only had the clothes of a homeless person, they refused to award the prize to the teenager with the sultry smooth velvet voice. This is what I mean about finding genius in the street. Fate, or fortune, found these two. Their talent, their focus, and their destiny delivered them to each other, and to us.

When I was ambling around the dictionary, looking for a strong and impressionistic word that at once expressed power, and spirit, and eternity, and gumption, and complexity—I found *eidolon*. Wanting to better define Morrison as ancestor led me to the enduring *eidolon*, which led me to Walt Whitman. Just as Morrison reminded me early on of what Paul

Laurence Dunbar meant when he referenced myriad subtleties, at the end, Morrison reminded me of what Whitman references with his call to seers, to entrance songs, to summits, to eidolons. In his poem "Eidolons," Whitman uses the word *atelier*; he references building wealth and strength and beauty; he nods to tendencies to shape and shape and shape. So Morrison.

Morrison's mind was crackling and crisp like poetry, and in the beginning and in the end, my image of her arc of life situates great poets, and their genius ideas.

Toni Morrison had a theory of genius that comported with what we believe as a society, as a culture. Genius is a gift of grace, a godsend. Genius must be treated as such. Genius must be recognized and pursued. In our society, Black genius is both acknowledged and denied—which creates, of course, a war of opposites. This unreasonable and untenable polarity can nullify or neutralize honest truth. People of all types and stripes show genius at particular skills and/or passions. Genius needs notice and nurture to thrive. Resistance to genius is like burial, like putting potential in a coffin while it screams.

I never heard Morrison use the term *Black genius*, but she recognized genius, and spoke of genius, and would not deny genius once observed. Toni Morrison was as serious about Black genius as she was about breathing.

In my experience, Morrison did not believe that we were any more genius than the next culture. But American culture crudely and ludicrously espouses that we have no genius, or less genius. Our society purports that we have little intelligence, in fact. Morrison proved and recognized that Black genius exists everywhere. She set out to do all she could with the wits she'd been given. Her social and intellectual strategy included surrounding herself with greats and experiencing and acknowledging other great minds that she found: passionate and studied artists, musicians, innovators who shared her era and her air. As is true for all of us, Morrison's community reflected her passions and energy and vibrations. Our friends and associates are part of the (human) environment we build for ourselves.

Black genius is both abundant and profitable in America. This is inarguable and obvious. But there are other Black geniuses, now and in history, who found the nurture—whether by grace or by grabbing—to develop themselves and thrive. Even these accomplished folks have names we might not know; their achievements might not have survived the whitewashing, the hiding, the suppression of truth. There are Black geniuses whose potential is wasted because their lives are discarded, treated as detritus. The soul-crushing waste of Black possibility is ongoing, brutal, and destructive of genius in general, and quite possibly implodes a potentially genius nation.

A whole collection of brilliant men and women have emerged from the very sites of our silencing. None will forever be denied. Morrison would suck her teeth, dispense quickly with erasures, demonstrate how little about us is known. Insist you call names.

Just go down the alphabet. Takes no time, because this is a truth we know. Any one of us can start the list, and we can all keep going. Any viable list about our standing will burrow deeply into intentionally buried truths.

Benjamin Banneker. Bojangles. Beauford Delaney. Paul

Laurence Dunbar. Henry Dumas. Sammy Davis Jr. Sam Cooke. Mahalia Jackson. Lucille Clifton. Langston. Micheaux. DuBois. Wells-Barnett. Cooper (Anna Julia). Matzeliger (Jan). Morrison. . . .

You could make a list. Hundreds long. Every day, you could arise and add more names. Geniuses. (Black.)

WE ARE OFFICIALLY AND FOREVER post-Morrison. Her works will live on, likely forever, but her impressive, legendary, irrepressible personality has moved beyond the performative, away from the curated, into the sustaining milieu of ancestry. She is absent of her aches and pains. Even if we stand, unmoving, at the gate of goodbye, she will not come sauntering down the hallway; she will not pull her Jaguar into a parking space; she will not change your schedule to what she has planned. She will not laugh aloud again. She will not cut her eyes again. She will not wordlessly disabuse you of whatever you are thinking. She will make no more demands.

Toni Morrison modeled what it meant to be demanding—of herself, of her language, of her genius. Of her country, of her readers, of her chosen friends. She responded to the pressure of her own expectations, and she never let up. If you read Toni Morrison, you will see many lives moving. You will see actions and responses you recognize from life. You will also see the miraculously imagined, the astoundingly impossible. You will likely be just like the rest of us—changed by Toni Morrison—if you read her work, if you consider what she taught us, if you observe her philosophies, if you follow her advice, if you rise up to meet her demands.

The Main Among the Many:
Lessons I Learned from Toni Morrison

Naming yourself is entirely within your power.

Becoming a whole person demands gracing your God-given gifts with fruition. This is not only your power, but your duty.

Grow what you have been given, own what you can access, and pass it on.

Language mastery is possible.

Language mastery can deliver infinite imagining to the page, and to reality.

Technique relies on repetition.

Focus and control.

Be brief.

Close the door on yesterday.

Start with a question.

Do not spend time defending yourself in your own country. Instead, develop your spirit and intellect and personality. Do not be distracted by pathological, illogical obsessions like racism (to call the elephant its name).

Don't repeat ridiculous insults about who you are or might be. Belief is the powerful outcome of repetition.

Let the work speak—not just work as outcome, but also work as energy, as your effort.

Answer no, and feel the liberation.

Mothers are fierce about their children, which is not the same as saying that their decisions, as mothers, can be universally understood.

Everyone must read James Baldwin.

Every library has its children, whose names only the future knows.

Insight comes naturally, and, like all that is natural, must be nurtured and must be managed to be of use.

You have the whole past to work with, and you have only now to work.

Don't be scared to cover your head.

Don't be scared.

Imagine.

. . . sky had packed
its scarves and gone over the hard blue hills.
. . . You stood
flicking ash onto the trampled grass.
I could smell the rain leaving, the sage
enthralled in a bitter virtue for hours.

Rita Dove
from "After Storm"

ACKNOWLEDGMENTS

Toni Morrison reached her hand out to me multiple times in my life. Reviewing the memories laid down here, letting stories fall to the proverbial cutting room floor, considering the intimacies too far—all these have felt like a gift. I hope I have been adequate to the task. Just as I tried to be clear in her lifetime that knowing Miss Chloe was a treasure, I have also wanted to offer a praise song—if prickly sometimes—here. Life is prickly sometimes. Living the days of our friendship was also awe-inspiring. Writing about the time we spent together would not have occurred to me but for Steve Ross, whom I thank for proposing the book and representing the book, and for agenting without drama. Black people in America need less drama in their lives. Lauren Norton—fellow toiler in the garden of words—brought this book back from the brink, bringing her organizational mind to my messy manuscript, reminding me of the outcome that could come. My two sisters—Brenda and Adrienne—have flanked me all my years, chattering advice and encouragement. My family continues to remind me that my history is fierce and not wordless. My former students and budding writers checked on me and cheered me on and brought me soup and made sure I was fine—I count them among the acknowledged, the village people who helped get this done. Tracy Sherrod, editor, brought unwavering perception of Black women's reaching and relationships and our place in the big sea of now and of the past. Even when time demands required cryptic communication, Tracy managed to lob magnanimous, if brief, directives, and to keep expecting me to stretch as a writer. My assistant Crystal Cain handled all she could to free me to concentrate on rememory. Imani Wilson and Julie Love are so reliable as friends and witnesses that I work with confidence they'll be there when I look up. Findings of fact are given new meaning by meticulous copy editor Jenna Dolan; the experience of answering her queries felt both epic and important. I wrote these recollections from memory, and those months re-examining our time together was like watching reels of film; my heart leapt and fell and whirled. In the end, I join the chorus: I applaud and acknowledge Toni Morrison's grandness, greatness, genius; I acknowledge her as American, as a Black woman, as explosive with her accomplishments. As this book goes to press, Toni Morrison's books are being banned, her significance being further imprinted; her name is spoken many times, every day. As is fitting, Miss Chloe has gone into ancestry blazing.

2022, Baltimore